BOTH SIDES
OF THE BORDER

MY AUTOBIOGRAPHY

ARCHIE GEMMILL

with
Will Price

BOTH SIDES
OF THE BORDER

MY AUTOBIOGRAPHY

HODDER

Copyright © 2006 by Archie Gemmill

First published in Great Britain in 2005 by Hodder and Stoughton
A division of Hodder Headline

The right of Archie Gemmill to be identified as the Author
of the Work has been asserted by him in accordance with
the Copyright, Designs and Patents Act 1988.

A Hodder Book

1

A CIP catalogue record for this title is available from the British Library

ISBN 0 340 89571 3

Typeset in Galliard by Hewer Text UK Ltd, Edinburgh
Printed and bound by
Mackays of Chatham Ltd, Chatham, Kent

Hodder Headline's policy is to use papers that are natural, renewable
and recyclable products and made from wood grown in sustainable forests.
The logging and manufacturing processes are expected to conform to
the environmental regulations of the country of origin.

Hodder and Stoughton Ltd
A division of Hodder Headline
338 Euston Road
London NW1 3BH

Dedication

I have been very fortunate in life. I have achieved things which the normal man in the street can only dream about. I have earned my living playing the game I have loved since I was a boy, I have experienced the kind of elation you feel when you win at Wembley, I have travelled the world and played in the most famous stadiums in the world, I have experienced genuine adulation from football fans and I even managed to get myself in the history books with a goal which I am beginning to think will never be forgotten, but I have to say, by far my greatest achievement in life has been to father two of the most wonderful children a man could ask for. That is why I am dedicating this book to them. They are genuinely good people who are always thinking of others, they are warm and generous with their love. Somewhere along the line I obviously got something right when I was raising them.

Of course I had a little help from my beloved wife Betty. She is the source of my strength. She is the person I turn to when I am happy, when I am sad, when I want a moan and when I want an unbiased opinion.

Obviously I also want to thank my Mum and Dad who gave me such a happy start in life and who continue to be there for me whenever I need them.

So, to all my family, I dedicate this book to you because I love you.

CONTENTS

ACKNOWLEDGEMENTS

Will Price, my ghost writer – I only met Will a couple of years ago but it turns out he has been a Derby supporter all his life and he used to watch me play at the Baseball Ground in my heyday. Thank you Will, this would not be happening without you.

Brian Clough – The biggest influence on my career. Brian sadly passed away shortly after completing the foreword for my book and I miss him so much. He was a good friend and his passing has left a huge hole in my life.

My fans – without them no-one would be remotely interested in my life. They allowed me to achieve some of my dreams. Thank you.

Hodder & Stoughton – I would like to thank Roddy Bloomfield, my publisher for his support at all times, Marion Paull, an expert copy-editor, and Gabrielle Allen for researching a wealth of interesting photographs.

Photographic Acknowledgements

The author and publisher would like to thank the following for permission to reproduce photographs:

Colorsport, Andrew Cowie/Colorsport, L'Equipe/Offside, Stewart Fraser/Colorsport, Getty Images, Nottingham Evening Post, Offside Sports Photography, PA/Empics, Popperfoto.com, Peter G. Reed, Peter Robinson/Empics, Neal Simpson/Empics, SMG/Empics, Sport & General/Empics.

All other photographs are from private collections.

FOREWORD

IT'S one of the puzzles of my life that Archie Gemmill is not in football at the highest level. It's such a waste to the game. I'm not saying he should be manager of Scotland, although I will say I've seen people in that job who couldn't lace his boots. I think Archie doesn't get jobs because of his physical stature. I believe that, I genuinely do. When he walks through the door the chairman, probably a great fat, six-foot three fella, sees Archie and says to himself, 'Well, he won't impress anybody.' One of the daft things about football is the number of people still in it who know so little about it. Archie knows more about the game than most of them put together.

He can be a miserable little so-and-so, and cantankerous, as awkward off the field as he was on it, but he's loyal. I've seen him practically every week of the ten years or so I've been out of the game, and that's the sign of a good friend. Perhaps I'm trying to make amends for some of the rotten things I did to him in my early days but, anyway, he's still here, sitting in my front room, having a cup of tea.

Bringing Archie to Derby from Preston was the hardest deal I'd ever done up until then. I never saw him play before I signed him but the second he arrived I knew I had a player. I had an obsession with heading the ball, you know. I was under the impression, and still am to this very day, that if you can head a ball you can play. It meant you were brave for a start. For somebody of his size to head a ball as well as he did was incredible. Inch for inch, he jumped higher and headed a ball better than anyone I knew in the game, and I had his mate Roy McFarland at centre-half. Roy was not very big, either, only five-foot eleven, but he could get up, too. One of the criticisms of McFarland was that he was too small to be a centre-half. What a load of rubbish!

I've seen players of six-foot three who couldn't jump as high as Archie, six-foot four some of them – couldn't get off their feet. To be brave in football, to head a ball, you've got to be able to get up to head it blind, when you've got your back to opponents. You've got to be prepared to take the bangs and most players duck, you know.

So that was Archie's great strength, his ability to head the ball. Then, of course, he had phenomenal pace. A lot of players got into football just because of their pace. If you could see somebody run like a gazelle, you might think, 'Ooh, what a player!' but pace wasn't enough on its own. Archie combined pace and his ability to head the ball with vision and heart, especially as he was competing against bigger fellas. It stood him in good stead on the floor as well as in the air because he was frightened of nobody. Now what other combination do you look for? What do you want? Goals? His famous goals for me are all on tape. He started one for Nottingham Forest against Arsenal in our penalty area and he finished by putting it in. He had all the qualities of a midfield player, simple as that.

Archie's great games for me were spread all over the shop. Inevitably, with a player of his type, he would contribute as much if not more than anybody but didn't capture the headlines. Goalscorers always caught the headlines and they always will until the game's finished. I'll tell you what Tommy Docherty was quoted as saying about him. Archie played an international on the Wednesday for Scotland and Derby County played on the Saturday at Manchester United and we either got done or drew. Docherty was in conversation with a pal of mine from Manchester and hc said, 'I knew they'd have trouble. I got every last thing out of that little shit on Wednesday night. He couldn't walk when he left us.' Archie hadn't got the headlines playing for Scotland but that's what the manager had said. In fact, he couldn't walk playing for us. I remember that type of thing in preference to him scoring three goals or anything like that.

The second time I signed Archie, for Nottingham Forest, it was the biggest con in the game. Docherty was Derby manager and I'd heard that he wanted a goalkeeper. Now John Middleton was supposedly the up-and-coming goalkeeper and I thought, 'Well, he's not as good as people say he is,' because I worked with him. He was as soft as my backside for a start and I'd got three or four goalkeepers. Docherty's tongue was absolutely hanging out for a goalkeeper and he came on to me for Middleton, asking, 'What do you want?' and trying to browbeat me. I thought about it and thought about it and eventually I said, 'Go on then, I'll take cash. Do you want to get rid of Gemmill?' I added, just as a daft thing.

'Yes, you can have Gemmill,' he said, just like that on the telephone. I thought he'd either had a drink or when I saw him face to face he'd say, 'Sod off, you're not getting him.' He didn't, though, and Docherty thought he'd got the better of the deal. In fact, he went round telling everybody as much. He used a terrible word, actually. He told people, 'I've sold Cloughie a pup,' but I knew Archie and that he'd do me for a couple of years. I'd formed a relationship with Archie by then, both off and on the field, and I dropped a clanger when I sold him on. It was too early. Money turned my head. I wanted money at that particular time and I must have had a surplus in midfield. He was thirty when I sold him to Birmingham but with his physique and his off-the-field behaviour he could have gone on for another two or three years at Forest and would have been ideal for me.

Did I try to get him back a couple of months later? I tried quicker than that. I rang him up and said, 'Come back,' but he wouldn't. He said, 'No, you got rid of me once and I'm not coming back.' That was probably his pride. He had pride as a player, you know. My first message when Archie came to Derby was to get his hair cut. He did have it a wee bit longer than we liked, and he got a trim, became smart and became part and parcel of the club and our success.

I didn't know he was such a good player as he was when I signed him – you never do, you know.

1
EARLY DAYS

I NEARLY didn't make it past the ripe old age of fourteen. My head felt ready to explode and the doctor didn't know what to do, which wasn't very reassuring. Nobody could discover why I was getting the most awful headaches. The local chemist's shop must have made a small fortune from all the painkillers my mother, Ina, bought for me, but nothing would rid me of the nightmare. It got so bad, I was physically sick and started banging my head on the wall in my bedroom.

The doctor finally decided I should be admitted to hospital for further investigation and so, with my mother in a flood of tears, I was taken into Glasgow General. Through all the pain I can recall hearing the dreaded words 'meningitis' and 'tumours', but I was suffering so much I could not react with the terror I felt. Fortunately, a lumbar puncture test for meningitis was clear, but that left the medical boffins even more perplexed.

Following numerous other tests, I was transferred to Killearn Hospital on the outskirts of Glasgow where the doctors decided to 'go in and have a look' as it was casually explained to me, as if they were thinking of browsing around a department store. I was told I would be awake throughout surgery.

Well, if I was scared before, my fear now reached mammoth proportions. I can still remember them boring into my skull with a hand-held drill. I don't rightly know what they found in there – over the years, friends have put several suggestions to me, not all of them complimentary – but they did not find a tumour. It has become a standing family joke that they didn't find anything inside. The operation was a success, though, because it relieved the pressure on my brain and I quickly recovered. I still bear the scar on my scalp, just above my right ear. The wee bit of hair I still possess just manages to cover it.

My mother demanded to know from the consultant exactly what had been wrong with me but he couldn't put his finger on it. He reckoned it was probably a build-up of pressure caused by either a kick to the cranium during a match, or simply too many headers, even by the age of fourteen. It was enough to make Mum plead with me to stop playing my beloved football. Fat chance.

When I was born on Monday, 24 March 1947 at home in Greenhill Road, Paisley, I should have had an older brother but, four years earlier, William, named after my father, had survived just twenty-four hours, and I was destined to be an only child. My earliest recollections are of moving house fairly frequently. From Greenhill Road, we went to George Street, Candron Road and then Langcraigs Drive. It was a rough and ready existence, I suppose.

By all accounts and evidence from about five of my uncles, my father, Willie, was a fairly useful footballer and played for Mossvale YMCA, Johnstone Athletic and the Maryhill club in Glasgow on the left wing before the war. Then he joined the Air Force, did a few parachute jumps, served his country – that sort of thing – and came home to settle down as a roofer and tiler who preferred a pint after work to training. I remember one summer, I must have been about eleven, having a whale of a time on Dad's building site, stacking tiles and mixing up the cement.

You grew up quickly in my part of the world. I think it's fair to say a lot of drinking went on, not that I was about to start complaining. A few pals and I made a cart with some pram wheels and went round collecting empty beer bottles from bins, or from where drunks had simply collapsed. We exchanged the bottles for a few coppers, and maybe some silver, at the local public house, and built up quite a lucrative round.

Football, of course, was what really interested me. I'd had a ball at my feet as soon as I could walk and I was soon developing my dribbling skills, kicking my football one mile to Langcraigs Primary School every day and one mile back again. In my last term there, Mr Hudson, the teacher who took the football team, thought I had some reasonably good qualities. He picked me on the left wing, made me captain and I scored the winning goal when we beat St Peter's Roman Catholic School to win the Paisley and District Cup final 2–1.

I didn't do brilliantly in the eleven plus and moved on to South School on Neilson Road. Standing four foot nothing in my short pants, I must have been an easy target for the playground bullies, and they weren't about to miss an 'open goal'. A group of kids were mithering me, tripping me up and stealing my dinner money. I didn't like to let on at home what was happening but Mum was, and still is, a remarkably astute and formidable woman. She found out what the score was soon enough. One day she suggested that I go to school and tell the bully boys I would meet them at four o'clock to settle things once and for all. They must have thought their Christmases had all come at once but their tune soon changed when the headmaster walked round the corner. I've never been bullied from that day on. Thanks, Mum. Good call.

Although I'm the first to admit I wasn't the brightest, I did have the great sense to make good friends with Andy Cassidy, the biggest lad in school, and that also undoubtedly helped keep the bullies off my back. Life improved, I had nothing to fear and I had enough money to get a hot dinner inside me, instead of relying on pals to get me an apple after I'd been robbed.

It wasn't long before I moved on to the new Stanely Green High School in Paisley, together with Andy Cassidy and most of my friends. The only change was that now it was two-and-half miles to school every morning with a football fixed to the end of my toe – and two-and-half miles back when the bell rang at the end of the afternoon.

That ball got me into some trouble, I can tell you. The local constabulary weren't very impressed to say the least and I had my football confiscated by a policeman a couple of times. On the second occasion, I marched down to the local police station to demand my property back. The duty officer refused to oblige unless I gave him my name and address. I must have been a stubborn little so-and-so even then because I wouldn't budge and simply insisted it was my ball and I wanted it back. I was only standing up for my rights, after all. In the end, I got my way only for a policeman to arrive on our front doorstep and inform my mother, 'Mrs Gemmill, we believe you are raising a thug!' He got short shrift, believe me.

One boy took my ball and wouldn't give it back – big mistake. I seized a friend's air rifle and fired a warning shot. Unfortunately, the pellet caught the boy on the top of his arm. His mother went screaming blue murder to the police and the next thing you know I'm being driven off in the back of a Black Maria with Mum chasing us down the road. It never went to court. Things like that didn't in those days. I just had to go round to the boy's house and make a proper apology.

School never held any great attraction for me. I was not academically inclined and studying for seven hours a day left me cold but, come Saturday, I was as keen as mustard, representing Stanely Green in the morning and Anchor Boy Scouts in the afternoon. Excited doesn't come near describing how I felt when I made the final trial for the Scottish Under-15 team and it is a great blessing that I have always been mentally strong because I was devastated to be turned down, purely on the grounds of my size. The game took place at Kilmarnock's Rugby Park and I played the second half on the left wing, scoring a couple of goals. After that performance I was pretty confident of being selected but my optimism drained away when the squad was announced and my name didn't appear. The official reason, and I have never forgotten these words, was that I was 'far too small ever to make a footballer'. Nothing to do with skill or ability, then. Well, how could it be? I had made the final trial, after all, and scored twice.

That made me more determined than ever to make a name for myself, even if I was Archie Gemmell to the press – and, especially in the Scottish papers, Gemmell I remained from the age of fourteen for more years than I care to remember. The mistake stemmed from a tiny article in the local paper, which stated, bold as you like, that I was related to Tommy Gemmell of St Mirren, my local professional club in Paisley.

Now Tommy was a bit of a local legend and had won a couple of Scotland caps, but he certainly wasn't connected to our family, and neither was he the Tommy Gemmell of Lisbon Lions fame, the Celtic team that won the European Cup in 1967. Confusing, isn't it?

My formal education came to a full stop in 1962. Often in life it's not a case of what you know but who you know and Mum knew the personnel officer at Kilpatrick's electrical company. Consequently, I got a start there as an apprentice electrician.

They were busy days. Money was tight and I was saving up for my first transistor radio, so I took another job as well. I would get up at 4.30 in the morning to deliver milk, for which I was paid the princely sum of one pound and ten shillings per week. After a bite of breakfast, I would catch the bus from the Glenburn estate to Erskine and take the ferry over the River Clyde before jumping on another bus, which would take me to the building site of some multi-storey flats in Dalmuir, where I was earning three pounds and fifteen shillings each week before tax. The journey could take up to two hours on a bad day.

After a full day's work I'd go training twice a week with

Drumchapel Amateurs, one of the leading boys teams in Glasgow, and not get home much before ten in the evening. I was also supposed to attend nightschool as part of my electrical apprenticeship and, needless to say, I didn't turn up very often. Boy, did that get me into trouble. It needed all Mum's powers of persuasion to prevent me from being kicked off the course.

We were not exactly a wealthy family but as an only child I was spoiled rotten when it came to food at home and I became a very pernickety eater. I would never eat fresh vegetables. It always had to be frozen peas or, my staple diet, baked beans on toast. My mother made a wonderful Scotch broth and she'd have to strain out all the vegetables for me. It wasn't until I played for Preston North End several years later that I started to eat properly.

Despite the Scotland Under-15 selectors' words of doom, my lack of inches was not proving a barrier to my development as a footballer. I had already signed provisional forms for St Mirren and I got an inkling of what the game had to offer in July 1963 when Drumchapel took me on an eleven-day pre-season summer tour of Iceland, where we played in front of crowds of 6,000.

At the time, St Mirren had a glamorous Icelandic star player, Therolf Beck, known as 'Tottie' to everyone at Love Street. Foreign footballers were very rare in Scottish football in those days and, as luck would have it, Tottie lodged with my grandmother, Mary Verner, for fifteen months. You can imagine how much of a thrill it was for a young football-daft lad like me to go round to my gran's, talk to Tottie and sometimes have dinner with him. Over in Iceland, I went to see Tottie's mother and later, when St Mirren got rid of him, I replaced Tottie in the team. It can be a small world sometimes.

That tour with Drumchapel was a wonderful experience for a young teenager, seeing the hot springs and glaciers. The most amazing thing was the length of daylight in that part of the world.

I think there was just about half an hour of dusk a day when the sun wasn't shining. We needed to pull the blinds tight shut in our dormitory to get any sleep. It seemed a far cry from getting up in the pitch-black on a winter's morning for that milk round back home.

2

EDUCATING ARCHIE

I HAD made quite a name for myself with Drumchapel, so much so that both Celtic and Rangers were interested in signing me. The Old Firm beckoned. So too did Manchester City and Falkirk, but I was registered as a probationary amateur player with St Mirren on 26 June 1963 because my dad argued that it was much better to be a big fish in a small pond, rather than a small fish in danger of being gobbled up in the big oceans of Parkhead and Ibrox. I understood his logic and it probably helped that the Buddies registered Dad as a scout and slipped him a few quid on the sly every week for me to spend on clothes for myself.

I suppose most people would say I should have jumped at the chance of joining Rangers when their chief scout Jimmy Smith came calling. My dad had always taken me to Ibrox but I took note of what he said about being just one of a handful of hopefuls. At times like that, when a big decision had to be made, I always turned to my folks. I played for my mother and father. Some people look down on folk like us. Dad didn't earn much and Mum supplemented the household income with the wages from her job as a school cleaner. We never had much money but no boy could have had a better childhood. My mother is a wonder. She told me that whatever job I did in life I would be all right as long as I gave everything I had to it. That stuck with me throughout my career.

Love Street was just five or six miles from home and I loved going there to train in the evening and to play on a Saturday. On weekdays, however, I was still locked into those marathon treks across the Clyde as an apprentice sparky. My first manager was Jackie Cox, a big, strapping chap who liked things done properly. That suited me perfectly and so did the trainer, Ernie Nash, an ex-Army officer who was always immaculately dressed. Everything had to be spot on for Ernie. There was never any slacking. If a drill lasted thirty seconds, then thirty seconds it was and woe betide any player who didn't come up to the mark.

Once people started to take an interest in me in St Mirren's famous thin black and white striped shirt, the inevitable nicknames and puns weren't long in coming. 'Educating Archie' was a highly popular radio comedy show, featuring a ventriloquist's dummy, which later transferred to television. Hell was going to freeze over before the newspaper headline writers missed the opportunity to associate me with the star of the show. I also became known as 'Crunch' or 'Crunchie' on account of my robust tackling – on reflection, I think this suited me better than being named after a dummy, even if Archie was a noisy, tiresome little so-and-so in a stripy blazer! My collection of nicknames grew along with my reputation – 'The Mighty Atom' and 'Tiny Terror' weren't too bad, I suppose, but 'Pint-sized Pixie' was cringe making.

I made my first-team debut in the 1964–65 season and must have set some kind of record because I was named the Buddies' Footballer of the Year at just seventeen and presented with a trophy and a gold watch at a dinner-dance in the Hunterhill Community Centre. My first senior match in October could hardly have gone better. We beat Dundee United 2–1 at home with a Tottie Beck winner, and one perceptive reporter, Joe Hamilton, was kind enough to write: 'Tiny tot Archie has everything it takes to become another Billy Steel . . . pace, power, shot, ball control and, above all, the cheeky confidence that all great players must have. After only one game, I am convinced he will become a hit in Scottish football.' Billy Steel? That was some comparison. Billy Steel was a great character and a Scottish international legend. He had a short spell as an amateur with St Mirren but was at his peak in 1947 when he signed for Derby County from Morton for what was then a British record transfer fee of £15,500. I was following in the great man's footsteps although, of course, I had no idea at the time. A while later I was chuffed to read an article on Billy in which he enthused: 'Archie is the sort of hard-working little player I like to watch.'

The press men also fancied that they saw in me more than a little of two superb wingers of the era, 'Wee' Willie Henderson and 'Jinky' Jimmy Johnstone. Willie was a Scotland great who had won every domestic honour in the game with Rangers by the time he was nineteen. He liked to get stuck in. Jimmy was a fiery redhead who enjoyed fabulous success with Celtic.

My reputation grew the afternoon Hearts came across from Edinburgh as league leaders and left with their tails between their legs after yours truly sparked a pitch invasion in the last minute. I just nipped in between two would-be tacklers and scored the winner in a 2–1 victory, dashing back to the centre circle, both arms held aloft towards the sky with hundreds of small boys spilling off the terraces and on to the pitch. The police had no chance. It's fair to say I was more popular in our camp than I was with the local constabulary but the only lasting damage was done to Hearts, because Kilmarnock pipped them for the championship in May on goal average.

Inevitably, the success I was enjoying was noted in high places – and by that I don't mean the Scottish Football Association. The dressing rooms at Rangers or Celtic were places where seasoned defenders of some repute did not take at all kindly to the prospect of little whippersnappers attempting to embarrass them and so it came to pass that I turned up with St Mirren at Ibrox to take on a Rangers side, which by now included my old pal Tottie Beck. Rangers had bigger fish to fry four days later – a European Cup tie against Inter Milan – but the minnows from Paisley almost lodged in their throats.

Two things stick out in my mind from this match. First, I 'scored' in the first half with a shot that struck the underside of the bar and bounced down clearly on the net side of the sawdust on the line. Result? Play on. Unbelievable. Second, I gave Davie Provan a thorough chasing for forty-five minutes and paid a hefty penalty. A few minutes into the second half I tried to go round Provan again and was summarily dropped right in front of the main stand. Quite how the referee, Hugh Phillips, didn't see that as an automatic sending-off offence was as bizarre as my goal that wasn't a goal. I don't consider myself a coward in any sense of the word, but I will readily admit to spending the rest of the afternoon giving Mr Provan a very wide berth and I'm sure he had the last laugh because Rangers won 1–0. I wouldn't be at all surprised if Davie dined out for a week or two on the fact that he had quite enjoyed 'educating' Archie.

I soon came down to earth with another bang. Before the 1965–66 season kicked off, St Mirren were involved in something called the Paisley Cup, a tournament involving Northampton Town among other clubs. It seems very odd now but at the time Northampton flickered briefly as really big news, having come all the way up from the old Fourth Division in England, and they were preparing to rub shoulders with the élite, such as Everton, Liverpool, Arsenal and Manchester United, for the first time. Unfortunately for me, they had a big, no-nonsense centre-half by the name of John Kurila who was built like a brick outhouse and he broke my standing left leg when he went right through me as I was turning on the halfway line. 'Kurila the Gorilla' opposing fans called him, and they weren't far wrong.

I was out of action for three months and my comeback match for the reserves against Kilmarnock proved to be another painful experience when I fractured my left leg again, this time in a different place. Just a kick, they said at the club, you'll soon be fine. Rest it. So Betty Maitland, who was my girlfriend at the time, and I took off for a weekend on a caravan site at Millport on Great Cumbrae, with another couple, Johnny and Irene. When the time came to catch the ferry back to the mainland, we were dashing to beat the clock and had to rush down the mile from the camp site to the terminal, me hobbling as fast as I could all the way. Not surprisingly, the left leg didn't feel too clever and when I next went in for training I expressed my fears that it was something more serious than just a knock. Still, St Mirren wouldn't have it and I trained Tuesdays and Thursdays for three weeks before complaining that things were getting really silly now. Eventually, an X-ray revealed the full extent of the damage.

My professional career could have been over before it had properly begun but word of my ability had started to filter south by now. Brentford put in an offer of £5,000 for me, which was rejected, and Bury, Leicester and Brighton were among other clubs reckoned to be interested. I just wanted to play and worked on my fitness like never before, especially bodybuilding exercises including practising my long-throwing technique. So I was a fit-again St Mirren player as the 1966–67 season approached, but it turned out to be bittersweet. Doug Millward, an American champion ten-pin bowler, had replaced Jackie Cox as manager. How on earth he got the job remains a mystery to me to this day. Let's just say he knew more about skittles than football. The record books will tell you that I became the first player in Scotland to come on as a substitute when I replaced Jim Clunie in a League Cup tie away to Clyde on 13 August but another match holds greater personal significance. On Christmas Eve, on a bone-hard pitch covered with a thin blanket of snow, which one pundit maintained was fit only for 'an eskimo with skates on', I scored a hat-trick against Ayr United. That became a collector's item because the only other time I achieved the feat was when Derby beat Boston United in an FA Cup replay in January 1974. I finished the season as St Mirren's top scorer with five goals, and if that tells you something about what a poor team we were, you probably won't be surprised to learn that we were relegated to the Second Division.

I was going down, too – down south. A new door was opening and, at nineteen, I was about to leave my home town for a place in Lancashire I had barely heard of – Preston.

3

LIPSTICK ON MY COLLAR

THE deal that took me from Love Street to Deepdale probably took less time to complete than the five hours it took to drive there from Paisley. Preston's Scottish scout Jim Scott had recommended me to North End, promising them that I could do a decent job, and their £13,000 bid was accepted by St Mirren. The only question remaining was did I fancy the move. I was an only child remember, England looked a long way away and this seemed a huge step, a big wrench not only for me, but also for my mother and father. They were both working but they promised to come to see me a couple of times a year and the close-season was much longer back in those days than it is now. It meant terrific upheaval all round but my mother is one of the most positive people you could ever wish to meet and she just said, 'Son, if you're ever going to make it as a professional footballer, you're going to have to take this opportunity.'

So that was my mind made up and I climbed into my green Hillman Minx, registration EAG 77D, and headed for Preston. That Hillman was the first car I ever bought, aged eighteen. It cost £780 and my parents gave me half the money. The registration turned out to be the happiest of omens, although I didn't have an inkling at the time – Elizabeth and Archie Gemmill, what a team!

From the day my transfer was registered, 24 May 1967, I was made to feel welcome at the club, which has a long and

14

distinguished history of links with Scottish footballers, stretching all the way back to the Invincibles of the 1880s. I wasn't what you might call a super scholar but I'd heard of the Invincibles, who dominated football when Queen Victoria and Charles Dickens were alive and kicking.

Preston's manager Jimmy Milne distinguished himself by always wearing a scone – better known in England as a flat cap – and the dressing room had more than its fair share of familiar accents with Scotsmen Alex Spark, Jim Forrest, Bertie Patrick and George Lyall, who was to become a great friend, in residence.

Betty and I were officially engaged on 15 July 1967 and I went back to Paisley for the party. Then it was time to concentrate on the new season and new opportunities. I went straight into the first team on the left wing and if I wasn't exactly the greatest thing since sliced bread on the pitch, the crowd quickly accepted me because I gave 100 per cent even when I wasn't playing particularly well. I ran here, there and everywhere and made my tackles. My involvement was total. To this day, whenever I return to Deepdale and go on the pitch before a match to make a presentation, I am assured of a marvellous reception, even from supporters far too young to have ever seen me pull on the famous white North End jersey.

Preston paid me £30 a week for starters and I earned a few more quid each week on Tuesdays and Thursdays, finishing my time as an apprentice electrician at a firm owned by Tom Finney. I like to think we've always had a practical streak in our family and kept our feet on the ground. It was a sensible precaution to have a trade to fall back on just in case the football went pear-shaped. Yet to this day, Betty will barely trust me to change a light-bulb, so perhaps it's a good thing that I did make it as a footballer.

My logic struck a chord with Mr Finney, of course – supporters of a certain vintage will know that one of the best players England has ever produced was also known as the 'Preston Plumber'. I often wondered if the great man would offer me any advice but he never did. A very quiet character, he seemed happy to stay in the background, content in his role as a director at Deepdale.

Life off the field and away from the wiring, however, was turning into one long struggle. There was more chance of Tom Finney pulling on his boots again to replace me in the number eleven shirt than there was of me finding somewhere I wanted to live. I'd been spoiled rotten at home, being provided with virtually anything and everything I ever wanted. At nineteen, I had still never eaten a fresh vegetable. I knew what I wanted to eat and my mother, bless her, always made sure I got it.

Preston found me digs, sharing a hotel room with Alex Spark. He went on to play for the first team but, tragically, lost a leg and died several years ago. The club were sure we would get on together famously but I liked my own space and just didn't enjoy the experience of having to share for the first time in my life, especially such a tiny room.

Next stop for Alex and me was a room in a house run by two young ladies – and that was even worse! They had loads of gentleman friends and hippy students hanging around all over the place. It was absolute turmoil and I couldn't put up with that place for very long either. After that I told Alex that I just had to get a room of my own and the club proudly boasted that they had found me the ideal digs just three or four minutes away from the ground. If I say it was a small semi-detached, typical of so many homes in the Preston-Blackburn area at the time, I'm being over-generous. This place was tiny and I walked in to be confronted by mother, father, son and daughter. My first thought as I was shown to my room was, 'How on earth are we all going to survive in this shoe box?' I'm sure they were a lovely family but when I came downstairs and found my lunch on the table that was it. A meat and potato pie floating in the middle of a bowl of tomato soup might cut it for some people, but I'd never encountered anything like it before. I'm ashamed to say, I went straight back upstairs, grabbed my belongings and fled, muttering something along the lines of, 'Awfully sorry, big mistake,' under my breath.

Back at Deepdale, the response from the long-suffering receptionist was an incredulous, 'Not you, again!' I tried several other places after that, which never suited me in any way, shape or form, when suddenly word reach the club that Derek and Dorothy, Mr and Mrs Grave to me, wouldn't mind having a couple of players again. Preston had successfully lodged some youngsters with them before but now they were adamant they wanted just two, so that was me and the long-suffering Alex again. I couldn't stand sharing though, and after four nights with barely a wink of sleep I told Alex I would go back to the club and find something else and he could stay. Then came a message from Mrs Grave that she and Derek had changed their minds. They wanted one paying lodger and they wanted it to be me. The upshot was two-and-a-half absolutely fabulous years at what swiftly became a real home from home. Dorothy's greatest success was getting one of the world's most adamant vegetable-haters to reform the habits of a lifetime. It started with a carrot, then a little bit of turnip and before you knew it there I was wolfing down cabbage and every other kind of greens you could buy on Preston market. I was a vegetable junkie!

Life with the Scots lads was good, as well. Each day we would go down to the Fairway Café after training for bacon butties and mugs of tea. The jukebox had great music by the Rolling Stones, the Beatles and Creedence Clearwater Revival, among others. Can you imagine suggesting unwinding like that to today's young professional footballers with their £50,000-a-week wages, night-clubs, London hotels and flocks of women? They'd laugh in your face. Looking back, we had so many genuinely good laughs and happy times with bacon butties and mugs of tea that maybe it's not surprising Preston weren't too successful.

Still, things were going well for me and I swapped my Hillman Minx for a very tasty MG 1100, which set me back over £1,000, and after Betty, it was my pride and joy. It looked good parked outside the Grave's house at No. 4 Kane Street and obviously represented a bit of a temptation to a couple of likely lads.

I got in late one Wednesday night after playing in a home match and was woken a few hours later by an alarm going off outside. I thought no more of it until Dorothy came charging into my room at ten past eight the next morning, all of a fluster, to tell me, 'Archie, Archie. Quick. You've got to get up. Someone's stolen your car.'

Now a man sometimes has to get his priorities in order and this was a day off for me after a hard night's graft on the pitch. Although I say it myself, I am a world champion sleeper and always have been. If Dorothy thought for one minute that the small matter of having my sports car stolen was going to rouse me from my pit, she was very much mistaken.

'Thanks very much, Mrs Grave. I'll sort it all out later,' was my casual response to the drama as I turned over and went blissfully back to sleep. I'm sure she couldn't believe quite what was happening. I must have finally surfaced at about 11.30 and reported the theft to the police. Three or four hours later they called back to inform me the car had been found safe and sound in Liverpool, so I just hopped on the train and drove it home.

Once I'd got my feet under the table in the Grave household, I settled to produce some useful football for Preston, although at first I got the impression from some fans that they would have preferred the club to have signed Tony Green, who moved from Albion Rovers to Blackpool, where he was a huge success. Preston and Blackpool being fierce rivals, the feeling was perhaps understandable. My new nickname was 'Go Go' and the papers in England were at least spelling my surname correctly – fame at last, even if I was still 'Gemmell' in the Scottish press. By Christmas 1967 I had emerged, according to one report, as a 'general of the highest order, not only with some intelligent midfield scheming but also with resolute defence and sharpness near goal.' General was over-egging the pudding a bit, I thought. I wasn't that far up the ranks by any means and felt much more like a humble foot soldier.

Preston were a struggling Second Division side virtually all the time I was there but every team we played had a character or two you might learn from, or try to outwit. Off the top of my head I recall playing against Ron Atkinson (Oxford), Tony Currie (Sheffield United), Eamon Dunphy (Millwall), Gordon Taylor (Bolton), Bruce Rioch (Aston Villa) and Tony Hateley (Birmingham). What seems like a lifetime later, Peter Shilton and I were lining up together for Nottingham Forest but I never let him forget the time I scored against him twice, outjumping the future England goalkeeper to head the first goal in a 2–1 win over Leicester – impressive, eh, for a small fella described as 'five feet four of bounce and belligerence'. That was me all right that afternoon at Deepdale because a few months earlier I had been booed after coming on as a substitute. On this occasion I felt I had something to prove and so, as one report had it: 'Gemmill declared war on Leicester in the twenty-fourth minute when he outjumped the City defence to beat Peter Shilton with a magnificent header.'

Unfortunately, I was in and out of the side like a fiddler's elbow, flavour of the month one moment, not to the manager's taste the next, but there were occasional treats in the FA Cup. In January 1968, the third round took us to Queen's Park Rangers and into the west London lair of Rodney Marsh. QPR were top of the Second Division and, with home advantage, no one gave us a prayer because they had beaten us 2–0 the previous week. The manager had done his homework properly on poor Rodney, who barely got a kick, and we won 3–1. A fading pink cutting in a dusty old scrapbook reads: 'When Archie ("Go Go") Gemmill in injury time sealed the surprise show with a goal that had a touch of Tom Finney about it, Loftus Road rose to him – and the others who had routed Rangers. Little Archie, a mini powerhouse of energy and running, laid on the first of Ray Charnley's two goals with a left-wing sprint that might have qualified him for the Olympics. Believe me, he has the makings of a GREAT player. Gemmill, collecting the ball in his own half and swerving zigzaggedly past the lunging legs of four defenders, twisted the knife when he slipped in the third goal. His somersaults of delight were understandable.'

Later that year came one of the most important, memorable and happiest days of my life. Betty and I were married in Paisley at 3 p.m. on Wednesday, 2 October 1968. We set up home in Lytham St Annes and the loneliness and homesickness that had been part of my life as a professional footballer became things of the past. It was a wonderful day. Betty's younger sister June was bridesmaid while my club colleague George Lyall played a blinder as best man. Since the football season was well under way, there was no time for a honeymoon and I was under strict orders to be back in Preston for training at ten the following morning. As we left the reception to travel back to Lancashire in a convoy of cars, I got a traditional Scottish send-off, being thoroughly manhandled by the male guests. We stopped for a coffee at a roadside café in Kirkpatrick, a village just outside Gretna Green. It was a greasy spoon job used by lorry drivers and packed to the rafters. Of course, it was already dark and when I walked into this brightly lit café all the truckers started laughing. One look in the mirror explained their sudden outburst of hilarity. I was covered in bright red lipstick with rude arrows pointing down to my nether-regions. My shirt was all over the place and I was covered in confetti. It was perfectly obvious that we were newlyweds and all the truckers cheered and wished us all the best, which was nice despite being quite embarrassing.

Betty and I headed straight to our brand new three-bedroomed semi in Tewkesbury Drive, for which we had taken out a huge mortgage of £5,000. We could hardly wait to see all the new furniture, ordered in Glasgow and delivered direct from the makers, but when we eventually arrived in the wee small hours, it was to find that everything had been delivered except any of the beds. Hence our first night of marital bliss was spent on the floor – very romantic.

It was easy for me to leave for training the next morning, but I felt very proud of Betty as I kissed her goodbye on the doorstep. She had just left her country, family, friends, job and everything familiar to her to come to a strange place where she barely knew a soul. She had such big plans to be a posh housewife and stuck it for three months. Then she went out and got a job as a secretary at Brookcorner Garage where she made some great friends and went on to settle nicely into her new life.

Things were changing at Deepdale, too. Jimmy Milne's time had come and gone and by November 1968, Bobby Seith was in the hot seat. He was another Scot, a former Dundee player and Rangers coach. We should have got on but rarely did.

In February 1969, Preston were back in west London for two epic ties with Chelsea in the FA Cup fourth round. Chelsea were a First Division team of all the talents, and the replays followed a 0–0 stalemate at Deepdale. We were on the verge of going out 2–0 in the first midweek replay when the floodlights failed with fifteen minutes to go and the match had to be abandoned. Back we went again to Stamford Bridge and after ninety minutes we were through to meet Stoke City in the next round, or so we thought. The referee somehow found enough stoppage time for Dave Webb to equalise after ninety-one minutes and Charlie Cooke to score the winner in the ninety-third minute – despite me desperately sliding in behind him and trying to boot him up the backside!

Seith had a reputation for being a defensive manager but I never understood why he didn't trust me, especially after one comment he made that same month. 'Many people down here have likened him to Billy Bremner, but I disagree,' he said. 'He's like Archie Gemmill and nobody else, and a natural if ever there was one.' Natural or not, the 1969–70 season dawned with the

Lancashire Evening Post Pink 'Un claiming: 'Gemmill has always looked a player full of potential, but it has never been fully realised.' I set about realising my potential that autumn with a vengeance. By October, the Pink reckoned: 'When Archie sets off, hurtling directly at the opposition, you can almost feel them quake and no one really looks capable of stopping him. His point of balance is such that defenders cannot knock him off the ball and his speed is quite devastating.'

That month we turned over Norwich 2–1 on their own patch and the Canaries manager Ron Saunders said something that still brings a grin to my face today. In the press conference afterwards, one journalist ventured timidly that, 'Gemmill looked very useful going forward,' to which Ron is supposed to have roared, 'And bloody sideways, backwards, diagonally and upwards.'

As for Seith, it's fair to say we didn't exactly see eye to eye and I clashed with him because he wanted to play me as an out-and-out winger. There was a stand-off because I told him quite plainly that I wasn't prepared to play out on the left, I didn't feel I was involved enough, so he didn't play me, and for six months I must have sat on the substitutes' bench about twenty times, getting splinters in my backside. I seemed to be the odd one out and you never improve your game sitting on the bench. Results weren't going particularly well but I had mixed feelings about that. I'm loyal but I've got my pride as well. Of course I wanted Preston to be successful but I wanted them to be catching the headlines with me doing my bit for the cause – not stuck in limbo land.

The battle raged on between Seith, me and the fans about my best position. One letter to the Pink 'Un argued: 'Gemmill in particular must never be allowed to revert to midfield as his sheer speed, guts and determination will worry the best defences. I'll stick my neck out by saying that wee Archie is the sharpest striker in the Football League today and Mr Seith deserves severely censuring for withdrawing him from the firing line.'

The new decade dawned unhappily for me. Brian Clough always swore blind that he signed me without ever seeing me play but he was wrong, although to be fair to the Gaffer, if he'd blinked he could have missed me. Preston pulled First Division Derby out of the hat at home in the third round of the FA Cup. Clough's team took us too lightly and we got a 1–1 draw on Saturday, 3 January. Two days later, Bobby Brown announced that he had selected me for the Scotland Under-23 squad and there was a chance I could make my first-team debut against Wales in Aberdeen later in the month. The squad also included such up-and-coming youngsters as Kenny Dalglish, Peter Lorimer, Willie Carr, Asa Hartford and John O'Hare. Delight turned to despair just two nights later when I damaged my thigh on a rock-hard, frosty Baseball Ground pitch and had to come off twenty minutes before the end as Derby strolled to a 4–1 win in the replay. Hoping against hope, I prayed I would recover in time to face Wales but it wasn't to be and with the deepest reluctance I had to cry off from the party training at Largs.

Bobby Brown promised he wouldn't forget me and proved to be as good as his word. On 4 March 1970 I won my one and only Under-23 cap for Scotland, against England at Sunderland. That freezing cold night, four young men out there on Roker Park were destined to play a significant part in Derby County's future. John O'Hare, who was already at the Baseball Ground, and I played for Scotland while Roy McFarland – another player signed by Brian Clough – and Colin Todd, then with Sunderland, represented England.

As far as I'm concerned, it was a totally forgettable game and the memories I do have of the night are about as welcome as the weather. We had been playing for about an hour when, with England leading 3–1, the referee brought a halt to proceedings because the snow was so heavy it was making a mockery of any sort of constructive football. That was tough on Peter Osgood, who had scored a couple, and Brian Kidd, who had stuck away

23

England's other goal. Our solitary reply was credited to Todd as an own goal.

Gordon Wignall, a lovely man who worked with Betty at Brookcorner Garage, had driven her all the way to the North East to witness her man's big night at first hand, so while the rest of the Scotland squad stayed tucked up snugly in the Roker Hotel that evening, I travelled home with Gordon and Betty and soon rather wished I hadn't. The snow was about six inches deep, making the roads back to the Lancashire coast treacherous. Virtually all the signs had been obliterated and we eventually limped home at 3.30 in the morning.

Despite the snow, I must have left some sort of impression on Wearside because within days the rumour mill was working overtime and I was suddenly being linked with a £100,000 transfer to Sheffield Wednesday, Everton, Sunderland and Tottenham Hotspur, none of which materialised, although after we were relegated to the Third Division at the end of the season, I nearly made it to Everton.

That summer of 1970 was a happy time. The Lytham St Annes branch of Preston North End FC was flourishing with team-mates living all around us – Graham Hawkins next door, Ken Knighton two houses away and Clive Clark just across the road – and Mum and Dad came down to stay.

One sunny day, Betty and I decided to take Mum and Dad to Blackpool. We were walking along the front when we came across a clairvoyant, Gypsy Rose Lee, and agreed that, just for a giggle, it might be fun if Betty had her fortune told. In she went with Mum, while Dad and I went to another fortune-teller further down the Golden Mile. When we eventually all met up again I noticed Betty was looking impressed and very flushed. Palms duly crossed with silver, Gypsy Rose Lee had taken one look at Betty's hand and told her that she was married to a professional sportsman and that she was having a child. That kind of took the wind out of Betty's sails. She was six weeks pregnant. How could the fortune-teller know these things? Betty was then plainly told that 22 September was going to be a very significant day in her life and that she would be moving to live in a place beginning with the letter D. It was not until I phoned her from Derby, having just passed my medical, that Betty said to me, 'Do you realise what date it is?' Uncanny! I signed for Derby on 22 September and have since always harboured a sneaking suspicion that Gypsy Rose Lee might have been Brian Clough or Peter Taylor in drag.

4

BACON, EGGS AND BRIAN CLOUGH

H OW charismatic was Brian Clough? How strong were his powers of persuasion? I would be an extremely wealthy man today if I had a fiver for each time I've been asked those questions. 'Very' and 'considerable' are two straightforward answers but they always leave those people seeking some sort of special insight into the Gaffer feeling rather short-changed in my experience. So for them and others with an interest, I am happy to provide the facts behind the transfer that took me from Preston to Derby for a fee of £66,000. Incidentally, Betty had a couple of choice words for me when she discovered the full details of the deal over which I eventually shook hands, especially as she'd married a man who considered having a telephone in his own home an unwarranted extravagance at that time.

My money had recently been doubled to £60 a week by Alan Ball senior, Preston's new manager, but in September 1970 I was definitely going to Everton. Months earlier, the men at Goodison Park had been crowned champions of England and here was their manager, Harry Catterick, generously offering me a four-year contract with a £5,000 signing-on fee and wages starting at £225 a week, rising to £250, £275 and then £300 in the final year. Yet I was to join Derby for £70 a week, no signing-on fee, a colour television and the promise I'd get my front room re-carpeted. Everton were preparing to play in the European Cup and were shortly to eliminate Borussia Moenchengladbach. Derby had just started their second season in the top flight with the Watneys Cup on their sideboard.

If truth be told, at first I had no intention of leaving Preston after my money had gone up from £30 a week. I don't care whether you play for Scunthorpe or Real Madrid, if you go in for a pay rise and get your salary doubled, you can't complain. I had already warned Ball, 'You can double my wages or I'm off', because I knew there were an awful lot of players at the club on considerably more than me – Alan Spavin, Derek Temple, Jim McNab and our Irish goalkeeper Alan Kelly, for example. My argument was that I didn't really want to display my talents, in which I still had the greatest confidence, in a lower league. If I had to, I would, but at a price. The three years I spent at Preston were remarkable for two things – the look on the manager's face when I asked for a rise after we were relegated, and the way my transfer from them came about soon after.

Ball arrived that summer with a reputation as a hard taskmaster and immediately lived up to that billing in pre-season training. I was to experience very demanding training later on at Derby and Nottingham Forest, designed to get you through a successful season, but what Ball put us through was something else. His so-called stamina-building was torture – run, run, run. I have always taken pride in my reputation for having a big lung capacity, a good engine some call it. I was extremely good at the short and long stuff but, although I wasn't physically sick, I was in a slightly distressed state after some of those sessions. Ball had the rest of the team literally on their knees. No one was complaining come the end of the season, though, as Preston were crowned champions of the Third Division. We were not too bad at the start, either, but after a couple of weeks Ball suddenly pulled me to one side and told me there was a bid from Everton on the table, it was good money for Preston and would I be interested.

Interested? I was delighted with the notion and Ball twice took me to visit his son Alan Ball junior who, along with Howard

Kendall and Colin Harvey, formed the 'Holy Trinity' in midfield for Everton. The young Everton player was impressive. Already a World Cup winner of course, he had been one of England's most impressive performers that summer during the 1970 finals in Mexico. Alan told me how good it was at Everton and how big the club was – not that he had to do a big selling job on me. You couldn't get any better than Kendall, Harvey and Ball in the middle of the park then. I was more than happy to sign for the league champions and I'd just have to take my chance on getting into the team. I also enjoyed a couple of interviews with Harry Catterick, a very nice, well-spoken man who expressed himself plainly and simply. He didn't have to lay anything on with a trowel because his achievements at Everton already spoke for themselves. We discussed wages and I could hardly believe what he was offering me. It was a different world from Preston. As I'm sure all keen students of the football pools know, Littlewoods have their headquarters in Liverpool and I came out of my talks with Catterick feeling as though I'd just got eight score-draws up on my coupon.

So the deal was set up and more or less agreed before what was supposed to be my final match for Preston. I expected to play but was suddenly told to watch the game from a seat in the stands. Ball also told me to come to the club the following morning. I knew then that it was either to sign for Everton or something had happened.

My mind was racing on the drive to Deepdale that Sunday and Ball didn't beat about the bush.

'Derby are in for you as well,' he told me. 'They've matched the £70,000 Everton are prepared to pay for you.'

I replied that I wasn't really interested in what Brian Clough had to offer. 'Let's get the Everton deal done,' I said, but Ball definitely wanted to meet Clough. Call it ego or just natural inquisitiveness, Ball was up for it. Like so many other managers in the game he probably wanted to experience the great man in action and then go home, taking great delight in thinking he'd beaten him. I was virtually an Everton player now, after all.

Betty was not so easily swayed. When I got home she was down on all fours, heavily pregnant with our son Scot, washing the kitchen floor. I told her Brian Clough was on his way over to talk terms and she replied in some distress, 'Oh, no, not that man. I can't stand him.' I wrapped a comforting arm round Betty to try to calm her down and told her we had no choice in the matter as he was already on his way, but with a bit of luck she wouldn't even have to meet him.

So the scene was set and that night we all met at the Pack Horse Hotel in Bolton – Ball, Brian Clough, assistant manager Peter Taylor, the Derby secretary Stuart Webb and me. There was no doubt who was in charge from the moment he swept into the lounge bar. Clough dominated the room, deciding exactly how he wanted the bar staff to arrange the table for our negotiations. Brash, big-headed, just as he had appeared to me on television, Brian had everyone running around after him. I think he even greeted me in time-honoured fashion with the phrase, 'Do you know who I am?' while the gist of what Ball tried to put across immediately was, 'Archie's got everything he wants – he's signing for Everton.'

The drinks arrived and I had an orange juice – I was teetotal in those days. It wasn't until I celebrated winning the league championship for the first time that I sampled alcohol properly with a glass of champagne. A couple of halves of lager and a bottle of wine arrived for the others.

Any thoughts Ball had that he might control the situation started slipping away and he began to look distinctly uncomfortable as Clough outlined his plans for the future with total conviction. It wasn't a case of him saying, 'With you, Archie, we will be a better team,' but the matter-of-fact way in which he stated that Derby would win the League and cups, and other great triumphs would follow. Ball started that evening convinced there could only be one winner and now he wasn't so sure as he summoned me into the gents for an urgent pep talk.

'Don't forget you're signing for Everton in the next couple of days,' he said as we stood together at the urinals, just as Taylor joined us.

'It doesn't matter what you do,' Taylor said. 'The boy will be signing for us,' and he calmly washed his hands and walked out. I do believe I saw the colour drain from Ball's face.

It was getting late, my head was spinning, I was tired and the only place I wanted to be was at home with Betty. I announced my departure and I think Ball retired hurt but the other three jumped up and said they were more than happy to come home with me. I led the way in my own car and Webb followed at the wheel of a big Mercedes with Clough and Taylor as passengers. As I said, we didn't have a phone in the house. When I wanted to call my mother in Scotland, I was happy to walk to the phone box at the end of the road. Consequently, I could not forewarn Betty and her face was an absolute picture of horror when I walked in closely followed by Brian Clough and the others. By this time I had told him what Betty thought of him and he walked right up to her and told her how 'radiant' she looked.

'I believe you hate me,' he added.

Betty, embarrassed, replied, 'Well, I hate the man I see on television called Brian Clough but I'll wait until I get to know you properly before I make up my mind.'

Neither of them could have known that night how fond they would become of each other over the years.

If somebody needed to get in touch with me urgently, Ken Knighton would always pop round with a message. So it was that Ken arrived about an hour later to announce, 'Your mam's on the phone, Archie.' I made my apologies to the Derby contingent and discovered Ball on the other end of the line, pleading with me not to sign anything. The 'opposition' might have got away with it once but I'm sure Clough and company twigged what was up when Ken came round again a few minutes later to inform me my mother needed to clarify something. This time I found Harry Catterick on the line, insisting urgently, 'Don't do anything. We'll sort everything out in the morning.'

I returned to tell the party, 'I'm away to my bed. I'm signing nothing tonight.' With that, Clough plonked himself down on the fireside rug, took off his shoes and announced he would sleep there for the night. Betty might have been six months pregnant but the Gemmills had certain standards when it came to hospitality and as it was perfectly obvious he was not going to go with the other two, Betty offered him the use of our guest room.

That night there was a serious conversation between Betty and me before lights out. She kept reminding me of the family plans we delighted in talking about all the time. How we would proudly walk our baby down the promenade in Lytham, a mere five minutes from our lovely home, and later let the toddler paddle in the sea in the warm evenings, and how much fun the three of us would have at Blackpool Pleasure Beach. Moving to Goodison Park didn't mean moving home and then, of course, there was Everton's fabulous offer. Betty kept reminding me of that amazing deal on the table. It must have looked a generous one to anybody in the game, let alone someone like me who was plying his trade in the Third Division at the time. Going to Goodison meant joining the English league champions and we could stay in our home with friends around who would help Betty through the childbirth, and Lytham was such a beautiful place to live. Later, Brian assured Betty the scenery in the Derbyshire Peak District was out of this world but when I did finally take her up there and she got out of the car to look, she said, 'Well, if he thinks this is fabulous, he's obviously never been to Scotland.'

I was prepared to fight for a first-team place at Everton, of course I was, but it pays to be realistic and how long would it have been before I broke up the Harvey-Kendall-Ball partnership? Getting his famous big head down in the bedroom downstairs was a man who really looked like he was going places. Derby had taken the Second Division title by storm in 1969, finished fourth in their first season in the top flight and here he was promising me my First Division debut at West Bromwich Albion at the weekend. Oh, and then there was the little matter of Cloughie guaranteeing me that I would win my first cap for Scotland within the year. Derby already had great players, he said, and there were more to come. The only way the club was heading was up, up, up. Titles, cups, Europe – it was all laid out there for me simply to reach out and grasp. I believed him. No, more than that, I believed *in* him. Such was the level of Brian Clough's power of persuasion, and his enthusiasm was catching.

Betty got up in the morning and started to prepare breakfast for the three us. She heard someone come into the kitchen and turned around, expecting to see me. Standing there rubbing his hands together and dressed in no more than his boxer shorts stood Brian Clough, the very man she had witnessed so many times on television, mouthing off at some poor sod. He was delighted to see that he was going to get some bacon and eggs and, after getting dressed, proceeded to sit down and eat a hearty breakfast. Before I had a chance to put my last forkful into my mouth he was dragging me into the sitting room to finalise our negotiations and to sign all the papers he put in front of me. Then I had to drive to Deepdale to pick up my boots.

It was a complete departure in several senses because I never saw or spoke to either Harry Catterick or Alan Ball senior again, although I did have to grin when I saw Ball quoted in the *Lancashire Evening Post*, complaining, 'I feel sick. We shouldn't have to sell good players.'

I drove to Derby, passed my medical and within days had moved into the Midland Hotel, which was to be my home for the next four or five months. The Baseball Ground and Derby's training headquarters in Sinfin Lane were no great shakes but, then again, Deepdale and where Preston used to train on the local recreation ground were hardly what you'd call opulent.

I'd made friends with John McGovern within about five minutes and the friendship endures to this day. Willie Carlin was another player who went out of his way to make me feel at home, even though I think everyone in the club, Willie included, already had a shrewd idea that I had been recruited to replace him. Derby lost 2–1 at the Hawthorns on 26 September and Willie was soon on his way to Leicester City, but for me the glory days were only just beginning.

5

WELCOME TO INTERNATIONAL FOOTBALL

T HERE was a vibrancy about the town and the club, a sense of excitement and anticipation you could almost taste. Derby should have been looking forward to playing in Europe, in the old Inter Cities Fairs Cup, which Leeds went on to win that season, but certain financial irregularities had led to them being banned from playing all foreign opposition for a year. I don't know what Juventus, Barcelona and Bayern Munich would have made of Dave Mackay but in Derby everyone looked up to the big man. He made you very proud to be a fellow Scot.

Clough had somehow coaxed him out of returning to Hearts from Tottenham in 1968 and converted one of football's great rampaging box-to-box midfield men into a centre-half who could read a game as easily as if it was a child's nursery rhyme. Mackay possessed a pair of immensely gifted feet to go with his magnificent physique, nerves of steel and the shrewdest of brains. Above all, Dave Mackay was a winner – whether it was five-a-sides, cards or tiddlywinks, Dave just had to win, and in 1969 he'd shared the prestigious football writers' Footballer of the Year award with Manchester City skipper Tony Book.

The man was a colossus both on and off the pitch, a larger than life character held in the highest esteem at every club he played for and idolised by supporters. A competitor from first minute to last, he simply loved playing football and he went out on the pitch every time to prove he was the best player on the park. He totally dominated a large percentage of opponents by his sheer physical strength. Some punters were misguided enough to think he wasn't much more than a bruiser but Dave was blessed with phenomenal talent. He could pass the ball like a dream with either foot and, for a converted midfield player, he read defensive situations as well as Bobby Moore. I think it's fair to say that Brian Clough's revolution at the Baseball Ground would have taken much longer without Dave Mackay at centre-half and the club would not have won promotion so quickly. He revelled in proving people wrong, that was Dave Mackay's pleasure.

The lads could have been forgiven for thinking I was a stereotypical little Scot with a chip on his shoulder after an early problem I had with Alan Hinton. I'd had enough of Hinton almost before I got to know him properly. He was the left-winger in the white boots who could put the ball on a sixpence, but would he give it to me? Would he hell. For two or three matches in a row I'd win possession, feed the ball out wide to Alan, make a forward run for the return pass and – nothing. Blanked, I wondered if my name was the Invisible Man rather than Archie Gemmill. If I wasn't constantly involved in the ebb and flow of the game, I felt awful. Hinton would look in my direction and, it seemed to me, elect to try to find any of the other available white shirts on the pitch. Frustration didn't even come close to how I felt.

Eventually, one half-time, I was determined to have it out with him. He had a kick on him like a mule on steroids, it was that powerful, but he was never the most combative of players. Maybe those famous white boots he wore didn't help. His nickname on the Baseball Ground terraces was 'Gladys' on account of his aversion to the rough stuff. Well, this confrontation threatened to develop into something a little more serious than handbags between 'Gladys' and me. We had a right set to.

Spit on the pavement in Derby town centre in those days and Brian Clough would get to hear of it, yet here were two of his first-team players arguing the toss right under his nose. Maybe it wasn't the most intelligent fight I've ever picked. I was a relative newcomer while Alan was a firmly established top name at the club. The immediate result was swift, emphatic and brutal.

'You,' said the Gaffer, pointing straight at my flushed face, 'can keep on running because that's all you can do. Alan can play, you can't. The minute you stop running, you're out of the team.'

I'd had my card marked, been told in no uncertain terms, but the funny thing is Hinton used to pass the ball down the line to me a lot more after that episode. I felt much more involved and we started to get along like a house on fire. I never did discover whether the Gaffer pulled Alan to one side and ordered him to pass to me but that little tale is another example of Brian's man management.

Unsavoury incidents like that were very few and far between, though. A sense of camaraderie flourished between the players and a strong bond developed as we changed at the Baseball Ground and shared lifts to what, looking back, I can laughingly call our 'training headquarters' at Sinfin Lane where the facilities were non-existent.

Back at the ground, between the players' entrance and the dressing room, we'd noticed a redundant area underneath the stand, no more than about twelve yards long, with a wooden wall at one end. One day the lads had the inspired idea of turning this dud cell into a shooting gallery and a craze was born. Someone would bang in a shot and get out of the way in time for the next man to seize on the rebound and try his luck. Okay, so it might not sound much in today's high-tech age, but suddenly players who normally pitched up five minutes before the deadline to get changed were arriving at the Baseball Ground an hour early in an effort to be crowned Derby's unofficial Top of the Shots. The competition was razor-sharp between Dave, Alan Durban, John O'Hare, Kevin Hector, John McGovern, Hinton and later Colin Todd. We'd happily spend hours sweating away in that cramped space, refining our shooting techniques. The Gaffer could often be found there, too, with his sons Simon and Nigel.

Training with Brian Clough was basic, although he'd happily run the legs off you in pre-season, arranging a small mountain of pre-season friendlies and then ensuring fitness and conditioning levels were topped up as and when necessary. He was big on building camaraderie between the players, splitting us into rival camps for ball games. The really serious stuff, apart from the matches of course, were our five-a-sides and they were treated as an important part of the training regime. Whether it was England v. Foreigners or Young v. Old, the atmosphere was intense and the games could last indefinitely. Today, five-a-sides at some clubs can end up with scores of 20–4. Who are they deluding? Who do they think is gaining any benefit whatsoever from a one-sided score of that nature? Sometimes, the youngsters, including McGovern, John Robson, Roy McFarland and me, would strain every muscle to put one over the old sweats Frank Wignall, Willie Carlin, Mackay and Durban, and then the Gaffer would casually announce, 'Next goal wins, lads,' and the atmosphere would get even spicier.

He was a great man for rest, though, and after a busy period of back-to-back matches his last words heading out of the dressing room for his tea on a Saturday night would often be, 'Oh, by the way, lads, see you all on Thursday.' At some big-city clubs at the start of the 1970s that might have been the green light for a four-day bender. A drink culture has existed in football throughout my career but while I did meet a few players at Derby who were fond of a pint, they were never remotely in the same class as Jimmy Greaves, George Best or the Chelsea set for putting it away. Ours was never what you might call a boozers' club for several very good reasons. Even though we were to finish only ninth in May 1971, the players sensed something special was happening on the mudheap at the antiquated Baseball Ground, tucked away behind row upon row of terraced houses in an impoverished part of town, and we all desperately wanted to be in on it: We were a bit too shrewd to toss it away on a raft of lager and spirits, and we respected Clough enormously. You would have had to be simple or have a serious drink problem to risk getting bombed out of the club. Let's face it, we'd never have got away with going on the razzle.

I was far too concerned with trying to establish myself as a First Division footballer, competing against internationals every week, ever to think about living the high life and, in any case, my marriage to Betty was rock-solid from day one. She was pregnant and living in Lytham. I had a quiet room at the back of the Midland Hotel next to the railway station and, by and large, my refuelling habits were fairly mundane and predictable – cereal and toast for breakfast, a sandwich and coffee with the lads in town after training and an evening meal back at the hotel.

The freedom Clough gave us was highly beneficial for me. There was no messing around with Sunday football, so after the match on Saturday night I was straight back to Betty and there I stayed until 6.30 on a Tuesday morning when I'd kiss her goodbye and start the next working week with the drive to training.

Derby may have grown somewhat – it's a city now – but back then it was very much a smallish, provincial Midlands town and we knew the Gaffer had his spies out all over the shop, or at least that's what we suspected. Anyone spotted out on the town a couple of nights on the trot being a bit, shall we say, loud was liable to cop for a serious ear-bashing. The Gaffer knew our watering holes and one of the favourites was a tiny little pub called Mr Jorrocks, just off the market place at the top of Derby's trendy Sadler Gate and near a nightclub or two. I was still happily teetotal but would sometimes go along with my good friends John McGovern and Willie Carlin to be sociable before going on with them for a meal. If Clough didn't know exactly what the score was, rest assured Peter Taylor would have his finger on the pulse.

The Dynamic Duo were simply the Gaffer and Pete to us – a good guy, bad guy relationship, I suppose, with Pete being the jovial member of the twosome. Taylor's job was to find the players for Derby, Clough's was to bring the best out of them. There's never been a double act in football to touch them and I doubt there ever will be. Pete could be extremely humorous, full of witty one-liners and always capable of breaking the ice, but it would be misleading to portray him as the one you'd turn to if you had a sense of grievance, rather than the Gaffer. If there was a problem, you had to go into the manager's office and tackle them both.

On a professional level, Pete was a master at unearthing any vice in a player, whether it be drinking, gambling or women. That certainly wouldn't put him off a signing if he believed the individual concerned could play and, sometimes, I even reckon Pete saw it as a challenge to pick up a so-called 'bad egg' and help turn him into a diamond.

Talking of diamonds, the Derby public were fantastic. It's a genuine football-loving town and they never gave us a moment's bother – apart from when fixtures against Nottingham Forest were on the horizon. Then we'd be left in no doubt about how fierce the rivalry was between the two clubs separated by a mere fifteen miles of the A52 dual carriageway. That rivalry was something I had never really experienced before and it brought out something near the very best in me two months into my career with the Rams.

The level of expectation and sense of excitement built steadily throughout that week at the end of November as the press and local TV cranked things up, and there was a full house at the City Ground, including the massed ranks of Derby fans, spread all over the East Stand terraces, creating a hell of a din. We didn't let them down either, recovering from 2–1 down to win 4–2. I scored for the first time for my new club and had a hand in all our other goals. Against hated rivals, that helped make me a great favourite with the Derby crowd.

It's always struck me as a bit odd, and unfair in some ways, that the fans will take to you if you run here, there and everywhere at 100mph, even if the end product is zero, whereas another player who doesn't run so much, John McGovern for example, can spend his entire career largely unsung, unloved and un-appreciated. Happily for John, one person was prepared to sing his praises, loved him dearly and did appreciate his talents – Brian Clough. John had such a terrible, lopsided running style, you'd think he had a broken shoulder. In fact, he was a far better footballer than people gave him credit for. He was the one who sat there in midfield, constantly breaking up opposition attacks with an uncanny sense of timing and anticipation before turning defence into attack with some deft footwork. Some creative midfield players of the highest calibre would arrive at the Baseball Ground with the opposition and, ninety minutes later, we'd be asking ourselves, 'Was so-and-so really out there today?' because John had done such a fabulous marking job. That was one of his greatest attributes as a player. McGovern was in the Derby line-up that day in Nottingham but I stole all the headlines.

I felt established by the time Christmas arrived but I was still star-struck when Manchester United rolled into town on Boxing Day with a forward line that read: Morgan, Best, Charlton, Kidd and Law. The previous year I'd been plugging away in a pretty nondescript Preston team and here I was facing George Best. At twenty-four, he was only a year older than me but he had been in United's first team since the age of seventeen and already had a list of achievements, honours, medals and international caps as long as your arm – or at least that's the way it seemed to a young man from Paisley who had been facing Bury in the Third Division three months earlier.

The game was a cracker on an icy pitch, finishing 4–4 when, in truth, it could have been anything there were so many thrills and spills and so much goalmouth action.

If I was thrilled to be sharing a stage with Best and 'The King'

Denis Law, that was nothing to the excitement I felt on Saturday, 2 January. We'd played at Chester in the third round of the FA Cup, I'd scored in a 2–1 win and had travelled back to Derby with the team. A few of us were settling down to watch 'Match of the Day' on the television in the public lounge at the Midland when a porter came to tell me there was a phone call for me – Scot had been safely delivered at 10.03 p.m. in Paisley. I can recall mumbling, 'That's great,' and going back to watch the football sporting a wide grin. The boss was there and noticed the look on my face right away. When I told him my great news he insisted that I take the overnight train to Glasgow, but said that he wanted me back on Monday morning for training. That sounded good to me, and it gave me time to watch the end of the football highlights and pack a bag.

It made perfect sense for Betty to have the baby in Paisley, rather than Lytham. For a start, both sets of parents were on hand to help and, just on the off-chance that it was a boy and he might possibly become a footballer, nobody would ever be able to question his eligibility to play for the land of his father. As a proud, new dad, I thought life couldn't be better but events were suddenly to take a rapid turn for the worse as Scot fell ill and needed a succession of operations.

Liverpool manager Bill Shankly once famously observed, 'Football is not a matter of life and death. It's much more important than that.' You had to be joking, didn't you, Shanks? If I had known how ill my son was, I would have said bollocks to my job and headed straight back up north to be with him. That's why I was kept in the dark. Why do women always think they know best? Between them, Betty and my mother decided that it would be better not to tell me that almost immediately after I left Glasgow to head back to Derby, Scot started to be violently sick and was unable to keep down even a sip of water.

In the middle of the night he was whisked away and put into intensive care because he had become extremely dehydrated and he'd dropped from a healthy, above average birth weight of $8\frac{1}{2}$ lb to a disturbing $6\frac{1}{2}$ lb. The only person permitted to see him was Betty, dressed up in germ-free clothing, and she could only look at him through a glass panel. He was on a drip and kept sedated so he appeared to be quite peaceful but the doctors could not tell her what was wrong with him. When I learned this, it felt likes shades of me at fourteen when I had that meningitis scare. Scot was put through a series of tests and Betty was told that she would be sent home without her new baby, but every time I phoned to see how Scot was doing, I was told he was just fine. Betty and my mother were such good actresses I reckon they missed their vocation in life and should have been on the stage in the West End or on Broadway.

At the end of a two-week stay in intensive care, Scot was finally allowed home and Betty looked forward to being able to show off her bonny boy but, in some ways, the nightmare was just beginning. On the second day at home, Betty lifted him out of his cot to give him a bath and he let out such a piercing yell she almost dropped him with fright. Not unnaturally, she thought she had lifted him awkwardly but when he screamed blue murder the next time she lifted him, Betty knew something was far from right. She stripped him down, carefully examined him as gently as she could with her fingertips and discovered a lump like a small egg on his neck. One rapid telephone call to the hospital later and Scot was heading back to intensive care.

This time Betty could not help but come clean. When I phoned that night I knew right away something was very wrong because she could not hide how upset and worried she was. Yet she still managed to convince me that it would do no good to flee up the motorway because I could not do anything, and it was more important for me professionally to cement my place in Derby's team.

After another extended stay in hospital, we were told Scot had a sterno-mastoid tumour in his neck, caused by trauma at birth, and that he would need an operation to remove it. Surgery could not be attempted until he was at least five months old, providing he progressed steadily. Having explained that by then we would be living in Derby, we were told how fortunate we were because the town could lay claim to one of the best children's hospitals in the Midlands, so that was quite reassuring.

The family was eventually reunited in March 1971 at home in Littleover on the western outskirts of Derby, when Scot was three months old. Scot's lump gradually increased in size until, at five months, he went into hospital for the operation to remove the tumour in his neck. Despite being reassured he would need just one operation, when he was brought back to the ward the consultant responsible for the surgery gently explained that he had been unable to remove all of the lump because it was more complex than he had anticipated. That was the bad news. The good news was that Scot was in no immediate danger as the tumour was non-malignant.

What a load that lifted from our shoulders – I felt as if a ton weight had suddenly been removed and at last I could attempt to get my mind back to football. Although I had not missed any matches throughout Scot's dreadful ordeal, I must be honest and admit my mind was elsewhere. My team-mates knew what was happening with Scot and I was thankful that they were extremely supportive.

After the first operation, the routine continued as before – training in the morning and straight up to the children's hospital in North Street to sit with Betty and Scot for the rest of the day. We were permitted to stay with him until he fell asleep at night and then Betty was back first thing the following morning. After Scot's third operation he was discharged but he had to have another two as an out-patient over the next few months. By the time he finally got the all-clear, Scot was coming up to his first birthday.

Scot learned to walk in a plastercast that ran from the top of his head down to his waist, with his head held slightly to the side to support the muscle on which the tumour had formed. As the plaster was so heavy, he could not stand on his own and needed to be supported by a baby-walker. My father-in-law has got cine-films of Scot running up and down our street in this thing, burning up the rubber. By then, Colin Todd and his family had become neighbours in Littleover. Their little boy, Colin junior, and Scot became firm friends and used to run everywhere together. Happy days, at last. Young Colin was a year older than Scot and the Todds soon had another son, Andrew, who has carved out a decent career for himself with Bolton, Charlton and Blackburn.

Despite the prolonged drama of Scot's illness, I managed to maintain my form and the Scotland cap that Brian Clough and Peter Taylor had promised me duly arrived. Mind you, Mickey Mouse could have pulled on a pair of size 18 boots and sloped out with us in a blue shirt for the second half and it would have been a fitting comment on my international debut – Belgium, 3 February 1971. The European Championship qualifier played on a Wednesday night in Liège had 'trouble' written all over it from the moment our plane landed and we learned the pitch was bone hard and icy. I was mortified to think my introduction to the full Scottish team might be cancelled and I went to bed early in the team hotel the evening before the game, offering up a few silent prayers for a thaw.

However, a handful of seasoned old pros in manager Bobby Brown's squad viewed the dodgy conditions in a different light – a green one, to go out on the town and paint it red! Some of them stayed out near-enough all night. Breakfast time arrived and I went into Charlie Cooke's room to discover him lying on top of his bed, fully suited with his tie still fastened around his neck. The celebrated playboys had more or less talked each other into believing the match was certain to be called off, so they were in for a nasty surprise when a thaw did set in and they had to go to work against the Belgians.

I had enjoyed the benefit of having played at Derby for five months by then and Brian Clough had very definite ideas about the beneficial properties of early bedtimes, rest and proper preparation for football matches – quite apart from his supreme tactical nous. Kick-off arrived and I remember thinking how proud Peter Taylor would be at that moment. In September, he'd told everyone who would listen that I'd be sure to win a full cap that season because I couldn't fail to become a better player at the Baseball Ground by playing in more illustrious company.

While the antics of our Liège Drinking Club members made me question their professionalism, nothing could have prepared me for what happened inside our dressing room in the Stade de Sclessin when we came in trailing 1–0 at the interval. We sat down in our numbered positions, one to eleven. Enter Brown, who took his place on the bench next to me. I waited eagerly for words of wisdom from a man at the very pinnacle of his career, an international football manager. I thought he'd be sure to know what to put right. Instead, I watched him put his head in his hands and let it drop into his lap before slowly turning to ask the Scottish team doctor, 'What shall we do, Doc?' He didn't address his assistant manager or Bobby Moncur, the skipper, or one of the other established figures such as Tommy Gemmell or John Greig. Bobby Brown actually asked a medical man for advice on how to retrieve a football match that was slipping away from Scotland. That made as much sense to me as if I'd asked Brown, 'See these blotchy red spots on my arm, Boss. Exactly what's wrong with me?'

To say I was a wee bit disillusioned by my welcome to competitive international football would be an understatement. There I was, young, fresh, keen – and suddenly wondering what the hell was going on. Needless to say, Belgium ran out comfortable 3–0 winners, Paul Van Himst helping himself to a couple more goals. Not too many months after that, Bobby Brown was looking for a new job.

I had represented Scotland the previous week on an occasion overshadowed by tragedy. On 2 January – the day Scot came into the world – sixty-six fans lost their lives at the end of an Old Firm match when steel barriers gave way on a stairway behind one of the giant terraces at the Rangers end of the ground. Jimmy Johnstone scored for Celtic in the final seconds, then Colin Stein struck a dramatic equaliser and supporters attempting to force their way back up the stairway met a tidal wave of jubilant fans coming in the other direction. That's pure detail, as far I recall, but what price football in the weeks to come compared to the abject misery of families grieving for lost fathers and sons?

The nation was mourning and it was eventually decided to stage a friendly between a Scotland XI and a combined Rangers/Celtic select in aid of the Ibrox Disaster Fund. I happened to be in Paisley at the time, visiting my parents, when word came through from Derby that I'd been picked as a replacement for Nottingham Forest's injured Peter Cormack, and Clough had given his blessing to my participation. My precious, well-worn boots were hundreds of miles away at the Baseball Ground but some kind soul at the club drove all the way to Glasgow to bring them to me.

Tinged with such sadness as it was, the occasion turned out to be a good night personally. The crowd at Hampden numbered over 80,000 and easily another 80,000 would have bought tickets if Scotland had boasted a big enough stadium to accommodate them. So many people wanted to pay their own tribute to the fans who died so cruelly.

I was on cloud nine after about as many minutes when I whacked a goal past Peter Bonetti, who was guesting for Rangers/Celtic alongside George Best and Bobby Charlton. My boyhood hero John Greig – who *was* Rangers for years and years – was also playing for the Old Firm select and I was overjoyed when he gave me his jersey after Scotland had won 2–1. I packed it carefully in my holdall, which I left unguarded for a few minutes in the reception area at Hampden. Those few minutes were all it took for some uncharitable so-and-so to have the shirt away for himself but I got word of the theft to Greig that same evening and, great man that he is, a replacement reached me in a parcel the following week.

Another of my cherished possessions is a short letter from the Scottish Football Association, thanking me for my participation in the match, which raised £37,500.

Disappointment followed the Belgium match, however. I waited and waited for another call-to-arms from the SFA's head-quarters in Park Gardens but I had clearly not impressed Bobby Brown as much as certain members of the secret Liège Drinking Club had, although I could hardly complain when players of the quality of Willie Henderson, an emerging Peter Lorimer and Jimmy Johnstone wore the number seven shirt in the following internationals.

6

WE ARE THE CHAMPIONS

I F Prime Minister Ted Heath had enforced a three-day week at the Baseball Ground in 1972, I seriously doubt whether Derby County would have been crowned champions. We couldn't have coped with a workload as heavy as that. I was one of several players nursing injuries, who needed injections purely to get from one Saturday to the next. I played the full ninety minutes in numerous games when I was nowhere near fit.

I was fuelled by a cocktail of fear, pride, adrenaline, cortisone and painkillers. Once you were out of a Brian Clough side – let alone one in contention for the Football League championship – there was no guarantee you would ever get back in again. We were on good wages, more than the average man in the street, but it was never what I would call great money. The big incentive was the extras. Appearance money in the first team was £10, which with a £20 win bonus gave you £30 extra. For some players, that was 50 per cent on top of their basic pay.

Roy McFarland, John O'Hare and I thought nothing of having a painkilling injection at 1.30 to numb everything down and another one at half-time. Roy seemed to collect quite a few injuries, John had awful trouble with weak ankles while I suffered with my hamstrings. On Sundays we would be back at the club for a cortisone injection to bring down any swelling and speed up recovery, and then it was frequently a case of being ordered to rest for four or five days before a gentle spot of light training and the next match on the following Saturday.

Roy was the England centre-half, John and I were representing Scotland, but the three of us were still concerned about losing our places in the Derby first team. We were happy to have those jabs; nobody forced us to have them. Clough kept Roy on his toes by insisting, 'If I can find a better centre-half than Roy McFarland, I'll buy him.' The needle was just part and parcel of the game in the early seventies. Much has been said about the long-term effects of having regular injections to treat sporting injuries and John has needed a couple of operations on his ankles, but I've been very fortunate that my general level of health and mobility has stood up exceptionally well.

There was nothing suspect about our mobility from the moment the 1971–72 season kicked off with a home game against Manchester United. I think we were on a roll even then despite being held to a 2–2 draw, although the results suggest we were solid rather than spectacular. We were twelve games in – five wins and seven draws – before we suffered defeat in October. A George Best goal at Old Trafford gave Manchester United the win, and we lost the last unbeaten record in the First Division to boot.

Earlier that week, I had returned to international duty. The new season promised brave new times for Scotland, too, and it heralded the dawn of the Tommy Docherty era. Bright, breezy and enthusiastic, the larger-than-life Doc talked a good game and, more importantly, he had the great sense to bring me in from the cold for his first game as Scotland manager. So it was that I collected my second full cap in another European Championship qualifier, this time against Portugal at Hampden, and marked the occasion by heading the winner. The Portuguese made a huge fuss of it, claiming I'd handled the ball but it was never a 'Maradona' and I reckon they were just cheesed off that such a little fella had made them look like mugs.

One player on the pitch that evening was capable of making any opponent look foolish. Eusebio was one of my idols, along with Pele, Cruyff and Beckenbauer and, with the exception of the 'Kaiser', I was extremely privileged to play against them. They were world-class players with phenomenal ability, everything revolved around them and they scored beautiful goals that lingered in the memory.

I came up against Eusebio a second time in the European Cup when Derby beat Benfica in the second round. Try as he might, though, for forty-five minutes against Scotland, before injury forced him off, Eusebio couldn't turn the tide against the Doc's rampant swashbucklers. I thought this was the start of something big for me and Scotland. Brian Clough was considerably less impressed when he heard the Doc boasting how he'd run the legs off me against Portugal, because three days later Derby went down 1–0 in the return match at United.

My sense of belonging in the Scotland team increased in December, despite a 1–0 defeat by Holland in a friendly in Amsterdam. Docherty said I could do the same sort of job as Alan Ball did for England. He said I could become a better player than Ball and that I would never be out of his plans. What a joke that turned out to be, Tommy.

Meanwhile, a miner's strike in January led to widespread power cuts throughout the country and brought in the three-day working week. The first thing I fancied us for was the FA Cup but that all went pear-shaped after three epic battles with Arsenal in the fifth round. Charlie George, later to become a valued team-mate, scored twice at our place and enraged the crowd, who had been baiting him throughout the tie, by racing over to our fans and flicking V-signs to all and sundry.

After that 2–2 draw that merited an X-certificate, we replayed at Highbury the following Tuesday and were obliged to kick-off in the afternoon instead of the evening because of the power cuts. Floodlights were temporarily off limits. So many people were off work, the replay in north London attracted a crowd of more than

63,000 and Derby schoolteachers were on overtime outside the Midland Station to prevent boys bunking off school to follow the Rams, after stuffing their satchels in the left-luggage lockers.

Neither side could score even after extra time and so the epic moved on to Leicester's Filbert Street where my friend John McGovern suffered the grievous misfortune of underhitting a back pass, which was gratefully seized upon by Ray Kennedy, soon after the kick-off – 1–0 to Arsenal and that's the way it stayed. If that was a moment of personal disappointment for John, he was to emerge in triumph in the most thrilling fashion imaginable in our final, decisive game of the season.

Derby won the First Division using just thirteen players plus Jimmy Walker, young Steve Powell and Tony Bailey, who made a grand total of six starts between them. Strangely, maybe a man who didn't sign for Derby played his part as well. Shortly after we had beaten Nottingham Forest 4–0 to complete the double over our neighbours, we were gobsmacked to read that the Gaffer had signed the Forest winger Ian Storey-Moore for £200,000 – and this despite the fact that Alan Hinton was playing out of his skin and enjoying an absolutely fabulous season. Alan was on his way to finishing our top scorer and must have been responsible for a good 60 to 70 per cent of our other goals. If Clough was prepared to pay top dollars for another left-winger of the highest order, it left more than a few of the rest of us in no doubt that we were only as good as our last performance.

As it happens, the Storey-Moore episode ended with the Gaffer on the wrong end of the punchline for once. Decked out in his massive great sheepskin coat and looking like a film star, Ian was introduced before the next home match against Wolves in March as 'our new player' – but his missus was far from impressed and Ian ended up signing for Manchester United instead the following month.

Each and every Derby player knew his job, and we could all play, as well. The record books may show that we lost eight times on our way to the title, but we went into every one of the forty-two matches thinking we could not be beaten, and expecting to pocket at least a point. Whether we were travelling down to London to face Chelsea or up to the North East to tackle Newcastle, it was a wonderful feeling, knowing everything was going right within the club, and we never changed our outlook.

The tactics that took us to the pinnacle of English football were devastatingly simple, yet effective. When we lost possession, everybody was expected to get behind the ball as swiftly as possible to make it difficult for the opposition to play through us. When we regained the ball, it was a case of all hands to the pump going forward, getting as many white shirts into the opposing penalty area as we could. The more players we had in their box, the better our chances of scoring. It wasn't rocket science. We played a disciplined 4-4-2 and it helped that Alan Hinton, as well as our two front men, Kevin Hector and John O'Hare, was a natural goalscorer. Hinton ended up with fifteen league goals, John got thirteen while Kevin weighed in with a dozen. The other three in midfield were Alan Durban, John McGovern and me.

John McGovern was one of the most underrated footballers there has ever been. He would always cover for me when I went on runs and the enormous amount of work he got through in ninety minutes was never truly appreciated by either the public or the press. The number of tackles and interceptions John made was astonishing and he very rarely gave the ball away. A tremendous professional, John's unselfish holding role meant Alan Durban and I could get forward at every opportunity, and I revelled in hustling up front.

Our central defenders, Roy McFarland and Colin Todd, were as good a pair as any in football throughout the seventies. Sol Campbell, Rio Ferdinand and John Terry would be lucky to get a sniff of an England cap today if Roy and Colin were in their prime.

Both of them were terrific players. Roy had a bit of nastiness about him while Colin could summon up electric pace, read situations brilliantly and was a tremendous user of the ball.

The two full-backs, Ronnie Webster and John Robson, never got the credit they deserved because Roy and Colin were such imposing figures, but both were strong characters with a good work ethic and no little flair.

Our goalkeeper Colin Boulton I would place in the good and steady bracket, rather than brilliant. He'd taken over when Les Green had a spectacular fall from grace the previous season at Christmas and handed Manchester United a 4–4 draw.

Christmas 1971 had brought a nasty shock in the shape of a 3–0 defeat against Leeds United, one of our bitterest rivals. The season was already shaping up into a titanic battle, with Bill Shankly's Liverpool and Malcolm Allison's Manchester City the other two clubs in contention for the title. There was never any love lost between Brian Clough and Don Revie, and Leeds had already stuffed us in the League Cup when we travelled to Elland Road on 27 December and got turned over by this line-up: Sprake (Wales), Madeley (England), Cooper (England), Bremner (Scotland), Jack Charlton (England), Hunter (England), Lorimer (Scotland), Clarke (England), Jones (England), Giles (Republic of Ireland), Eddie Gray (Scotland).

Allan Clarke could be a nightmare. Once, we beat them at our place and how I didn't stick one on him I'll never know. The England striker felt it necessary to spend ninety minutes abusing me and informing me that Betty was having an affair with Brian Clough – but he used much more graphic language than that. I knew it was nonsense but Clarke was so persistent he had me wound-up tighter than a coiled spring, goading me to turn round and punch his lights out. I was in such a foul mood until midnight that Betty was convinced Derby had lost but when we climbed into bed and I explained what had happened, we collapsed into a bout of hysterical laughter with Betty wondering just where and when she could fit in clandestine meetings with one of the most famous men in the country.

Leeds could certainly play a bit – as you might expect of a team of internationals – but we played just that little bit better than them over forty-two league matches and I've got the medal to prove it. Confidence was undiminished after that painful trip to Yorkshire because Clough teams invariably became stronger in the second half of a season due to his wise policy of giving players the maximum amount of rest and recuperation whenever the schedule allowed, and also throwing a mid-season break into the equation. Pre-season training could be very harsh but once you got into the regular programme of playing matches, the Gaffer knew how to keep things ticking over smoothly with the minimal amount of work on the training pitch.

New Year's Day was something of a personal triumph because I scored – one of the three goals I managed during the whole campaign – and it was enough to see off Chelsea at the Baseball Ground. I remember collecting the ball on the halfway line and running on and on and on while a sea of blue shirts kept backing off. In the end, it was just an invitation to shoot, so I stuck the ball past Steve Sherwood.

Going to the top of the table for the first time on All Fool's Day was especially sweet because we did it by beating Leeds 2–0. It was obvious to everyone by now that the championship was going to be an exceptionally tight affair and would probably go right to the wire. The only thing nobody could agree upon was in which order Derby, Leeds, Liverpool and Manchester City would finish.

With two games left we had to face City in front of 55,000 fans at Maine Road. We fancied the job, as usual, having already beaten them 3–1 at home, but we didn't play particularly well and went down 2–0. City were a very good team. Colin Bell and Mike Summerbee pulled the strings while Rodney Marsh caused havoc, scoring a cracker, and Francis Lee came away with his customary penalty after Terry Hennessey had wiped out Rodney in the area.

This was the City team for their last fixture of the season that bright April afternoon: Corrigan, Book, Donachie, Doyle, Booth, Jeffries, Lee, Bell, Summerbee, Marsh, Towers.

Big Mal and his City team were left sitting on top of the League, but it must have been an uncomfortable seat because the lead was a single point. The one game to go for us was absolutely massive – Liverpool at our place on a warm Monday evening. It's worth recalling Shankly's team that night: Clemence, Lawler, Lindsay, Smith, Lloyd, Hughes, Keegan, Hall, Heighway, Toshack, Callaghan.

The famous old ground was packed to breaking point with 39,000 officially inside and thousands locked out, many of them having travelled down from Merseyside without tickets. This was our Cup final. We had a terrific home record and, although we were playing against a fabulous Liverpool team shot through with experience and quality, we were still confident of beating them.

You could have cut the tension with a knife before John McGovern ran across the face of the Liverpool box after an hour and connected with the sweetest of drives into the top corner – 1–0 and it finished that way. Now we were top again, by a point, and swiftly on our toes for a well-earned spot of relaxation therapy in Majorca. The pressure was all on Liverpool and Leeds, both of whom would require points from their last matches. Suddenly, Leeds were red-hot favourites to do the double after beating Arsenal 1–0 in the FA Cup final thanks to Allan Clarke's diving header.

Everything was decided the following Monday night, which kicked off with Peter Taylor and the players having a drink in our hotel bar in Cala Millor – the Gaffer was enjoying a holiday with his family in the Scilly Isles – and Leeds needing just a point at Wolves but Liverpool having to win at Arsenal.

I suspected the Gunners might do us a favour because Bertie Mee's men were a proud bunch and stung by performing so poorly in the big Wembley showpiece two days earlier. It finished 0–0 at Highbury but not without some drama when Liverpool had a goal disallowed for offside. Wolves, meanwhile, performed absolute heroics at Molineux. Leeds simply couldn't find an equaliser and went down 2–1.

Peter had been keeping in touch with events over the phone elsewhere in the hotel and he suddenly marched into the bar with a huge beam on his face to announce, 'You've won the League, lads. Now where's that champagne?'

My immediate reaction was to recall my first meeting with Brian Clough back in the Pack Horse Hotel in Bolton, when he had promised, 'Sign for Derby and you'll have a league champion-ship medal within two years.' Man of his word, the Gaffer. He actually believed that would happen – no ifs or buts or maybes. Derby were going to be champions of England. It was black and white in Clough's view, just like our kit.

One moment I was a twenty-three-year-old teetotaller who had never touched an alcoholic drink in his life, the next I was sipping a glass of bubbly. There have been the occasional few during the intervening years, but none that tasted quite as good as the fizz in Majorca that evening – or that had quite such an impact! The booze flowed, the lads hit the hotel disco dancefloor and, just for once, I didn't have one of my trademark early nights.

Of course, the biased northern press were quick to belittle unfashionable Derby's achievement. 'You won the League in Cala Millor,' they taunted. What rubbish! We all played forty-two league matches and we ended up with more points than anyone else – simple as that.

This is my take on the best team in England in 1971–72:

Colin Boulton – Colin was a bit of a dour character and small for a goalkeeper, but nobody could ever doubt his consistency. 'Bernie' played every league match. An abso-lutely fabulous five-a-side player, he could almost shame the strikers with his ability to score goal after goal with either foot. He always had to have a cigarette before training.

Ronnie Webster – An exceptionally good full-back with a bit of pace, he covered the centre-halves very diligently but was always happy going forward. Ronnie scored once all season and I can still see his brilliant header when we beat Manchester City 3–1 at home in December. A very quiet lad, you wouldn't know Ronnie was at the club. He was from Derbyshire and did a bit of farming with his family in his spare time.

John Robson – Tough and very steady for such a young lad, John was only twenty-two when he collected his championship winners' medal. Like Ronnie, he loved to join in the attack. John died at the age of fifty-three in May 2004 after a lengthy battle against multiple sclerosis, which is a desperately sad loss. His great sense of humour is what I always remember.

Colin Todd – A tremendous footballer with electric pace and a ball winner's mentality, he had a tackle like a steel beartrap. Colin, who took over from Dave Mackay, was a terrific reader of the game and a superb passer of the ball to boot. He formed the perfect partnership with Roy McFarland. Colin had the pace, intelligence and awareness while Roy supplied the aggression and aerial power. Another player who didn't make a song and dance of it on or off the pitch, Colin had a wonderful dry wit.

Roy McFarland – Roy had a little streak of nastiness that let opponents know they were in a game. He could look after himself on the pitch but he also had tremendous footballing ability. Skipper and very clearly the leader at the club, I admired him greatly but I thought he got preferential treatment. Maybe he'd get an extra day off here and there, and the Gaffer tended to back him in an argument or dispute. I resented that, but I'm glad to say that my personal relationship with Roy is considerably better these days.

Alan Durban – A terrific footballing brain in and around the box allowed Alan to score more than his fair share of goals from midfield. 'Taffy' was a top man and our social secretary, guaranteed to liven up any night out with a quiz or a party.

John McGovern – A terrific player, John went on to captain Forest to the European Cup twice, the side containing such players as Larry Lloyd, Kenny Burns, Peter Shilton and me. John was known as 'Border', nicknamed, somewhat bizarrely, after a horse! On tour in Germany, John was in a party returning noisily ninety minutes after the curfew time of 11 p.m. He had the presence of mind to run ahead of the pack and slip unnoticed up to his room, so when the bollockings from Brian Clough were duly handed out the following morning, John escaped with a lie about the time he'd got in. Now Les Green, who loved a bet, had taken a fancy to a horse called Border Mask and gave the name to John because he thought that, on this occasion, John had shown two faces. The Mask bit was soon dropped as non-applicable. John is a man I would trust with my life. He is one of my best friends.

Archie Gemmill – I never scored enough goals. If there's one regret I have, looking back at my career, it's that my goals-to-games ratio was pathetic. I would love to have scored a lot more and then I think I would have been classed as a better midfield player. I was always a willing workhorse, though, prepared to go back and do my share of the donkey work helping out in defence, winning the ball and playing it upfield.

Kevin Hector – A terrific awareness of where the ball was in and around the penalty area led to him scoring twelve league goals that championship-winning season. He wasn't the bravest, but he was the fans' favourite, known as 'The King', and he became something of a Derby County legend, playing over 400 games and scoring 200 goals. A very quiet person, Kevin tended to stay in the background.

John O'Hare – Big, barrel-chested John always fronted up for us, as they say in basketball. We might be taking awful punishment from behind but he would make it his business to be available and give us an out, and he was renowned for a wonderful knack of being able to take the ball with his back to goal from virtually any height or angle, control it and lay it off nice and simply. Lacking pace, John was a really good finisher, scoring thirteen league goals. He was called 'Solly', after Luis Del Sol, a great Real Madrid and Juventus star of the sixties. Socially, we got on extremely well, which is just as well because we spent a lot of time in each other's company on Scotland duty.

Alan Hinton – Not interested in physical confrontations, Alan was one of the best dead-ball experts there has ever been. England fans can rave all they like about David Beckham, but Alan was far superior, and he could do the business with both feet in those flashy white boots of his, half the time on a tight Baseball Ground pitch that often resembled a ploughed field. Brian Clough was a firm believer in the best striker at the club taking every free-kick, corner and penalty, so Alan saw a lot of action. He was top scorer with fifteen league goals.

Terry Hennessey – A terrific competitor, Terry called his right foot 'The Glove' because he reckoned he could wrap it around the ball and make the ball do anything he wanted it to do, and he wasn't far wrong. Equally at home in midfield or at centre-half, Terry had a good footballing brain that made up for his lack of pace, and he was a very pleasant person.

59

Frank Wignall – An old-style British centre-forward and as tough as they come, Frank was exceptional in the air and very physical – perfect for when the Gaffer thought we needed a bit of malice up front. Frank was another very nice man, but then again I probably would say that because he was on my side!

My season didn't end on a disco floor in Majorca, far from it. The international season had a sting in the tail. After Scotland's routine 2–0 win over Peru at home in April came the Home International Championship in which we had the considerable advantage of playing all three fixtures at Hampden. Northern Ireland were beaten 2–0, Wales 1–0 and then came the crunch – 27 May 1972 goes down as a black day in the Gemmill household. On that day, against England, I was made a scapegoat and publicly humiliated in front of a jam-packed crowd of 119,000. Defeat, and a little humility never did sit easily on Tommy Docherty's shoulders and I felt like the fall guy who was to take the blame on this day.

In the first half, Alan Ball did his job, scoring the only goal of the half. When we came in, the Doc was on my case in a trice. He had a real go, blaming me directly for failing to pick up Ball's run for the goal. Scotland were losing 1–0 and it was all Archie Gemmill's fault. It was obvious to everybody in that dressing room that Docherty was going to take me off but instead of making the change there and then, he made me sweat for five minutes of the second half before giving me the hook and introducing Jimmy Johnstone as substitute. The crowd naturally took this to mean that I was at fault.

I was not in the Doc's good books. He was starting to fancy Asa Hartford more than me after Leeds initially offered West Bromwich Albion £155,000 for him, although the move eventually fell through on medical grounds. Tommy always was impressed by big money but he did at least want me for the squad heading off to

Brazil the following month to play in the Independence Cup against Yugoslavia, the Czechs and the host nation. Brian Clough had other ideas.

'You,' said the Gaffer, pointing to John O'Hare and to me, 'have just had one hell of a busy season. You have worked hard for nine or ten months, just won the league championship, and now I want to see you both in the sand with the sun on your backs, relaxing with a few bottles of beer if you fancy them. If you think you're going to sweat your bollocks off in Brazil, you've got another think coming.'

Obviously, I was disappointed because I was eager to consolidate my place in the Scotland team, but I understood the Gaffer's argument and accepted his logic without question. His loyalty was to his family and Derby County. He owed Scotland nothing but he had let me make my debut in Belgium at very short notice, three days before an away match at West Ham.

I thought Tommy Docherty would accept the explanation behind my polite refusal to join the tour to South America. Never did I imagine it would be three years, five months before I next pulled on the Scottish jersey, and Willie Ormond had taken over by then. It rankles with me that the Doc must have known I was good enough to play for Scotland yet stubbornly refused to pick me.

7

PADDLING IN PORTUGAL

MIGHTY Juventus were clearly worried about facing Derby County in the European Cup semi-final in April 1973. So worried in fact that Peter Taylor suspected they may have tried to influence the referee. Before the game he noticed that some of the Italian club's people, not to mention substitute Helmut Haller, were in the referee's room. Haller was the beefy, blond lad who scored West Germany's first goal in the 1966 World Cup final against England at Wembley. Well, here he was again, and Peter caught him having a laugh and a joke with the referee, Herr Gerhard Schulenburg, who also happened to come from West Germany. Roy McFarland and I were carrying bookings from the quarter-final against the Czech club Spartak Trnava, so another caution would mean an automatic one-match ban and rule us out of the potentially decisive second leg against Juventus at the Baseball Ground.

It is impossible to know exactly what went on in the referee's room but having known the Italian club's people had been in the dressing room prior to the game, we were especially aggrieved to be on the wrong end of what we considered to be two outrageous bookings. Biased I may be, but I don't believe either of our challenges could be construed as fouls, let alone anything remotely worthy of a caution. I was just chasing the ball to the byline to try to keep it in play, while Roy jumped for a high ball and was involved in an innocent, if unfortunate, clash of heads. My booking didn't inhibit me in any way. If I got sent off, so be it. I was not going to play any part in second leg, anyway.

Kevin Hector created a little bit of history when he equalised past the legendary Dino Zoff and became the first man from an English club to score in Italy in the European Cup, but we got turned over 3–1 and then the fun and games really kicked off. All hell broke loose with Taylor beside himself at the injustice of the bookings and what he thought he had seen going on between Haller and Schulenburg. He was desperate to make his point to UEFA officials through an interpreter and the odd thing is, suddenly, nobody could speak English at all.

I have noticed this strange phenomenon in Italy and other European countries. When it suits them, the people around all appear to understand perfectly and speak English well but when it doesn't suit them, all you get is a load of old 'no comprendo'. Poor Pete, bless him, ended up getting arrested and we feared he was going to be carted away and put in prison. Inevitably, the boss put his two penn'orth in as well but the mood in the dressing room was far from down. We thought we still had a good chance, never mind that the Juventus side was full of such famous names as Causio, Altafini, Capello and Marchetti.

Scoring an away goal was very important and we felt we could reach the European Cup final provided we didn't concede a goal at Derby and had managed to score one ourselves with half-an-hour still to go. If that was the scenario, we knew there was enough backbone about us to score again and go through 2–0 on the away goals rule.

A fortnight later, I was sitting in the main stand watching the lads batter Juventus, who were defending like demons, when we were awarded a penalty early in the second half. This was it. I don't think anybody in the Baseball Ground that night thought Alan Hinton would miss it. He was a magnificent penalty-taker, no question about it, his record of success was extremely high – but Alan had been out injured for a month and maybe that made him a little less composed than normal. Nine times out of ten, he drilled the ball like a daisy-cutter, inches inside an upright. You could have heard a pin drop when Hinton missed the target. Several minutes later, big Roger Davies got himself sent off for a headbutt and there was a definite sense that this was the end of the road for our European Cup campaign.

In the dressing room afterwards, Alan must have been sick to death hearing so many of his team-mates telling him not to worry about the one that got away and not to blame himself. We'd all been in it together, it had been a marvellous experience, we had just come up a little bit short and we were all optimistic that better things were still to come. The belief within that Derby team was awesome and we were definitely good enough to have won the European Cup in 1973. Yes, I would have fancied us to take the great Ajax side that completed a hat-trick of European Cups that season, but we never had the luck – or the barefaced nerve to attempt to influence the referee. Having said that, Brian Clough may have pulled a stroke or two in his time but nothing more devious than watering the pitch. Certainly, nothing as extreme as what we suspected had happened deep in the bowels of the Stadio Comunale in Turin.

Earlier in the competition we had landed a plum tie with Benfica and the Gaffer must have had the firehoses on the pitch all night because the surface was as slick as anything. Benfica are one of those magical names in European football, on a par with Real Madrid and Juventus, and we really didn't know whether we'd have enough in our locker to beat them in the second round. In addition, they had the legendary Eusebio – even if his glorious career was coming to a close – and a young Portuguese lad called Toni, who was supposed to be Eusebio's heir apparent. Against the odds, we absolutely paralysed Benfica 3–0 with all the goals coming in the first half on one of the great evenings in the history of Derby County. We were irresistible and the only frustrating thing was that we didn't score more goals. As for Toni, John McGovern and I did a job on him in midfield.

For the second leg, the Gaffer was at his best. We flew out to Portugal on the Monday, fresh from a horrible 4–0 defeat at Manchester City, a match for which Kevin Hector, John O'Hare and I were all rested. Peter Taylor was friendly with a car dealer, Ernie Clay, who later became Fulham chairman, and we stayed in Ernie's small hotel in Estoril. Training for one of the biggest matches of our lives consisted of walking the entire length of the beach, a good three-quarters of a mile, with our bare feet in the sea. The Atlantic that November was absolutely freezing and a couple of the more reluctant players had to be asked twice by Clough if they wouldn't mind just rolling up their tracksuit bottoms and joining the rest of us for what he called 'a little paddle'. Nobody needed to be asked a third time – it would have been professional suicide.

I could barely feel my feet or legs beneath my knees, let alone my toes, during that walk in the sea but nobody was complaining when the boss marched us into a brilliant seafood restaurant for lunch. That was it; that was our entire training for the match – a walk in the freezing sea, followed by prawns, lobster and squid. Highly recommended, I can tell you.

Come the day of the match and we had a little saunter after breakfast, followed by lunch and an afternoon kip. When we boarded the coach to take us to the Stadium of Light, Clough brought on a crate of beer and a couple of nice bottles of rosé wine. He just told us, 'Help yourself if you fancy a drink.' A couple of the players had a beer to relax and the boss never batted an eyelid. His team talk was brief and to the point: 'Just go out and enjoy it. You may never be in a position like this again in your lives. I know you're better than Benfica. Now prove it.' It was a real backs-to-the-wall job in front of a packed crowd of 75,000 for long periods but we were very regimented and defended with great discipline. We couldn't repeat our goalscoring heroics from the first leg, but that scarcely mattered because Benfica didn't score either. By the end of the ninety minutes, very few home fans were left in that fabulous, famous stadium but those who stayed until the bitter end clapped us off the pitch. I like the Portuguese. They love their football and appreciate good teams, and we were very good.

The great adventure had started in a low-key way when we were pulled out of the hat first to entertain Zeljeznicar Sarajevo, the champions of Yugoslavia, and the first leg at home was noteworthy personally because not only did I score a rare goal but, rarer still, I whacked it in with my right foot to clinch a 2–0 win. We'd beaten the Yugoslavs quite comfortably and, unless there was a disaster, we were through.

We stayed in the lovely city of Dubrovnik for the return leg but the fiercely partisan 60,000 crowd were in an ugly mood with sirens and firecrackers going off all over the place. Our response was perfect, two early goals silenced the Kosevo Stadium and a 4–1 win on aggregate sent us strolling on to meet Benfica.

It was back out to eastern Europe for the third round to tackle Spartak Trnava in Czechoslovakia and, after the fun we'd had in Portugal, this was a definite straight-in-and-out job according to the Gaffer. More than one day's acclimatisation to the dull, featureless black and grey landscape of Trnava – so typical of Iron Curtain cities in those days – and we might all have died of boredom. The boss took us out on Tuesday, we got a good night's kip and then proceeded to lose 1–0 despite being arguably the better side. Still, I suppose it was a reasonably good result to take back to East Midlands airport, even if we hadn't managed a precious away goal.

Spartak surprised us at the Baseball Ground and we struggled for some time to break them down before Kevin Hector did the business with a couple of goals. Tense and too tight for comfort at the end, we knew that one slip and Spartak would go through on away goals. The relief at the final whistle was immense.

Juventus awaited with skill on the pitch and dark acts off it. It was scant consolation to me but justice, of some kind, was done in the European Cup final when Ajax beat the Italians 1–0 in Belgrade.

As for the First Division in 1972–73, injuries and inconsistency took their toll and it was bitterly frustrating to finish in seventh spot, just one place outside a UEFA Cup place, which was the least I believe our efforts deserved over the campaign. There were some calls for Sir Alf Ramsey to pick our entire back four to play for England, but the defence proved strangely fallible at times and we conceded far too many goals in the League. We would lose 4–0 to Manchester City one week and beat Arsenal 5–0 virtually the next.

David Nish joined us from Leicester for £225,000 – a new British transfer record – and settled in at left-back although he was such an accomplished footballer he could have played in any position on the park. He was so elegant and comfortable off either foot and would shine like a beacon in the Premiership today because of his outstanding natural ability. David's arrival meant someone had to go, and the break-up of the championship-winning team started with the departure of John Robson to Aston Villa for £90,000.

A lesser side with weaker characters might have faded into oblivion once the European Cup dream had been laid to rest but we simply went out and won our last three matches, all at home, against Everton 3–1, when I tucked away a successful penalty, Ipswich 3–0 and Wolves 3–0.

Brian Clough would happily have throttled any player feeling sorry for himself and after that Wolves victory on a Friday night, a real sense of achievement pervaded the team because we were more or less convinced we would be playing in the UEFA Cup. The only thing that could prevent it was if Leeds, our old foes, failed to win either the FA Cup final the following afternoon or the European Cup Winners Cup, and Leeds were absolutely nailed on to win the FA Cup again at Wembley, having beaten Arsenal the previous season. This time their opponents came from the Second Division and nobody outside the North East gave Sunderland a prayer. Unfortunately, those prayers from Wearside were answered in the most dramatic fashion and Leeds somehow lost 1–0.

That started the butterflies flying around stomachs in Derby and it was a sickening bodyblow when Leeds lost the European Cup Winners Cup final, 1–0 again, to AC Milan. Their consolation prize would be 'our' UEFA Cup place.

Just when we'd needed a favour from Don Revie's lot, they had failed to oblige. It was almost as if Leeds were mocking us because in March, when we'd met them in the last eight, there was a real feeling about the place that it could be us going to the Twin Towers for the FA Cup final.

The season was notable for the emergence of Roger Davies, a gangling 6ft 3in striker Taylor had spotted at Worcester City. Derby's board took some convincing that it was worth spending £14,000 on a non-league player, but I imagine they enjoyed the big cigars and double scotches in the boardroom after Davies stole the show in a fourth-round replay at Tottenham. Roger had already scored the only goal in the previous round at Peterborough and he was on target with a precious late equaliser against Spurs at home, but our luck appeared to be right out at White Hart Lane under the floodlights a few days later. A bumper crowd of almost 53,000 packed the famous old terraces and the 'Glory, Glory' chants were starting to roll around the ground with Spurs 3–1 up with twelve minutes to go. That scoreline was a travesty, however, and the tune soon changed as Davies went to work, carving out a hat-trick for himself alongside two goals from Kevin Hector as we roared back in astonishing fashion to turn the tie on its head and triumph 5–3 in extra time. Spurs had a couple of seasoned internationals in their defence, goalkeeper Pat Jennings and centre-half Mike England, but it looked as if nothing in their lives had prepared them for Roger Davies as they trooped off the pitch thoroughly shellshocked.

It was Hector's turn for a hat-trick with Davies settling for one goal in the fifth round as we blasted a very talented QPR side 4–2 at our place to book a ticket for the quarter-finals and prepared for the visit from Leeds. They had murdered us 5–0 at their place in October and 3–2 earlier in March to complete a league double in highly controversial fashion when they were given two penalties. Leeds could certainly play, but they could also play up to the referee, put him under pressure and generally make his life a nightmare, which made Brian Clough dislike Don Revie's way of doing things all the more. Now a fortnight after our last fruitless meeting, we had the chance of revenge but Leeds played it by the book this time and Peter Lorimer scored to shoot them into a semi-final date with Wolves.

The season ended with Leeds and Derby supporters united for once and crying into their beer.

8

CLOUGH OUT, MACKAY IN

PRIDE myself in having always been a ferocious competitor. I never quit and I never hid but I've seen my fair share of players, opponents mainly, go missing in action. For me, that's a crime. Even if you're having the biggest stinker of all time, you have to keep at it. Nine bad passes might go astray but the tenth could set up the winner. You might be shattered but you still chase a ball in the ninetieth minute because you might stir a move to snatch the vital goal.

I came across defenders who took one look at my size and reckoned a quiet word early on would sort me out but I knew I was strong enough to take them on. If they whacked me, I would get up and skin them again. I was a typical Scot – flat out to win. I didn't have a nasty streak, certainly not compared to some notorious characters in the 1970s such as Norman Hunter at Leeds or Chelsea's Chopper Harris, but in my early days at Derby I refused to take a foul lying down. As soon as I'd been fouled, I'd be up like a jack-in-the-box to take a swing at the man who had just done me. It won me no favours with Brian Clough. One day I copped the biggest bollocking of my life off him and I never had an inkling it was coming.

I was getting booked time and time again, and had already served one three-match suspension for six cautions. Now I was well on the way to another ban. This time, I seem to recall, there was a danger I would be out for six matches. I was summoned to

70

the Gaffer's office where he proceeded to peel the paper off the walls with the telling off he gave me. I was letting down myself, the team, the supporters, him, Peter Taylor, everyone, and if I didn't pull myself together I was on my bike. He didn't want me. Brian said it was a waste of time him paying me my wages if I was going to be missing six to ten matches every season through suspension.

I never knew such a single-minded, abrasive character but he was also capable of acts of great warmth and charity. He would fine us for being improperly dressed and there was an automatic £100 deduction from your wages if you were booked for dissent. On one occasion when he dropped me, he said, 'You're not in the team – now get out of my sight.'

The great thing about the Gaffer was that he understood professional football so well. He knew my retaliation wasn't malicious, and he didn't want to curb my enthusiasm. His parting shot on the day of the bollocking was a pointed reminder to bite my lip and use my head.

'Don't be a pillock and take a swing right in front of the referee's nose, Archie,' he said. 'There will always be a time when the ref's forgotten everything and you can get a little bit of your own back. So wait twenty minutes and *then* do the bloke!'

By October 1973 the lesson had sunk in. At Old Trafford a lad called Tony Young took me out with a big dig and succeeded only in getting himself booked. Kevin Hector popped in an early goal as we notched up our first away win of the season. The fact that it was against Manchester United made it especially sweet. Winning there was always a very good result, even if United were in decline and on their way to relegation. Two points took us to third in the table and I felt Derby were well on their way to winning another league championship. If only life at the club had been so sweet off the pitch.

There had been one or two little rumblings for some time that the chairman, Sam Longson, was unhappy with the Gaffer's extra curricular activities. The boss said some outrageous things on television, which certainly didn't please Sam, and Clough was just as forthright, outspoken and opinionated in his newspaper articles. Then the board issued an ultimatum, ordering Clough to pipe down. Well, you can imagine just how that was received by the Gaffer – talk about a red rag to a bull. He had a very big ego and didn't like to be told what to do. In the world of Brian Clough, he told other people what to do.

The Gaffer returned from that Old Trafford game to the humbler surroundings of the Baseball Ground to discover his drinks cabinet had been emptied and office cleared of several items. It was war now between two very strong-willed individuals and Sam sent the Gaffer a letter telling him to discontinue his newspaper and television work. Longson was scared stiff the club would get into trouble with the Football League or the FA because of what the Gaffer was saying.

Like just about everybody in Britain, I first heard that Brian and Peter Taylor had resigned when the news broke on the television and radio on the Monday – and it seemed as if all hell had broken loose. Most of the players were in Derby but Colin Todd, Roy McFarland, David Nish and Kevin Hector had already left on international duty. They were with the England team that drew 1–1 against Poland at Wembley, the killer result that meant Sir Alf Ramsey's side failed to qualify for the 1974 World Cup. By the time the England boys returned, our trainer Jimmy Gordon had been put in charge and I felt particularly down in the dumps and depressed. The club was geared for even greater successes. I felt sure they were just around the corner and Derby would go on winning competitions and trophies for years to come, indefinitely. Suddenly, I felt as if my football had come to an abrupt halt and my mood did not improve when Longson came out and crowed pompously, 'We will go into the Second Division with our heads in the air rather than winning the First Division wondering whether the club will be expelled from the Football League.'

Jimmy took charge on the Saturday and we beat Leicester 2–1 at home, but the result was almost incidental compared to the demonstrations at the ground and an appearance in the stands by the Gaffer before he left early for the drive down to London to appear on the Michael Parkinson show that evening.

Events gathered pace rapidly. I was one of the prime movers, along with Roy, Todd and Colin Boulton, in getting up a players' petition, insisting that we would not play again until Brian and Peter had been reinstated. Every single member of the squad signed apart from Henry Newton, who had joined from Everton the previous month and didn't have such strong feelings about the boss. Everybody else was totally behind him.

While all this was going on, we also had two meetings with Brian and Peter, the first at the Kedleston Hotel just around the corner from the Gaffer's house in Quarndon. The second took place at the Newton Park Hotel near Burton-upon-Trent to which all our wives and girlfriends were invited. Typical Clough, he had champagne at the ready to meet and greet the girls on that occasion. He explained to us that he had every right under freedom of speech in a democratic country to say whatever he wanted to whomever he wanted. To be honest, we didn't really give a toss what Brian said on the telly or wrote in the papers unless it affected us directly. What did concern us deeply were results on the pitch.

I could possibly have understood Longson's logic if Derby County had been struggling against relegation with a poorly motivated team, but nothing could have been further from the truth. We were champions and European Cup semi-finalists. It seemed to me that Clough had only just tipped his big toe into a whole ocean of achievements at the Baseball Ground.

Everybody had a chance to have their say at the hotel meetings – democratically, in the manner the Gaffer approved. The business end was tied up fairly swiftly and the occasions developed into social events, with a jar here and there. We felt he would come back, he wanted to come back and we reached the ludicrous position of deciding that unless we got what we wanted, we were not going to play that Saturday at West Ham and would all fly off to Spain for a weekend in the sunshine instead. Then the Professional Footballers' Association stepped in and warned us in no uncertain terms that if we carried out our threat, we would be in breach of contract and the club would be within their rights to stop our wages.

Word reached us that Dave Mackay had been sounded out about replacing the Gaffer. Dave had slipped away from Derby in May 1971, sold to Swindon Town as player-manager for £20,000, and following that he'd had eleven unremarkable months in the hot seat down the road at Nottingham Forest when the call came.

One or two cracks started to appear in the ranks. I was quite willing to say, 'Sod Derby. If Clough's not coming back, I'm off to Spain,' but others had bigger mortgages and more financial commitments than I had.

The Gaffer slapped in a libel writ against the club, claiming they had sullied his character, and the cloak-and-dagger stuff continued with a team meeting at my house in Dean Close, Littleover, from where Roy phoned Dave and asked him not to take the job. That call came from the heart but it was a waste of a tanner if ever there was one. Dave had been offered a four-year deal worth a very reasonable amount of money. He told Roy his plea had come too late because he had already signed the contract and would most certainly be coming to Derby.

Somehow we pulled ourselves together and went down to Upton Park on 27 October. We were unfortunate to come away with just a single point and it certainly rankled with me that Longson felt it necessary to state afterwards, 'I could manage this lot.'

Dave was installed as our new boss but that was not the end of the story. Mike Keeling had resigned from the board and was a leading light in a supporters' protest movement. The players also believed there was still a fighting chance of getting the Gaffer back. That first month for Dave and his enthusiastic assistant Des Anderson must have been hell. In happier times to come, a motivational poster appeared in our dressing room. 'It's a crime to give the ball away' was the punchline, to which one wag added, 'to Des!' At first, though, we certainly were not playing ball with Dave Mackay. The atmosphere between management and players was strained, results were not good and, frankly, Dave's working conditions were very poor. We wrote another letter, demanding Dave went and Brian returned. Roy had it in his possession and was on the point of dropping this bombshell on the Baseball Ground when the PFA intervened and warned us that if the letter was delivered, the club would be perfectly entitled to cancel all our contracts. Eventually, it dawned on us that the Gaffer wasn't coming back and results started to pick up.

After being thumped 3–0 at Sunderland, Ipswich and Sheffield United, as well as losing 2–1 to QPR in Dave's first home match, we steadied the ship with home draws against Leeds and Arsenal before travelling up to St James' Park on 15 December and remembering how to win again. A spot of personal glory in the FA Cup showed how swiftly fortunes can fluctuate in football. In January 1974, Boston United travelled over from Lincolnshire as sacrificial lambs for the Rams in the third round and went away with a 0–0 draw, but the non-league team had run themselves to a standstill. Four days later I scored my one and only hat-trick in English football in a 6–1 romp at York Street, with a penalty sandwiched between a couple of tidy finishes.

Hindsight is a wonderful gift. We were totally wrong to treat Dave Mackay the way we did. He had been a colossus on the pitch for the club and was a colossus off it, too. He had honesty, integrity and a sense of purpose, yet we tried to undermine him. It was hardly Dave's fault that the lines of communication between Brian Clough and Sam Longson became so bitterly confused, yet

Dave was forced to carry the can while we went through the motions of being a professional football team for a little spell. At the time we were convinced we were doing the right thing, we had such blind loyalty to the Gaffer, and our feelings were whipped up by the media every day.

To Dave's eternal credit he never harboured any grudges, and in the circumstances Derby recovered brilliantly to finish the 1973–74 season in third place behind champions Leeds and Liverpool, securing a UEFA Cup place along the way. Now it was Dave Mackay insisting we could progress to become league champions again – and he was soon to be proved spot on.

9

THE REAL MACKAY

I F Dave Mackay was fortunate to inherit a fine team with the capacity for improvement, you've still got to take your hat off to him for his signings. Some first-class buys made us stronger, more formidable opponents. Significantly, we were well rid of all our complexes from the fallout surrounding the Gaffer's messy end at the Baseball Ground the previous season, thanks in no small measure to the two most influential of those signings – Francis 'Franny' Lee and Bruce Rioch, strong characters and leaders, the pair of them.

Franny was an instant hit. He had an abundance of talent and proved to be an outstanding acquisition from Manchester City. I knew he'd always score goals, even though he was in the twilight of a marvellous career, and he retained the ability to be a right pain in the backside for defenders, especially Norman Hunter at Leeds with whom he had several run-ins.

My Scotland pal Bruce, acquired from Aston Villa for £200,000, was a very good footballer who could kick the ball as hard as anyone in the game. He took over from Alan Hinton as our dead-ball expert. Bruce had the added advantage of being as hard as nails.

Scoring goals was never going to be a problem that season with those two. Bruce weighed in with fifteen, a fabulous return for a midfield player. Kevin Hector notched up his usual quota while Roger Davies was particularly effective at times, notably in the 5–0 home win over Luton when he scored all our goals, had a couple disallowed and might, with luck, have ended up with ten. I swear that's no exaggeration.

Welsh international Rod Thomas arrived from Swindon to play right-back. A big, gangling lad, he loved to get forward, but it was in defence that he stood out, those long legs of his snaking out to nip any crisis in the bud. He enjoyed a couple of terrific years with the club.

I, for one, remember kicking off in August with the slate wiped clean and in the frame of mind to win the title again. If there were reservations elsewhere, it was because everybody knew we would have to cope virtually all season without our captain Roy McFarland at centre-half. Playing for England against Northern Ireland at Wembley in May 1974, Roy had ripped his Achilles tendon very badly and recovery was going to be a long job. In his absence until the last handful of matches, I led the side and like to think I made a reasonable success of it.

Many punters expected Dave to splash out on a top-quality replacement for Roy but he didn't need to. Peter Daniel, from Derby's Central League team, had been at the club for ten years. Peter was salt of the earth, a diamond. He was quiet and a genuinely nice person with a quick, dry sense of humour. He filled Roy's shoes to such an extent that Roy wasn't missed at all – and Roy McFarland was an exceptional player. Forgive me one little Michael Caine moment when I tell you, and not many people know this, that the Derby fans' player of the year that season was Peter Daniel.

Peter had made his first-team debut as far back as 1965 and we were all thrilled for him when he scored his first goal for the club against Servette Geneva in the UEFA Cup. We outclassed the Swiss side 6–2 on aggregate, winning both legs, and our hopes of success in Europe soared after the following round when we came out on top of a very tasty Atletico Madrid side. It was 2–2 at Derby and 2–2 in the Spanish capital after ninety minutes and extra time. Sixteen spot-kicks later we were through, 7–6 after a sudden-death penalty shoot-out. It was my 200th game for Derby and one of my best, although you don't have to take my word for it.

Afterwards, it was quite embarrassing because Atletico's Argentinian manager Juan Carlos Lorenzo grabbed me in a great bear-hug outside the dressing room and shouted, 'Magnifico,' before going on to tell the press boys that he rated my perform-ance just about the best he'd ever seen from a midfield player, anywhere, any time. Looking back now, I shouldn't have been embarrassed. I should, instead, have given Lorenzo credit for his very generous praise, considering what must have been a very difficult result for him to stomach.

With Atletico out of the way, I thought we were on a roll, despite the fact that class acts such as Juventus and the German pair of Cologne and Borussia Moenchengladbach, the eventual winners, were progressing in the competition. That feeling was reinforced when three goals in the last quarter of an hour brought us a 3–1 home win over Velez Mostar, but in the return leg in Yugoslavia the European dream turned into a nightmare. I might have been a hero in Madrid, but I was a mug in the fireworks and smoke of Mostar. I let the ball run away from me and gave away an early penalty, which put us on the back foot. Velez established a 3–1 lead and extra time was looming again when the highly respected Dutch referee Charles Corver awarded them a dubious spot-kick and we were out 5–4 on aggregate.

More rough justice came our way in the FA Cup. We beat Orient after a replay and Bristol Rovers before falling at home to our old nemesis Leeds United in the fifth round, the only goal cruelly bouncing in off David Nish's shin. I found that particularly hard to take for two reasons. We outplayed Jimmy Armfield's side and I was kicking my heels in the stand, missing the tie because I was suspended.

Now all we had to play for was the title. In December, you would have had to be a brave man, or a diehard Derby fan, to have wagered much of your hard-earned cash on us winning the championship again. We lost 1–0 at Kenilworth Road in the week leading up to Christmas, to a poor Luton team that had won once all season, and found ourselves stuck in mid-table, about the same distance away from Ipswich at the top as we were from Carlisle down near the bottom. Our odds lengthened to 12/1. Results improved, however, and it was anybody's championship until a crucial spell around Easter. In quick succession we polished off Wolves, West Ham and Manchester City at home with a rush of goals from Rioch and Lee while Kevin Hector rescued us with a last-minute equaliser when all seemed lost at Middlesbrough.

Seven points out of eight was a killer burst that left the others gasping. We were up against top-class rivals in Liverpool, of course, Everton and Bobby Robson's fine Ipswich side. It was almost all over on the penultimate Saturday of the season when Derby fans virtually took over Leicester and swarmed all over the dusty Filbert Street pitch at the end of a 0–0 draw. Liverpool, in Bob Paisley's first season as manager, lost at Middlesbrough while Everton got turned over at home by Sheffield United, and Ipswich went down at Leeds. Unless Ipswich could win at Manchester City in midweek, we believed Derby County would be champions for the second time in four seasons, even though we had one more game to play against Carlisle. On that Wednesday night, the squad were safely ensconced in Bailey's nightclub in Derby town centre for presentation of the club awards. It was almost like a re-run of 1972 when we were in Cala Millor with our work done, seeing if anyone could catch us, but with one significant difference. Even if Ipswich were successful in their game in hand at Maine Road, we would need just one point from the game against bottom-of-the-table Carlisle at the Baseball Ground to take the title.

When the final whistle sounded on a draw in Manchester, shown on a big-screen television in Bailey's, the party could really start and I was delighted that so many of our supporters joined us in the champagne and dancing on one of those nights that live with you for ever. Maybe one or two of us overdid it because three days later we could manage only a 0–0 draw against Carlisle, but I was presented with the Football League championship trophy and I didn't think life could get much better. Then it did.

If I leave it any longer to mention my beautiful daughter Stacey, she will never forgive me. Stacey was born on 3 June 1975 and lit up my world. As I had been unable to attend Scot's birth, I made sure I was not going to miss this one.

Betty had not been feeling too well during the pregnancy, fainting a couple of times. It was markedly different from when she was carrying Scot and felt as fit as a flea, which raised our hopes that the new arrival would be a girl to complete the family nicely.

Betty had a couple of weeks to go when her gynaecologist, concerned that she was slowly losing weight instead of gaining it, decided to induce the birth. All went according to plan and at 9 p.m. Stacey was born, weighing $6\frac{1}{2}$ lb. It was wonderful to witness, but when the baby did not make a sound and the doctor whisked her away and put her under some warm lamps, I became a little concerned. Suddenly, feelings of total elation turned to panic and fear. The minutes ticked away and still there was no sound, no cry. The doctor kept reassuring us that there was a strong heartbeat. What we weren't told was that infants are 'scored' out of ten at birth and our little bundle had managed a meagre one.

After what seemed like an eternity, Stacey opened her lungs and let out such a wail we all joined in and shed a few tears for good measure. Thank God, she was responding at last and after lots of cuddles and kisses she was settled into her tiny plastic cot and wheeled away into the nursery for the night.

I was back half-an-hour later with my friend and neighbour Fred Hovey, to show her off. Fred and I retrieved her from the nursery and went into Betty's room to wake her up and tell her how happy we were, before retiring to Fred's house to polish off a bottle of brandy.

Stacey is grown up now and a source of great pride to me, as is Scot. She did well at school and went on to university to gain her degree in Politics and European Studies. If she had been a brother for Scot, she would probably have been a footballer because she was always good at sport. As it is, Stacey represented Derbyshire at swimming and hockey and is one of the few women in my world actually interested in football. She has a fighting spirit and a huge competitive streak. Yes, you are right in thinking she has inherited her dad's personality and we clash quite a lot but, God, do I admire her!

While I doted on our new daughter, Mackay reinforced the squad for 1975–76 by bringing in Charlie George to give the attack greater bite, and Charlie proved to be one of Dave's most inspired signings. The manager had considered it well worth cutting short his summer holiday in Scotland in order to fly down to London to conclude the deal with Arsenal. Charlie came for a bargain £100,000 with what the media today call 'baggage' but I took to the confident, long-haired Cockney straight away. When it came to respecting others in my line of work, there really was only one question I ever needed to ask myself – 'Can he play?' In Charlie's case, the answer was emphatically 'Yes,' and I might add, 'Superbly.'

Obviously, his greatest asset was his goal-scoring, but he possessed magnificent all-round talent. He held the ball up well at the focal point of attack and had two good feet. Never underestimate that basic strength – plenty of Premiership players today get by on one foot to kick with and the other purely for standing purposes – but perhaps what made Charlie such a special player was his awareness. I've seen some players with a breadth of

Above: Armed with a football, it wasn't long before I got on the wrong side of the law.

Right: On parade in best bib and tucker, here I am with Mum and Dad at a family wedding.

Below: Class acts in the Langcraigs School team – that's me in the front row, far right.

Time for tea as an apprentice electrician in 1966.

Whenever Peter Shilton got above himself at Nottingham Forest, I always reminded him of the afternoon in October 1969 when I scored twice against him for Preston against Leicester. This is the second goal.

My queen of hearts Betty and I enjoy a game of cards with Preston pal George Lyall and his blonde girlfriend Linda.

My perfect match – marriage to Betty in October 1968.

Ready to rumble for Scotland against Portugal in a European Championship qualifier under Tommy Docherty in October 1971. I scored the winner at Hampden Park.

The King and I – pre-season training with Kevin Hector at Derby County.

Up and away – rising to the occasion against Leeds United's Billy Bremner as Derby County win 2–0 to close in on the 1972 First Division championship.

Derby bounty – the 1972 champions show off their silverware, (*left to right*) the Central League, League Championship and Texaco Cup trophies.

My finest hour? I rarely played better than in my 200th game for Derby – our UEFA Cup tie against Atletico Madrid in Spain.

Behind this painted smile I had mixed emotions about being recalled by Scotland in October 1975, the morning after that magical night when we beat Real Madrid 4–1 at the Baseball Ground.

Fresh fields as I run out for my Nottingham Forest debut in 1977.

Leading by example, I opened the scoring and skippered Scotland to a 3–0 victory over Northern Ireland in the Home Internationals in May 1976.

Dynamic duo Brian Clough and Peter Taylor were reunited at Forest and better than ever.

Striker light – I was pressed into emergency service to lead Scotland's attack against Brazil in Rio on the summer tour in 1977.

Mission Impossible against Holland in the 1978 World Cup and a Ruud awakening for Krol, the Dutch master defender, as I give him the slip.

Looking back at danger, Poortvliet is powerless to prevent my mazy run.

Golden goal delight seconds after scoring arguably the most famous goal in Scotland's history.

Lion Rampant – I celebrate my greatest ever strike, in Mendoza v. Holland.

On the run to outpace Trevor Hebberd in Forest's 3–2 League Cup final victory over Southampton in March 1979.

Singing our 1978 World Cup song with Scotland fan Rod Stewart – strange that he hasn't adopted my sartorial elegance.

vision not much further than the end of their noses, or a simple six-yard pass, but Charlie seemed to absorb what was happening within a fifty-yard radius.

We all knew he'd had one or two little blips during his career at Highbury but Charlie delivered for Derby from the word go and took the team on to a higher plane. Strangely, for someone who was as chirpy as can be, he suffered terribly with his nerves in the dressing room before kick-off. A large percentage of the time he would be physically sick and emerge from the toilet looking as white as a sheet. Once on the pitch, though, Charlie was right as rain, and he looked as if he'd been playing for Derby for years in his first match of any significance – the 2–0 Charity Shield triumph over West Ham. If there was an extra spring in our step on that boiling hot August afternoon it's not surprising because Brian Clough had denied his championship-winning Derby team their Wembley date in 1972 when he was at loggerheads with the authorities, and preferred to take us to Holland for a meaningless friendly against a Dutch club in The Hague.

In November, Dave signed Leighton James from Burnley for £300,000. Shortly afterwards, we came back from two goals down to beat Middlesbrough – I scored the winner – and Des Anderson, wrapping an arm round Leighton, wheeled him into the press conference, announcing, 'It was like riding pillion to Evel Kneivel.'

Clough and Taylor were a famous partnership, of course, but nobody should underestimate Des's contribution to Derby's continued success. He had a razor-sharp brain and a perfect sense of humour for keeping the atmosphere bright and bubbly. He also knew the game inside-out and could be as strict and serious as was necessary when the occasion demanded it.

Derby were up and down that season but, crucially, we never got the rub of the green when we needed it most. There were no broken bones when we crashed, just shattered dreams and bruised pride.

Our European Cup trail began in September against the Czech champions Slovan, who possessed a couple of marvellous players in Marian Masny and Novotny, and we needed plenty of defensive nous to escape from Bratislava just one goal in arrears. Back home, Franny Lee might have scored a hat-trick in the last quarter of an hour but he missed a penalty in between two late goals as we won 3–0. Still, Slovan were quality opponents to be respected and they thoroughly deserved the round of applause we gave them as they trooped off at the end.

Then the whole of Derby seemed to be grinning from ear to ear with anticipation when the draw paired us with Real Madrid, the most evocative name in European Cup football, winners of the competition for the first five years and again in 1966. Real were the most glamorous visitors ever to set foot inside the Baseball Ground, yet they could not live with us and we demolished them 4–1 in possibly the best ninety minutes in Derby's history.

Bill Shankly was particularly impressed and said, 'When Liverpool reached the semi-finals of the European Cup in 1965, they met Inter Milan, then technically the best team in the world. We won 3–1 at Anfield, and it should have been four. That was Liverpool's best night in Europe – and Derby were as good in this game.'

Charlie George stole the headlines with a hat-trick, including a pair of penalties, but several shrewd judges, including the Spaniards' Yugoslav manager Miljan Miljanic, made me their man of the match and I wasn't about to argue. I had, in truth, put in an excellent performance against Real's two German superstars Gunter Netzer and Paul 'The Frightener' Breitner.

Miljanic predicted, 'Our task is now formidable but not impossible. Nothing is impossible at the Bernabeu.' Sadly, he was proved correct. Injuries and suspension cost us dearly and that handsome three-goal advantage was whittled away in Spain as we went down 5–1 in extra time. Charlie scored another goal in front of a 125,000 full house at the Bernabeu and must have set some kind of record for scoring four times in a European tie and yet still ending up on the losing side.

Meanwhile, I had been sitting in the bath at the Baseball Ground with a cup of tea, surrounded by photographers, the morning after the first leg, when I learned Scotland wanted me again. The physio Gordon Guthrie rushed in and broke the news that Willie Ormond, the Scotland manager, had called me up for the squad to face Denmark in a European Championship qualifier at Hampden at the end of the month. Was I delighted? Was I thrilled? Was I hell! My immediate reaction was, 'They can get stuffed.'

Three years and five months of bottled-up hurt came to the surface. Tommy Docherty had dropped me in May 1972 just after Derby had become champions under Brian Clough. Since then we'd made an impact in the European Cup, found ourselves criminally cheated out of a semi-final by Juventus, and the club had been crowned champions of England again under Dave Mackay. I had not exactly been wasting my time or frittering away my career. Some kind soul once totted it up for me – during those three years and five months Scotland had played thirty-three internationals. I'm not saying I would have played in them all but, barring injuries, I was good enough to play in each and every one of them. I could not have been plying my trade at a higher level for my club. Now Ormond wanted me and I stubbornly told Guthrie and the press lads, 'They can do without me.'

Mackay was unimpressed and said simply, 'You cannot turn down your country, Archie,' and that was the precise reaction I received from Betty, my mum and dad and a couple of close non-footballing friends I'd met in Derby. They all thought I was being pig-headed and daft. Fortunately, it didn't take too long for the penny to drop before I realised how silly I was being and, by another good stroke of fortune, Willie never got wind of my initial reaction.

I'm mighty glad I accepted that invitation to return to the fold because I found a very happy camp. Willie was a good international manager, very easygoing but people had great respect for him and never took any liberties. He didn't rule with an iron fist or feel the need to be domineering. Most of us were always tucked up safe and sound in our beds by ten at night in the squad hotel – or, at least, that's what I assume, what with my ability to stick my head on a pillow at the earliest available opportunity.

I didn't confront him on why it had taken him so long to recognise me as an international player. Willie made me captain and explained that he felt it was just a natural extension of what I'd been doing successfully at the top of the League and in Europe. He had this endearing quality, similar to Jack Charlton, of getting a bit mixed up with players' names, and he could come up with the odd turn of phrase from time to time. After one trip to spy on Denmark, Willie's team talk to us went something like this: 'I've just watched the Danes and I'd like you to know they play 4–4–2 with great discipline and are a studious, physical team. And one other thing I've noticed about them . . .' Here he paused for dramatic effect and to make sure we were hanging on his every word, before continuing, 'they always take their corner kicks from wide positions.' With that, the room just erupted in stitches as the lads burst out laughing. Willie hadn't got confused in what he was attempting to portray, it was just his way of keeping things nice and easy.

He played another blinder, which brought the house down, before we met Romania at home in the European Championship, my second match back. A bit of tension was in the air because we knew they were a more than capable side, which they proved by drawing 1–1 at Hampden. Willie came into the dressing room before kick-off and started on this long, sombre warning: 'I've seen them and the Romanian captain is really special. Plays midfield, incredible pace, fabulous in the air, two great feet, covers every blade of grass, tackles like a tiger, passes like a dream and he scores goals.' One or two heads went down and we were just wondering if it was worth our while running out on to the pitch to tackle such an immense figure when Willie casually signed off, 'And oh, by the way, you don't have to worry about him because he's not playing tonight.'

Happily restored to international football, I soon found myself with another target. I was desperate to reach an FA Cup final, always had been, and we really did believe we'd cracked it that season at Derby. You can never win enough in football, it becomes addictive, and while the team I skippered to the championship in 1974–75 was the best in the land, it was a travesty that the vintage crop of 1975–76 ended up with nothing. Blame Charlie George's dislocated shoulder, and blame me, too. Derby were looking a decent bet to do the double in late March before Charlie suffered the cruel injury that ended his season prematurely one night in a very costly home draw against Stoke.

Three weeks later on the Saturday morning of our FA Cup semi-final against Tommy Docherty's Manchester United, I could be found at Hillsborough with Des Anderson, undergoing a fitness test. The date was ominous – 13 April. I had been given an injection three days earlier but now came the moment of truth. Des watched me do a few sprints and turns, then asked, 'How does it feel, Archie?' I remember looking Des straight in the eye and replying, 'Fine.' If I had been truthful, I'd have told Des, 'Fine, but then I've only given it 75 to 80 per cent. If you think I'm going to risk breaking down at this late stage with so much at stake, you must be crackers.'

Crystal Palace and Southampton were contesting the other semi-final at Stamford Bridge and, with all due respect, neither were expected to trouble either Manchester United or us. The afternoon started with a bad omen when a set of players wearing

BOTH SIDES OF THE BORDER – MY AUTOBIOGRAPHY

white tops ran out to warm up and hundreds of blue and white balloons were released by our fans, packing out the giant Kop End at Hillsborough. The supporters obviously thought they were greeting us and I'm given to understand a few sheepish grins appeared when those white training tops were peeled off to reveal red United shirts.

By ten past three I knew I'd blown it, too – big time. My hamstring hurt like hell and I wasn't anything like 100 per cent fit. It's a miracle I managed to disguise the injury sufficiently to last the ninety minutes. I should have been big enough to tell Dave before the match that I was hiding the injury, but I'm not the first player to have pulled a trick like that.

If you are looking for the supreme irony, fast forward to Munich in 1979 and Nottingham Forest's European Cup final victory over Malmo when I swear I *was* fully fit after an injury but Brian Clough decided otherwise and our bust-up cost me my job at the City Ground.

'Doc's kids will cry' proclaimed one banner in Sheffield but it was our supporters crying into their beer that night after Gordon Hill scored twice to carry United to a Wembley date with Second Division Southampton.

David Nish had a perfectly sound equaliser chalked off. He chipped the ball high in the air and ran through to beat Alex Stepney but the referee reckoned one of our forwards was standing in an offside position. It was a wretched decision. We were totally gutted. It's one of my few regrets as a player that I never figured in an FA Cup final. Nine times out of ten we'd have fancied ourselves to beat United and now we weren't going to Wembley.

There was time for a glorious swansong – a 6–2 win at Ipswich in our final league match, Franny Lee's final game in professional football – before my attention switched back to Scotland. May 1976 was particularly sweet because we won the Home International Championship for the first time in ages, beating Wales 3–1,

Northern Ireland 3–0 and England 2–1. I skippered the side after the farce of seeing Scotland led by six different players in as many matches – Sandy Jardine, Gordon McQueen, Billy Bremner, John Greig, Martin Buchan and Tom Forsyth.

10

TOMMY'S NOT MY CUP OF TEA

T HE summer of 1976 proved a pivotal time for Derby County. Franny Lee called it a day to concentrate full time on his lucrative paper manufacturing business, Alan Hinton left to try his luck with Vancouver Whitecaps in the North American Soccer League and Roger Davies went to Bruges in Belgium for £135,000, helping them to win the domestic double. In one fell swoop, Dave Mackay lost what could still be a more than useful attacking trio in its own right and by November he'd lost his job as well.

Eighteen months after winning the League, Dave was out on his ear, despite finishing third, first and fourth in the First Division. He was treated so shabbily. Look at his record. Dave came into the club from Nottingham Forest and coped in circumstances possibly only he could have lived with.

Dave thought I was something of a physical phenomenon. He once told a pal, 'We have a training routine that involves a series of sprints between poles. It's a real killer but Archie will finish yards in front of the rest every time and he has hardly broken sweat.' I was always ready to go the extra mile for him. As a manager, Dave revelled in attacking football, which is why he recruited such exciting talents as Charlie George, Franny Lee and Bruce Rioch. He also knew the precise value of a clean sheet, however, and defensive discipline was never overlooked.

We had some crazy results at the start of the 1976–77 season, and nobody would have guessed we had a problem in the goal-scoring department had they witnessed our 12–0 beating of Finn Harps in the UEFA Cup in September, or the 8–2 annihilation of Tottenham the following month when Bruce Rioch, operating as an emergency striker, scored four goals as we grabbed our first league win of the campaign at the ninth attempt in spectacular style.

Dave was having trouble at boardroom level and his problems intensified when we bowed out of the UEFA Cup in the following round, 5–2 on aggregate to AEK Athens, losing both legs. Injuries and suspensions meant we struggled to make the best of Leighton James's crosses, everything appeared to be unravelling at a rate of knots and the next thing we knew, Dave had been handed his P45.

To the surprise of nobody, the new management team of Colin Murphy and his assistant Dario Gradi were unable to recreate the championship-winning formula patented by Messrs Clough and Mackay. Murphy and Gradi were an honest, hard-working pair but the magic simply wasn't there, although Murphy had considerably more success than Mackay when it came to getting the board to stump up hard cash for a new striker. It seems incredible that a championship-winning manager was denied resources, yet his replacement was given the green light to go ahead and splash out £330,000 on Derek Hales, a forward at Second Division Charlton.

Derby were crying out for a new John O'Hare, a target man who could keep possession and bring others into the frame, but Hales was ill-suited to this style of play, much preferring to feed off a diet of crosses, which had brought him such a rich supply of goals at The Valley. Hales made his debut in December and thirty games later he was gone, knocked out at the start of the following season to West Ham for a cut-price £110,000. He was a costly failure for the club in every sense. Murphy's other major signing, midfielder Gerry Daly, proved a great success, however, scoring seven goals to keep the spectre of relegation at bay.

As far as I was concerned, it was a very uncomfortable campaign from the moment I was sent off in a pre-season tournament game against Athletic Bilbao. Most of the anguish was mental but not all of it. I thought nothing could ever rival the pain I felt as a fourteen-year-old back home in Scotland when mysterious headaches drove me to the brink of a breakdown, and nothing did until February 1977 when I suffered a depressed fracture of the skull. I can laugh about it now but it was a nasty injury and immediately raised fears I wouldn't play again that season. That would have gone down like a lead balloon at the club because we were locked in a desperate battle against relegation.

It was a bloody cold spell of winter, I do remember that, and the training pitches were totally frozen but we were fortunate to have reasonably large indoor facilities at Raynesway. Unfortunately, someone decreed it would be a bright idea for the first team, reserves and youth team to all pile in together. So it was we were playing something like sixteen a side one morning. Time and space, as you can imagine, were at a premium and I vividly recall jumping to head the ball, only to connect with the back of another lad's head. I heard an ominous crack and collapsed to the floor in a heap. It must have been one of those rare periods when we didn't have half the team on the treatment table because Gordon Guthrie was watching from the sidelines. He came over straight away to find me dumped on my backside, fingering a hole in my head above my right eye. I was carried out, laid down in the back of Gordon's car and off we sped to the Derbyshire Royal Infirmary.

Shock gave way to the most severe pain I've known in my life. Two broken legs were a mild inconvenience compared to the agonies I was going through now. I was cursing and swearing fit to burst in casualty for something, anything, to relieve the pain. It was absolutely excruciating. The medical staff were brilliant and I was operated on that afternoon. A surgeon sliced me open under the eye, with a cut requiring eight stitches, popped in an instrument and pushed out the dent in my head.

I was allowed home the following day and soon returned to training. Four weeks after the accident I made my comeback for the reserves in a 2–1 Central League win over Blackpool at home. My specialist was not particularly impressed because he wanted me to leave it another fortnight before playing again but relented when he saw how determined I was.

I was under instructions not to head the ball that day but I did just the same. He was amazed at how quickly I recovered but, in truth, it turned out to be not as serious as first thought. The surgeon told me that, in essence, the depressed fracture was a bit like breaking your nose. The injury heals very quickly and once it does there's no need to worry about future problems.

My future problems were worrying about how, and if, Derby were going to pull out of their nosedive down the First Division table. The club finished the 1976–77 season in fifteenth place out of twenty-two clubs, just three points away from relegation, having won only nine matches – the worst record in the First Division.

One of those victories sticks vividly in my mind because it involved The Incredible Case of the Missing Penalty Spot. We didn't need Sherlock Holmes to sort this one out, though, just groundsman Bob Smith, armed with a tape measure and a bucket of whitewash.

The omens didn't look too encouraging that spring day when Tony Book's championship-chasing Manchester City, with Peter Barnes, Joe Royle and Brian Kidd in attack, came to town. We were so short because of injuries that Murphy got me to play up front with Kevin Hector. I must say I loved every minute of it, and the only way I didn't beat big Dave Watson on a bog of a pitch was by running through his legs, although I was in such form that thought half-crossed my mind!

I opened the scoring in the second half and it was soon 3–0 before I went charging into the box at high speed and fell under minimal contact from Gary Owen. On another day, I admit the referee would have been quite within his rights to have waved play on, but he awarded a penalty. City were not at all happy with the decision but what followed entered the realms of farce.

The spot had disappeared. Our penalty-taker Gerry Daly looked for it and then just plonked the ball down as near the goal as possible. Joe Corrigan, the City keeper, already far from pleased at the way his afternoon was panning out, marched out to confront Daly, angrily demanding to know, 'Who's taking this bloody penalty, then, a kid?'

'What are you moaning about now, Joe?' said Daly, grinning.

'That ball – it's almost on my effin' six-yard line!'

Corrigan summoned the referee to plead his case and got booked for his trouble, while Bob measured out twelve yards and painted a fresh spot from which Daly duly made it 4–0 – a bizarre end to a rare happy day that season.

At the same time, things were changing for me on the international scene, and not automatically for the best. Willie Ormond's reign as Scotland manager came to an end that spring when the SFA decided they fancied a more forceful, charismatic personality and appointed Ally MacLeod, but not before Willie bowed out on a high note with a 3–1 win over Sweden in a friendly at Hampden. When Ally took over the reins, I wouldn't have got anywhere near the budding World Cup squad, let alone another dark blue jersey, if I hadn't buttoned my lip and swallowed my pride.

At the end of May we were preparing for a wholly forgettable 0–0 draw with Wales at Wrexham in our opening Home International fixture, when Ally decided he wanted a little chat with the lads after one particular training session. This point was made, that point suggested and then Ally looked at me and said in front of the assembled group, 'And, Archie, you will not be captain any more.'

That was my introduction to Ally MacLeod, who decided Martin Buchan would make a better Scotland skipper with Bruce Rioch as his vice-captain. In the hours that followed, a great many players came up to me to sympathise, shake their heads and say they couldn't believe the manager's decision. Even Martin came up and apologised, even though it obviously had nothing to do with him.

That was the mark of a big man and Martin was no wet-behind-the ears kid because he was captain of Manchester United at the time. I had no argument with Martin. In fact, I had to feel a bit sorry for the guy because he was unlucky with injuries at important times and the armband passed to my Derby team-mate Bruce.

I was thirty and less than impressed by Ally, but experience had taught me a thing or two. Sometimes I knew I had let my true feelings surface, spoken up and it had caused all sorts of problems throughout my career. Hand on heart, I have never been the type to stir up trouble but I do have strong points of view. If I think something is wrong or unjust, I have never been afraid to say so.

Many times Brian Clough and I argued, most notoriously in 1979 over his decision to leave me out of the Nottingham Forest team that defeated Malmo 1–0 in the European Cup final. If I had only kept quiet then, I would have stayed at Forest and in all probability lined up in the side that beat Kevin Keegan's Hamburg 1–0 in the European Cup final the following year.

In Wrexham in 1977, I was seething at the injustice of it all. Quite apart from the captaincy issue, I suspected Ally fancied Asa Hartford as a player more than me but, equally, I knew I was still in with a good chance of making the World Cup squad, so I decided to stick with it and go with the flow. If the situation had been different and I couldn't have seen much of an international future, I would have told Ally immediately to stick it where the sun don't shine! Ultimately, the Scottish captaincy and who played was his prerogative, I knew that. However much I might have disagreed with him, I accepted the situation. You simply have to be professional about these things.

I fretted away the remainder of that Home International series against Northern Ireland and England on the substitutes' bench, determined to convince the manager of my value in the forthcoming mini tournament in South America. We flew there in June to play Chile, Argentina and Brazil in an effort to prepare for the 1978 World Cup finals in Argentina, in case we qualified.

I started a 1–1 draw with Argentina in Buenos Aires and then, because we were so short of strikers, I was pressed into service as an emergency striker against Brazil in the Maracana and turned in a terrific performance to take the plaudits, even though we lost 2–0. Talk about a bucketload of sweat! I ran until I almost dropped that day.

This was a very challenging period of my life. With my Scotland future unsettled, to say the least, despite my best efforts in South America, I discovered on my return to the Baseball Ground a distinct fear that things were on the slide. Chairman George Hardy's patience ran out after five matches of the new campaign. We had won just two points and been stuffed 3–0 away by Brian Clough's newly promoted Forest. Colin Murphy and Dario Gradi were out and Tommy Docherty swept into the manager's office while I was away with Scotland, on the bench, for a midweek World Cup qualifier against Czechoslovakia at Hampden.

Back in Derby, I clocked on for training and was given a message that Docherty wanted to see me at the Midland Hotel, where he had taken up residence. Nothing sinister in that, it was a fair enough request. I thought he maybe wanted to have a natter about the Scotland match or discuss what he expected of me in

the team for that Saturday's difficult trip to Liverpool. I felt sure
he'd want me in the team because I had played well the previous
weekend and scored in a 2–2 home draw with Leeds.

I went up to Docherty's room and he was nice as pie. 'Archie,
how are you?' he greeted me. Some general small talk followed
and he asked me if I would like a cup of tea. Then came the
bombshell as the Doc was kind enough to inform me, 'It's quite
simple – you're finished here. You're too old, your legs have gone,
you're basically a has-been and that's it. I'm bringing in a young
keeper from Nottingham Forest. I've done a deal for John
Middleton and you're going to Forest as a makeweight.'

'Is that it?' I replied.

'Yeah.'

My parting shot as I headed for the door was, 'Thanks and, by
the way, you can stick that cup of tea up your arse!'

I wish I could have thought of something more original but in
the heat of the moment that captured my mood perfectly ad-
equately – and that was the last I ever saw of Tommy Docherty.
Our paths have never crossed since that day. I should not think he
was put out in any way, delighted rather to have attempted to
humiliate me again.

Later, I was tickled to hear from a fan that when Docherty was
manager of Aston Villa in the Second Division, he'd boasted that
all Clough's Derby would get from Villa Park was a cup of tea at
half-time. Derby won 1–0 on their way to the title in 1969 and
15,000 or so travelling supporters took great joy at the interval
informing him precisely what he could do with that cup of tea –
and sideways, at that!

Still, all my anger was swiftly offset by the knowledge that I
would be having another meeting in the Midland that same night
with a football manager who did rate me – Brian Clough. I didn't
need any persuading whatsoever to join Forest, although I
suppose it was flattering to hear the Gaffer, accompanied by
Peter Taylor, tell me, 'Come and join us, Archie. You're the last

97

little thing we need in the team. Then we will win the League this season.' Typical Clough – no ifs, not buts, no maybes. Sign for Forest and celebrate with the third championship winner's medal of my career. What could be simpler?

Apart from not being exactly one of the greatest judges of football talent the world has ever known, Docherty had a mean streak. I don't know, maybe it was all a throwback to 1972 when he was Scotland manager and held me personally responsible for a defeat by England at Hampden. Anyway, in the deal involving Middleton I was valued at around £62,000 and as I had been fully expecting to play for Derby at Anfield on the Saturday and a transfer request was the last thing on my mind, I was entitled to ten per cent of the deal. Imagine my anger and disgust when Docherty tried to twist the knife already stuck in my back. It felt like he had enjoyed every second of telling me I was washed up as a professional footballer and the next thing I knew he was telling all and sundry that at our meeting at the Midland Hotel I had shouted the odds about a transfer because I didn't want to play under him.

What utter rubbish! I'm nothing if not loyal. I was a Derby player and I would never ever consider running out on a manager without giving him a fair crack of the whip. It made no sense. It was getting messy now. Docherty was adamant that Derby would refuse to release me unless I signed a form indicating that I had requested a transfer. My initial reaction to that was, 'Over my dead body,' but Clough, eager to get me bedded in at the City Ground and never a man to be messed about, was becoming more than a little fed up. I felt a principle was at stake but he just leaned on me and said, 'Get it signed, Archie. There's no way on this earth you will lose your argument on appeal.'

Derek Dougan of the Professional Footballers' Association got involved in trying to get the £6,250 due to me and when the case was heard in Birmingham I think it took less than five minutes for

Docherty's evidence to be thrown out and my side of events to be accepted.

I don't know why Docherty was so professionally incompetent. I picked my boots up from the Baseball Ground, wondering, 'Am I daft or is it him who's daft?' I went on to win a bit at Forest, play in the 1978 World Cup finals and collect another twenty-one Scotland caps, so that perhaps indicates just how stupid the man was.

While Docherty will never exactly rank as my favourite Scot, Rod Stewart will always be my favourite Scotland fan. I once drove Betty wild with jealousy by phoning her from my hotel room to ask, 'Guess who's lying on my bed?' It was Rod, of course. He'd popped in for a chat while he was helping us with the 1978 World Cup song and I do believe we were both a little bit starstruck for a moment. Rod was 100 per cent rock and roll in those days, to my mind. He ordered a bottle of Bacardi plus one bottle of Coke as a mixer when he asked for a drink, and put it on my bill. I couldn't believe it.

One day I was out at training when Rod's agent telephoned our house, wondering if I might possibly be prepared to exchange an authentic Scotland shirt for one of Rod's platinum discs. It's a good thing the guy only requested one of those famous dark blue shirts because Betty would probably have traded the lot of them for such highly prized Rod Stewart memorabilia. Did I have any say in the matter? Did I hell!

That deal led to an invitation to attend Rod's concert at the NEC in Birmingham where the TV cameras filmed me swapping the shirt for a disc. We watched Rod sing from the VIP area with our friends, Derby commercial manager Stuart Robinson and his wife Christine, before being ushered back stage at the end of the concert. Rod came bounding off in his leopardskin top and black lycra tights to greet me again with a massive bear-hug. Betty received a kiss on the cheek, which took her on to cloud nine, and we ended up in Rod's dressing room. I remember Alana

Hamilton sitting there, pretty as a picture, but she didn't approach until Rod invited her over. He was down-to-earth and involved everyone in the conversation, not just me, asking about our kids and everyday, run-of-the-mill stuff.

Rod's manager had to remind him it was time to go. 'Sorry Rod,' he said, 'we really must make a move because we're due back in London soon.' At that, a young girl, who couldn't have been more than nineteen, stepped forward and Rod held his arms out by his sides as he was stripped right down to his underpants. Well, Betty and Christine watched this performance wide-eyed, giving each other a little look that said, 'If I come back in another world, I want that job!'

Rod was dressed in his outdoor clothes and during all this, he never once stopped talking or halted our conversation in any way. Then, talk about temptation, Rod's next invitation was for us all to travel in his limo to a party in London. Unfortunately, the real world kicked in – we had a babysitter to consider and I had training in the morning. Betty has a platinum disc of 'Foot Loose & Fancy Free' hanging in our dining room and wouldn't part with it for all the tea in China.

Mrs Gemmill and Mrs Robinson could be a dynamic duo when they got going, footloose and fancy-free. One happy day and night, by the sound of it, resulted in Betty reading some lurid headlines about herself, which still give us a giggle. My parents came down from Paisley to mind Scot while Betty took off on a long-overdue jolly with friends to Ragdale Hall health spa in Leicestershire for the weekend. Alcohol was strictly forbidden but the girls managed to smuggle in a few bottles of wine. They were on just 1500 calories a day and starving come bedtime. The girls all piled into the room Betty was sharing with Christine. Although the wine went down a treat, I'm told, the girls were having hysterics and couldn't sleep a wink because their stomachs were rumbling so loudly.

Sunday morning dawned and the party gathered for breakfast

of half a grapefruit and the newspapers, one of which stated bold as brass that Betty was suffering from a nervous breakdown and I'd packed her off to a clinic for treatment! What a hoot! She was having the time of her life.

11

FOREST ON FIRE

ONE of the Gaffer's greatest strengths was his total unpredict-ability, the fact he always kept you guessing. A few eyebrows were raised in the Nottingham Forest dressing room and whispers heard among the players when the skipper, my great pal John McGovern, was unceremoniously dropped so I could make my debut against Norwich at home in a 1–1 draw on 1 October 1977. It was just Clough's way of letting the team know that nobody was safe.

The teamsheet read: Shilton, Anderson, Barrett, Bowyer, Lloyd, Burns, O'Neill, Gemmill, Withe, Woodcock, Robertson – and it's fair to say I didn't play particularly well. In fact, I had a stinker and Clough was kind enough to let the world and his wife know. 'Gemmill has picked up some bad habits recently down the road,' he said, 'and I'm not putting up with all his sideways and backwards passing.'

Maybe the shenanigans with Docherty and dispute over my pay-off from Derby had affected me. In any case, I was the new boy on the block. The management would understand and be sympathetic, despite the Gaffer's public utterances. After all, when we'd shaken hands over my move at Derby's Midland Hotel, Peter Taylor had told me, 'That's it, that's the last piece in the jigsaw we need. You'll be picking up another winner's medal this season, Archie.'

I was promptly axed for the next three matches and left to stew against Ipswich, West Ham and Manchester City as the Gaffer made another point to anyone who cared to listen – 'Favours? I don't do favours.'

When he deemed it fit for me to return, we whacked Sheffield United 6–1 in a testimonial match for John Harris at Bramall Lane and after that I was more or less ever-present in the number eight shirt as Forest seized the First Division title by storm. Knowing the boss so well, I fully expected to win trophies at Forest. I knew that any of his teams would have very good players individually and that 99 times out of 100 they would gel as a unit. We never felt any different playing home or away. We had immense belief.

I swear I'm not being deliberately controversial or perverse, but my abiding memories of the 1977–78 season when Forest became champions of England are the matches I didn't play in. Forest also won the Football League Cup, with Peter Shilton and me sitting on the sidelines, ineligible to play any part in proceedings because we were cup-tied. I had helped Derby beat Orient back in August in the second round and that was enough to turn me into a hugely frustrated spectator as Forest battled past Leeds United in two epic, high-scoring legs of the semi-final. Forest were on fire throughout the competition as we beat West Ham 5–0, Notts County 4–0, Aston Villa 4–2 and Bury 3–0 before seeing off Leeds 7–3 on aggregate. Truth be told, Liverpool thoroughly outplayed us in the final at Wembley but Forest produced a gutsy backs-to-the-wall effort to draw 0–0. Shilton's eighteen-year-old understudy Chris Woods made some unbelievable saves.

In the replay at Old Trafford, Forest lifted the trophy on the back of a 1–0 win. John Robertson scored a penalty after John O'Hare had been pulled down by Phil Thompson. I thought the offence took place outside the area and the referee, Pat Partridge, missed it, but I didn't have too much sympathy for Thompson because John was clean through on goal when he was tripped. It would be a straight red card today, no messing.

Forest were magnificently defiant that evening. I was very proud to be a member of the club, even though I was almost cracking up with frustration at not being out there, going head-to-head with Jimmy Case and Terry McDermott. Sitting in the stands with Shilton and me were David Needham, who was also cup-tied, having joined from QPR, plus Colin Barrett and John McGovern who were injured. Forest were missing five main players, yet their spirit was still strong enough to beat this Liverpool line-up: Clemence, Neal, Smith, Thompson, Kennedy, Hughes, Dalglish, Case, Heighway, McDermott, Callaghan.

Fitting in at the City Ground was as easy as slipping on a new pair of slippers once I'd got my feet under the table, so to speak. I'd been through a lot at the Baseball Ground, played with some terrific players in really good squads, won two championship medals and featured in a couple of exciting European Cup runs. There had been lots of highs and lows but I've never been a great person for yesterdays and I was quickly absorbed into the here and now of life fifteen miles east along the A52 dual carriageway.

Derby had come out of the Second Division under Brian Clough and taken to the First Division like ducks to water and it was no coincidence that Forest did the same. Forest had won promotion in less emphatic fashion in third place when nerves overcame Bolton, but my new team-mates were soon at home in the top flight. I was immediately taken by how similar the team was to Derby's championship-winning line-up under Clough and Taylor. Big personalities and quiet, unassuming professionals, they all knew their jobs to perfection. The mixture was ideal and still I found the Gaffer playing to everybody's strengths, and playing it simply, asking nobody to do anything unfamiliar or foreign to them.

We'd all drive to work and then walk or jog to the training ground down along the river embankment. I would happily run back afterwards as often as not and, after a shower, we'd walk round the corner to McKay's café to feast on hot sausage and bacon sandwiches and chip butties, washed down with cups of tea. Plain working men's grub was on the menu for the championship-winning class of 1978. It's a million miles away from the pasta, green leaf salad and mineral water enjoyed by Thierry Henry and Patrick Vieira today. I don't expect they pop into a café with the rest of the Arsenal lads after training at London Colney, either. Those sessions at McKay's should not be dismissed lightly because they did help to foster a tremendous team spirit.

There were never any trouble-makers on the playing staff. Clough and Taylor saw to that in the way they probed into the lifestyle and character of the men they recruited. Rows blew up because we were only human. As a group of professional sportsmen, you can't live in each other's pockets without the odd flare-up. Take an individual in training whose mind is elsewhere. He's under-perfoming on the pitch, he's got a problem with the missus, his kid is ill, that sort of thing. He is distracted and an overzealous challenge comes in, bang. The next thing you know punches are flying and blood is spilled. That happened but nothing ever festered at Forest. There was too much mutual respect. I took on Larry Lloyd more than once, verbally I hasten to add. Physically, it would have been a bit of a mis-match. It was always soon water under Trent Bridge.

Just before Christmas I knew for sure that we were good enough to lift the championship. The previous month we'd gone down 1–0 at Leeds before embarking on that fabulous, record-breaking run of forty-two league matches without defeat, which eventually came to an end the following December at Anfield. Now we had a little trip to Old Trafford, which always concentrated the mind and quickened the pulse a bit, and although the record books show we beat Dave Sexton's side 4–0, it could have been ten. The FA Cup holders included players of the quality of Sammy McIlroy, Steve Coppell and Brian Greenhoff, yet we played them off the park and I took satisfaction in setting up three of our four goals.

Sexton summed up Forest at their best that day when he said, 'They don't play with eleven men. They seem to have sixteen or seventeen. When they attack, about seven of them come at you, and when they are defending, there are about nine of them.'

Sexton must have hated the sight of me because I'd popped up in November to beat United 2–1 at the City Ground with a cracking header from sixteen yards.

I had another rare goal to celebrate in January, one that I treasure to this day despite all the attention focused on my effort against Holland in the 1978 World Cup. We were 1–0 up against Arsenal at home and under the cosh when I intercepted a pass from Liam Brady just outside our penalty area, fizzed a pass out wide to Peter Withe on the left and set off on a run, haring sixty-odd yards down the pitch like a mad thing. Peter sent in a killer low cross and I slid it into the net. Job done. That clinched a 2–0 win and the Gunners manager, Terry Neill, said, 'I think I know Brian's secret. He just goes out and buys a few good players and then makes them work harder than they've ever done before. Good luck to him and his team – they deserve to win the title.'

My performance caught the eye of our goalkeeper and Shilton generously declared, 'Archie has really matured now and for my money he's one of the best in the business. When most midfield players get the ball they try to play it out wide. Archie doesn't. He looks forward and if the pass is on to cut out three or four opponents and leave us with one forward against one defender, he'll play it, no matter how tight it looks.'

Shilton had signed from Stoke for £270,000 a fortnight before me and he made sure we were crowned champions at Coventry on a boiling hot April Saturday, with four games in hand. Ironically, it was one of our least impressive displays and my abiding memory is of Clough doing his best to get all the players to have a good drink in the hotel at lunchtime – not water, mind you, but wine and beer.

I had to play in attack because we were so short-staffed with Larry Lloyd suspended and both John McGovern and Tony Woodcock injured. We took an absolute battering but Shilton pulled off two or three incredible saves to keep it 0–0 and win the precious point we needed to make sure Liverpool couldn't catch us. That same day, Derby beat relegated Leicester 4–1 to ensure Tommy Docherty would still be in charge of a First Division club, for now, but the balance of power in the East Midlands had swung decidedly in favour of Nottingham and there it would stay for years.

The final margin of victory in the championship race was seven points, impressive by any standards. Forest lost just three matches – six fewer than runners-up Liverpool – and conceded twenty-four goals – ten fewer than the Anfield club.

At Derby, I had enjoyed playing alongside Roy McFarland and Colin Todd, who were probably out on their own for sheer class as a central defensive partnership in the seventies, but when it came to getting the job done, stopping forwards and protecting the goalkeeper, I can't praise Larry Lloyd and Kenny Burns too highly. We were very strong defensively, impregnable at times, worked extremely hard in midfield and scored a fair few goals with John Robertson, Peter Withe and Tony Woodcock responsible for half our sixty-nine league goals. Forest were champions because we had a very good manager with an eye for talented players who knew precisely what was required of them.

That championship medal is very important to me, although I think your first is always the one that sticks most in the memory. The Manchester United boys who won the Premiership title eight times in eleven years have a particular soft spot for their first one in 1992–93.

In all, Forest played seventy first-team matches that season and I don't think a single one of the lads would say they were tired at the end. We were delighted to play that many matches because we believed it meant we'd be there or thereabouts when it came to winning trophies. Shilton picked up the PFA player of the year award and I was runner-up. The lads had put in a very hard, typical Clough pre-season stint in Switzerland, Austria and West Germany before I joined them. Sometimes the Gaffer would give us a day off in the week and he arranged little breaks to Israel and Benidorm to keep us fresh and focused.

These were the Forest heroes in 1977–78:

Peter Shilton – He never conceded a goal in his career that was his own fault! Shilton could always pinpoint a mistake by someone else, sometimes up to eighteen moves away, that was directly to blame for the ball ending up in his net. This would have been a tiresome trait in anyone other than this incredible goalkeeper. Stoke's chairman warned Clough, 'He'll bankrupt you, for sure,' when the transfer went through, but Shilton was worth every penny of his hefty wages at the City Ground. Peter was a big personality, even if you did sometimes smell him coming before you clapped eyes on him. Almost surgically attached to his bag of toiletries, Peter was heavily into shower gel, perfumes and hairspray – and that was before he went out on to the pitch. He went off the rails a couple of times through a combination of drink and gambling, but he was a driven man on the training pitch – absolutely magnificent. He had an incessant need to win, win, win at all costs and a pathological hatred of losing at anything. His tally of clean sheets in a career that encompassed a record 125 England caps and over 1,000 league appearances marks Shilton as one of the top keepers in the history of the game.

Viv Anderson – Another terrific footballer with energy to burn, Viv got up and down the line with enough pace and grace to make him an England regular in the years to come as he progressed through the ranks from the youth team. Personality-wise, I always enjoyed Viv's company. He had a great, dry sense of humour and although he took a bit of stick here and there from the other lads, he was perfectly capable of dishing it out as well. Viv was a very pleasant person and a credit to his profession.

Frank Clark – Frank arrived at Forest at the age of thirty-two from Newcastle having won next-to-nothing apart from the Inter Cities Fairs Cup in 1969, and could scarcely believe his luck as he went on to stockpile the silverware. He played with unbelievable enthusiasm, as if every match would be his last, and never gave a moment's trouble. He was another very nice character.

Colin Barrett – Colin spent most of the season competing with Frank for the left-back position. He was very quiet.

Larry Lloyd – Larry couldn't be ignored. He always had something to say and could argue the back legs off a donkey, given half a chance. He might know he was wrong but would still claim he was right and knew best. Larry could not run to save his life and frightened opponents half to death instead with his sheer physical presence and power. He did very well in the air but was not exactly comfortable with the ball at his feet. Larry arrived at the City Ground with three England caps from his Anfield days in the early seventies and added one more to his collection, against Wales in 1980. Lack of international recognition rankled with him and his reply to the taunt, 'How many England caps have you got?' was invariably, 'How big's your bank balance?' He'd spent a fair few years at Liverpool, who were top payers, and was on an extra few quid compared to most of the other lads. The arguments Larry and I had tended to revolve around money but we respected each other and professionally, on the pitch, we had a perfectly good working relationship. I have no axe to grind with Larry and like him even more these days.

Kenny Burns – A wonderful character who was crowned Footballer of the Year in 1978, Kenny was a very accomplished player. He read the game intelligently and could also pass the ball. He had played centre-forward at Birmingham and that experience helped him at the back with us. He frequently knew where strikers would threaten, anticipated their runs and got there first. Kenny always stuck up for himself and stood his ground, on and off the pitch, and could be a bruiser. He liked to gamble on the dogs, and he liked a drink.

David Needham – Bought from QPR for £150,000 at Christmas as back-up when Larry broke his foot, David always gave his best when selected. He was extremely steady and very brave, never reluctant to stick his head in where it hurt.

Martin O'Neill – Martin would speak his mind and, even then, I had a feeling he was a good bet to go on to bigger and better things, which of course he has as a manager, most notably with Celtic. A great trier who made the most of his ability, Martin thought he never got the credit he deserved or the recognition for his contribution to the championship at Forest but, to be quite fair about it, he was what you would call a workhorse who scored a goal here and there. The intellectual one of our party, Martin read a lot and was knowledgeable on several subjects.

John McGovern – Forest had some big personalities but the Gaffer chose my best pal in football to skipper the side, and that tells you everything you need to know about his strengths as a player and leader. He was Captain Fantastic,

110

as far as I was concerned. John's awkward running style made him look ungainly but appearances were deceptive. A smooth operator, he loved rock music and still does.

Ian Bowyer – Totally underrated and far better than people gave him credit for, Ian was a textbook professional, never hid and always wanted the ball. Another thing he never did was moan when dropped. Ian scored several important goals during the League Cup run plus an absolutely massive one for the club to win the European Cup semi-final in Cologne. He was terrific in the dressing room with his dry wit.

John Robertson – Collar turned up on his grubby white raincoat, cigar in hand and one eye closed, Robbo perfected an hilarious impression of TV cop Columbo. Clough famously described him as a tramp when they first met and he still looks like a tramp to me, albeit a little bit wealthier since his success as Martin O'Neill's assistant at Celtic. With a terrific sense of humour, he was a jack the lad who loved the good life but when it came to playing football that great brain of his would be switched on in an instant. He was always available for a pass, even when worried opponents put two men on him, and his crossing ability was world-class. A fantastic player with either foot, he could do anything with a ball. Robbo made it look simple.

Peter Withe – Peter could be relied on to lead the line, keep things going up front and ensure defenders never had a moment to relax. He had terrific stamina and would run all day if you let him. When it came to clocking up high mileage, Peter and Viv Anderson were as good as anybody in the business. It seemed totally effortless to them.

Tony Woodcock – Off the pitch, Tony was a quiet, unobtrusive individual. On the pitch it was a different story and he scored his fair share of goals, earned himself transfers to

Cologne and Arsenal and ended up with over forty England caps – not bad going for a local lad who came through the youth team and was sent on loan to Lincoln and Doncaster because the Gaffer didn't fancy him to begin with.

12

TROUBLE IN ARGENTINA

THREE other Scotland players were on the same pep pills that got Willie Johnston sent home from the World Cup in Argentina in June 1978. I know who they are and I know they brought the stuff with them from their clubs. It's not my job to expose the trio more than twenty-five years later and I have no inclination to cause them any embarrassment. Let's just say I hope they have had time to consider the dreadful damage they might have caused Scottish football and learned the error of their ways.

I'm glad it's not a guilty secret that has ever cost me any precious sleep. It's all water under the bridge, much like the evidence, which was flushed down the toilets when we returned to the team hotel in the wake of a dreadful 3–1 spanking by Peru. It was like Niagara Falls, there was so much rushing water that night. Any casual guest would have thought we were all suffering from Montezuma's revenge after a particularly spicy South American supper.

We'd been kicked in the guts anyway by a Peru side written off by manager Ally MacLeod as 'old men'. After that, Willie's positive drugs test left us reeling. The fuss kicked up was bad enough, as he was sent home, reputation in tatters. What the outcry would have been if four Scottish internationals had tested positive and landed back together at Glasgow airport doesn't bear thinking about.

The gear was Fencamfamin which, apparently, contained

similar properties to amphetamine and cocaine. Willie whined about innocently taking a flu tonic and some stuff to combat hay fever. He was banned from playing for Scotland for life although his professional career continued for some years with various clubs. I believe he's now running a pub in Fife.

Yet the 1978 World Cup had started on such an upbeat note, with MacLeod beating the drum so loudly and consistently that I'm sure many legions of the Tartan Army were genuine believers as they sang: 'We'll really shake them up when we win the World Cup.' Even a 1–0 home defeat by England in front of 88,000 fans in our final match before flying off to the tournament couldn't dampen the enthusiasm and national fervour. After all, England had failed to qualify for the World Cup – again – after Don Revie jumped ship and Ron Greenwood took over. The delighted Scotland fans were only too happy to gloat: 'We're here to show the world that we're gonnae do or die, 'coz England cannae dae it 'coz they didnae qualify.'

Scotland's team for the game against England on 20 May was: Alan Rough, Stuart Kennedy, Kenny Burns, Tom Forsyth, Willie Donachie, Bruce Rioch, Don Masson, Asa Hartford, Kenny Dalglish, Joe Jordan and Willie Johnston. I got on for the last fifteen minutes as a substitute alongside Graeme Souness as we chased victory only to fall to a late goal from Steve Coppell.

Also in the party itching to get to Argentina were Sandy Jardine, Martin Buchan, Gordon McQueen, Jim Blyth, Lou Macari, Derek Johnstone, John Robertson, Bobby Clark and Joe Harper.

Maybe the England result should have sown a few little seeds of doubt, but there were no shades of grey with Ally. He saw everything in black and white – and tartan, of course – promising we'd come home with at least a medal. MacLeod had pumped everything up to a crescendo and there must have been over 30,000 people at Hampden the following Thursday, paying 50p for a seat and 30p to stand on the terraces for a gala farewell show complete with comedian Andy Cameron, massed pipe bands, majorettes and us on the back of a big open truck. Andy went from being a club comic to appearing on Top of the Pops with his catchy anthem, 'We're on the March with Ally's Army'. I heard they had to increase the original press run of 2,000 singles to 350,000, such was the extent of the World Cup mania. Hours after we drew with Iran, a fan in Dundee was reputedly selling that single for one penny and the free loan of his hammer.

The send-off was terrific, a once-in-a-lifetime experience and, to some, it must have felt as if Scotland had already won the World Cup. MacLeod had every reason to believe Scotland would put on a show in Argentina, considering the players at his disposal. It was an extremely talented squad, by anyone's standards. Right at the start of the qualifying campaign in the autumn of 1976, I had led Scotland to a 1–0 win over Wales after a 2–0 defeat by the Czechs, but on a dramatic night in October 1977, with over 50,000 partisan supporters shoehorned into Anfield for a play-off with Wales to decide which nation would go to the World Cup, I was marooned on the substitutes' bench. Don Masson, with a penalty, and Kenny Dalglish secured a late 2–0 win and, from the noise, you would have thought all of Glasgow, Edinburgh, Dundee and Aberdeen combined was on Merseyside. By the time we came to fly to Buenos Aires, I had won a third league championship medal, with Nottingham Forest, only to become a bit-part player on the international stage, unable to crack the now-established midfield trio of the Derby duo Don Masson and Bruce Rioch alongside Manchester City's Asa Hartford.

Normally, we travelled with sportswriters and senior football reporters but this time our huge party contained two or three unfamiliar faces from the press. I knew that was ominous and spelled trouble. They weren't along for the ride to inform an army of tabloid readers back in Britain that all was lovey-dovey in our camp. We would need to watch our step. The merest whiff of

115

scandal and the heavy-boots brigade would trample all over us with their brief to 'sod the facts, get stuck into Scotland'.

I don't know what went off between Ally and the press, but there was a suggestion that he had reneged on a promise to provide exclusive material for one paper. Certainly, some people were trying to stitch him up and more than a few would have liked to have seen him stitched up. Some folk didn't like the idea that he'd already made a few bob out of advertising carpets in TV commercials.

Things began to go wrong on the coach from the airport. It broke down and we were left to walk the last leg of our journey, carrying our bags half-a-mile to our hilltop hotel in Altagracia. Even at that early stage, I thought to myself, 'Here we go again, the usual Scottish disaster,' but nothing could have prepared me for the trouble that dogged our footsteps during the following weeks.

We arrived hot, bothered and thirsty after a journey of virtually twenty-four hours to discover painters in residence, dabbing here, there and everywhere. It was a joke. It's a good thing the hotel didn't require an electrician, otherwise I'm sure some bright spark would have volunteered me.

MacLeod certainly didn't endear himself to the press when we arrived by telling what seemed like 200 assorted journalists they could not interview us and to 'get lost', or words to that effect. He did, however, appreciate that our chances of getting some welcome sleep were about zero and informed us that there was a casino next door where we were welcome to wind down for a few hours with a beer or two.

The bulk of the lads needed no further encouragement but it was sheer laziness on our part that prevented us walking past reception, through the main entrance of the hotel and round the corner to the casino – 500 yards all told, if that. The most direct route was more like ten yards, into the garden and straight over a low wire-mesh fence that was held up by wooden stakes. No sooner had this plan of action been put into effect than the place was swarming with a dozen or so guards armed with machine guns. They burst out of the bushes, pointing their guns at us. Quite why they were lurking there I'll never know, particularly in such numbers. It was like a scene from a James Bond film and the atmosphere was tense. Ally was summoned to vouch for us, the guns were reluctantly lowered and we continued on our way to a welcome spot of liquid refreshment and a few spins of the roulette wheel.

We thought no more of it because it was basically a 'nothing' incident. Imagine our horror, then, at finding out about the front-page headlines back home, which accused the squad of breaking a curfew to go on the booze. That was such a load of cobblers. Suddenly, we were being made to feel like criminals.

To make matters worse, the facilities at Altagracia were not very good at all. Shame we didn't have Roy Keane along for the ride. He'd have loved it. There was no water in the swimming pool and the painting and decorating never ceased. The hotel was a shabby two-star job. That much could just about have been overlooked had our training facilities been up to scratch when we got down to the serious business of trying to win the most prestigious football tournament in the world. Tempers were not improved on arriving at the pitch where we were supposed to refine our skills and plan our tactics. It was rutted, like a ploughed field, and rock-hard. Shocking! No one was going to put their boots on and attempt to train on a surface like that. You could have broken an ankle the first time you turned. We went back to the hotel and found some fields nearby that were more suitable for a squad of international sportsmen.

That night the little matter of a dispute over bonuses arose. To my mind, that business should have been done and dusted before any of us set so much as a foot out of Scotland, but here we were, on the eve of the World Cup, arguing the toss about money. To be honest, I didn't feel that strongly about it at the time and I can't shed any light on the figures being bandied about. I had more important things to worry about – such as would I ever get on the pitches of Mendoza and Cordoba? Led by Dalglish, Macari, Rioch and Buchan, the lads kicked up a stink when the Scottish FA officials told us we weren't going to get anything like the amount we'd been led to believe we would receive. In the end, a compromise was reached, as always happens in situations such as this, but it wasn't the happiest of solutions and left another sour taste in the mouth. I was getting so used to it by now I might have been sucking lemons full time.

Still, the hills were alive with the sound of Scotland getting down to business at last and after a couple of days in the heat, working hard, Ally suggested we might like to take ourselves down into the village for a glass or two of cold beer. Nine or ten of the lads, myself included, took the manager up on his kind offer. Showered, changed and chatting away happily, we were hardly the Wild Bunch about to hit town. We settled in the square and were just having a beer in one of the bars when a handful of pretty girls came and sat round our table with us. The next thing you know, it's flash, bang, wallop, what a picture. Some photographers appeared from nowhere and fired off a load of shots before jumping into a little white car that went screaming off at high speed. We had been set up good and proper but the pictures on the front pages back home revealed only footballers, women and beer.

We had been caught in a very unfavourable light – Scotland players on the booze and on the pull, which was a million miles from the truth. After that, it seemed to be open season with tales of our supposed wild behaviour, discos and drinking until six in the morning. The papers were all on our backs now, day and night, making things as uncomfortable as possible.

Given the disastrous build-up, we desperately needed to start the World Cup on 3 June with a decent display, not to mention victory, against Peru in Cordoba. Buchan in place of Donachie was the solitary change from the side that had started against England. The midfield trio of Rioch, Masson and Hartford was playing really well, so I just sat on the bench, waiting to see what happened.

Scotland played particularly well to start with, Joe Jordan scoring after fifteen minutes. It was 1–1 at half-time but then Masson missed a penalty and I replaced him for the final twenty minutes. The next thing we knew, Teofilo Cubillas weaved some magic, scoring twice, and we ended up losing 3–1 – the sort of start we needed like a hole in the head.

Sometimes I wonder if the whole episode of Scotland in Argentina in 1978 wasn't cursed from the word go. Certainly, plenty of curses and oaths were muttered within the camp after what happened in the hours following that beating by the Peruvians in the Estadio Chateau Carreras. Kenny Dalglish and I were selected to provide a urine sample straight after the final whistle, but you know how it is sometimes, when you're dehydrated after expending a lot of physical energy on a hot day. It takes a good while before you feel the urge. I was struggling to oblige the testers and after six or seven minutes Willie Johnston walked through the door into the specimen cubicle.

Apparently, there had been a case of mistaken identity. Kenny and Willie, who both started the match, should have been the pair up for a pee, and it was nothing to do with me. Had I been able to produce a sample in time, perhaps they wouldn't have bothered with Willie, but the rest, as they say, is history. I felt sorrow for him more than anger. It was such a silly thing to do. Willie Johnston didn't need anything to assist his performance. He was such a naturally bubbly character, a very good player who could run like the wind and who was as tough as could be. I got to know Willie better in years to come when we played together at Birmingham City, and taking those pep pills was something he bitterly regretted.

Poor old Ally was now in the depths of despair, savaged for our surrender against Peru and having to face the consequences of seeing his first-choice winger sent home in disgrace for taking illegal substances.

Bruce and I were sharing a room and a few nights later there was a knock on the door, and in came Ally. The three of us had a lengthy chat about the next match, against Iran, and Ally admitted he'd made a mistake from the word go. He said he could see how much respect I commanded from the rest of the squad and he should never have taken the captaincy off me in the first place. You have to respect someone big enough to make a confession like that, especially in such an ego-driven profession as ours. He could just as easily have spoken to me in private, but he chose to be open about the matter, although I wondered about Bruce's feelings because he'd led the side against Peru. However, Ally had known about my strengths, guts and determination for at least a year.

Anyway, there he was, shrugging and saying sorry. He said he had been told that I was a very strong influence within the squad, like a Billy Bremner figure, and he didn't originally want someone like that. In my book, that was not a valid reason for stripping me of the captaincy. Billy was a colossus, despite his size in terms of feet and inches. When he walked into a room, everything stopped and only one man was the centre of attention. Billy got a terrific reception wherever he went. It's nice if some people think I have certain strengths, but I didn't have Billy Bremner's charisma. Ally feared – because I had been outspoken in team meetings – that I'd try taking over.

I rated Billy a magnificent player and I think we would have complemented each other in midfield. It's true we used to be tigerish against each other at club level, but that was par for the course whenever Derby and Leeds met. The players carried on the ill-feeling that always seemed to exist between their managers, Brian Clough and Don Revie

I may have played an unwitting role in the Johnston drug

scandal, but I was definitely guilty of the error that cost us very dearly against Iran back in Mendoza, four days after the Peru débâcle. Sometimes in life you have to hold your hands up. I'm 99.9 per cent certain that the team who played against Peru, with my Forest pal John Robertson a natural replacement for Johnston on the left wing, would have put Iran away with little fuss, but Ally seemed to panic. He dropped Masson and brought me out of nowhere to skipper the side, replaced Rioch with Macari, Kennedy with Jardine, put Donachie at left-back in place of Buchan, and gave the Manchester United captain Forsyth's role at the heart of the back four.

In front of a long-suffering crowd of under 8,000, we took the lead with a joke own-goal shortly before the interval, and that was probably more than we actually deserved. For reasons best known to myself – and even I can't remember what the hell I was doing there – I ended up at right-back against one of their lads, who twisted and turned me a couple of times inside the penalty area and managed to slash a shot across the face of Alan Rough's goal. Alan was anticipating the centre being cut back but he was deceived and it went in at the near post – Iran 1 Scotland 1. I should have defended much better while Alan's positional sense was not all it might have been. Afterwards, all of us – manager and players – knew exactly where we were heading – home.

The Tartan Army knew it, too, and were not best pleased. They spat at us as we left the pitch and threw their drinks at us – so things must have been really bad! To be fair to Ally, he did his best to rally the troops at a time when it was difficult to imagine the depth of hurt and despair he must have been feeling. The players could form little cliques and groups based around their clubs, moaning about everything and everyone else. Ally MacLeod had nobody to pass the buck to. He had promised the Scottish people the world and the world had turned round and kicked him in the teeth, and laughed in his face for good measure.

In our qualifying group of four, we'd needed to finish second to progress to the next stage of the tournament. In what should have been a two-horse race between ourselves and Holland, the odds now had us finishing third, or even fourth. With just the Dutch to come in Group 4 – a side including Johnny Rep, Rob Rensenbrink, Johan Neeskens, Wim Jansen and the van der Kerkhof brothers – our World Cup chances ranged between slim and nil, and slim had just left town, or so we thought.

The arrogant Dutch paid me and my Scotland team-mates the ultimate insult after we whacked them 3–2 in Mendoza. I have it on good authority that the match is remembered by many for a rather fine goal I scored, but my abiding memory of 11 June in the Estadio San Martin is the haughty manner in which Holland refused the traditional exchange of shirts at the final whistle. As we sat in our dressing room, totally drained but with a small glow of satisfaction at a job well done and some honour restored, a knock came at the door and in walked one of the Dutch trainers. 'Oh, good,' I thought. 'They've seen sense and brought their shirts in. Fair play to them.' I picked up my dark blue number fifteen jersey from the floor and moved to make a swap, only to discover Holland were offering us some training gear and most definitely not the shirts we'd made them sweat in during a gripping encounter. It was a total insult. The Dutch official was told in no uncertain terms where to stuff those training tops and he beat a hasty retreat.

I thought Holland were bigger than that. They might have lost the battle that day, but they'd won the war against us because Scotland had kicked off needing to win by three clear goals to progress to the knock-out stages. Their reaction seemed petty and spiteful to me after one of the most memorable matches of the 1978 World Cup. Maybe they got the needle because we were all fired up and a bit physical, but what do you expect in a World Cup when it's your last chance to show you can play a bit and you feel you've let down an entire nation watching on television at home, not to mention the supporters who had paid a small fortune to be with us in South America? Perhaps Holland would have felt more kindly disposed towards us and given us their shirts if we'd fallen at their feet and said, 'After you, Claude.' Fat chance!

A few weeks earlier, Graeme Souness had helped Liverpool beat Dutch coach Ernst Happel's Bruges team 1–0 in the European Cup final at Wembley when Kenny Dalglish scored. Souness was a great midfield operator, a fact that eventually dawned on Ally before the Holland match, when he belatedly brought Graeme into the side. It was all change again on the magical mystery tour as Stuart Kennedy, Tom Forsyth and Bruce Rioch were brought back while there were no places for Sandy Jardine, Kenny Burns, Lou Macari or John Robertson.

As for the Dutch, they kicked off with no fewer than eight of the team beaten 2–1 by West Germany in Munich in the 1974 World Cup final, and utilised an offside trap they had got down to a fine art. The late afternoon sun was soon casting long shadows over the pitch in the vast bowl of a stadium. Our cause wasn't harmed inside the opening ten minutes when I challenged Johan Neeskens and he had to go off with a rib injury. Souness organised us superbly and an early cross from him resulted in Rioch thumping a header against the bar before Dalglish had a goal cruelly chalked off. Kenny reacted first to toepoke the ball in when a huge clearance from Alan Rough bounced off the top of a defender's head, but the Austrian referee Erich Linemayr penalised Dalglish for a push. Then Joe Jordan left Wim Rijsbergen hobbling and the big, strong Dutch defender was later replaced.

Disaster struck shortly before the half-hour mark, however, when Johnny Rep stormed into the box and went down under a challenge from Kennedy and Rough to win a fortunate penalty. We were convinced it was a legitimate tackle by Kennedy and argued long and loud, too long in my case. Linemayr booked me – the second, and last, caution of my international career – before Rob Rensenbrink did the honours from the spot.

Trailing 1–0, we now had to score four goals without reply to go through. As tall orders go, it was as realistic as asking us to climb Mount Everest in carpet slippers. Still, this Scotland team on the day was nothing if not supremely game and we gave ourselves the faintest glimmer of hope on the stroke of half-time when Joe headed a centre from Souness back across goal for Dalglish to hook the equaliser under the angle of bar and post.

Right at the beginning of the second half Souness tried to get on the end of a header and the Dutch were panicked into chopping him down. I was our designated penalty-taker and had not the slightest doubt where the kick I was about to take would finish up.

So much rubbish is talked about penalties. If a player doesn't fancy taking one, I wonder whether he's in the right profession. You make up your mind which side of the goalkeeper you're going to kick the ball, put it on the spot, walk back, turn, run and do your job – all from just twelve yards with one opponent on the line. What could be simpler than that? It's an open invitation to score and I learned from watching an absolute master of the art at Derby, Alan Hinton.

Of course, once in a while you're going to end up with egg on your face – the keeper will guess correctly and make an inspired dive, or you will make a hash of the kick – but any footballer worth his salt should always be confident of scoring a penalty. Sometimes, when it all boils down to a shoot-out in a cup competition, you'll see certain characters, even strikers, slide away and try to hide. They are weak individuals and I have no sympathy for them, only contempt.

The Dutch keeper, Jan Jongbloed, guessed correctly, diving low to his left, but my penalty was too powerful, too accurate for him. Anyway, twenty minutes later Scotland were leading 3–1 and believing miracles could happen after I scored The Goal. If I had a fiver for every time I've been asked to describe the effort, I would be an extremely rich man today, but those few seconds of action have brought me something more satisfying than material wealth

– the satisfaction of being able to lay claim to a little bit of fame for doing something with a certain panache.

People who have a loose grasp on my career are liable to approach with a smile, go to shake my hand and ask, 'Aren't you that player who scored that goal . . .' I'm sometimes tempted to end the sentence, '. . . for Scotland against Argentina in 1978?' and then reply, 'No, you must be confusing me with another Archie Gemmill!' But I won't deny it has been fun down the years, never more so than in November 2003 when Scotland were drawn against Holland in a play-off for a place in the European Championship finals. I could hardly answer the telephone for a week without the call coming from some TV station or radio show in Holland or Scotland requesting an interview and, in-evitably, my memories of Mendoza. The goal had seemingly come back from the past and taken on a fresh life of its own. I'm not sure whether I strictly approve because of the subject matter, but in *Trainspotting*, a cult film about young low-life Scots on heroin, which came out in 1996 starring Ewan McGregor and Robert Carlyle, one of the characters remarks after sex, 'I haven't felt that good since Archie Gemmill scored against Holland in 1978.'

On a healthier note, I wonder if the goal inspired many boys to kick a football. I have a suspicion that it has maybe nudged one or two in to taking up ballet and becoming Scottish Billy Elliots. You could have knocked me down with a feather-duster a couple of years ago when I learned that Andy Howitt, the Scottish Youth Dance company's artistic director, was getting 200 school-children to Hampden Park to give a choreographed rendition of the goal, complete with feints, turns, shot and my celebratory punch in the air. It's very strange that a goal in football can attract so much attention. The modern dance was a great compliment to me. Dance, film, whatever next – the Gemmill Rap?

In a FIFA poll, my effort was nominated as the seventh best goal scored in a World Cup, while in the run-up to the 2002 finals in the Far East, BBC Sports Online selected it among their five most memorable World Cup goals. I'm in truly exalted company here, alongside Diego Maradona's run and finish from inside his own half against England in 1986, Michael Owen against Argentina in 1998, Brazil's Carlos Alberto and the forty-yard Arie Haan special in 1978, which took Holland past Italy to the final itself.

Channel 4 set themselves the impossible task of ranking the 100 Greatest Sporting Moments, ending up with Steve Redgrave's record-breaking fifth Olympic goal medal in poll position, while I crept in at fifty-one, sandwiched between Arsenal's 3–2 FA Cup final victory over Manchester United and Mike Tyson's illegal piece of the action when he bit a lump out of Evander Holyfield's ear. Fame indeed!

Somewhere along the line someone kindly made it 'officially' the greatest Scottish goal ever, although who makes these things official is quite beyond me. In the Scottish Football Museum in Glasgow you can even walk past several life-sized sculptures of defenders in orange and white and follow the path in my footsteps towards the goal.

A drama of a less palatable nature was unfolding back in Derby. Betty was at home, lying on the lounge floor, watching the game on TV, with the children tucked up in bed asleep upstairs. She had chosen to put Scot to bed at his normal time because he had school in the morning and, after all, she was not to know I would make my mark in such a memorable fashion. To this day, Scot has not forgiven her. Betty had her back to the patio doors, and no sooner had she recovered from the shock of my goal and regained her composure, than there was a tap on the window behind her. She turned to find an ugly, distorted face pressed flat up against the glass. Fortunately, she remained calm, checked the doors were locked and called one of our close friends who lived at the top of the road. He came straight away and checked the garden but the nutter had fled. Betty suffered some sleepless nights for some time after that. One of the drawbacks of playing in a match on the other side of the world is that unsavoury customers can try to take advantage.

A much more amusing story makes me grin every time it springs to mind. Two Scottish travellers were hiking through remote and barren areas of South America in the 1980s. At an isolated border crossing, they were accosted by some guards who patiently drew them out a diagram. Puzzled and bewildered, the pair later learned that the border guards weren't giving them directions or sketching out a request for a passport, but reconstructing the goal.

To be honest, far better goals than mine have been scored, but they don't get constantly repeated every time Scotland are drawn against Holland or when the big championships come round. Damien Duff's goal for the Republic of Ireland against Canada was ten times better than mine but you'll struggle to see it on television again because the match was a friendly. False modesty? No, opinion, mine.

I got a tape of the match a few years ago and since then I've watched it maybe twice. At the time, everything was totally instinctive, a blur of orange, white and blue. The ball broke to me fifteen yards in from the right touchline when Dalglish was tackled on the edge of the penalty area, and I skipped past Wim Jansen before sending Ruud Krol the wrong way with an outrageous dummy. Next up, across came Jan Poortvliet with a despairing lunge. I nicked the ball between his legs and when Jongbloed committed himself, it was a simple task to flick a shot over him. In total, I touched the ball six times – all with my trusty left foot – in maybe as many seconds. 'That is a goal in a million for Archie Gemmill,' cried the ITV commentator Brian Moore.

For three brief minutes, it must have seemed to all 40,000 fans in the ground, both sets of players and the millions glued to their television sets that Scotland were on the brink of pulling off the impossible dream. Moments like that emphasise why football is the greatest game in the world. However, if I was suddenly feeling on top of the world, my emotions plunged just as rapidly because I also played a part in the next goal – the one from Johnny Rep that brought all those dreams crashing down around our ears.

As he burst forward, I moved to close him down but I only succeeded in getting a toe to the ball. As a result, Rep's shot took a slight deflection. I've often wondered what would have happened if I hadn't got that touch. Did my intervention deflect the ball far enough out of Rough's reach and into the net? 'Football, bloody hell!', as Sir Alex Ferguson was to remark in 1999, in somewhat happier circumstances, when Manchester United completed the treble. Rep's balloon-buster left us with twenty minutes in which to score twice. In the circumstances, the task proved to be beyond us.

The whole Argentinian episode had one more bum note to sound. Before our flight home, the squad were taken to another rather shabby hotel and by now, the lads had taken more than enough of this second-rate treatment. The disappointment we felt at leaving the tournament combined with staying in distinctly average facilities all came to the surface when we arrived at our dodgy airport accommodation for our last night in South America.

Top brass from the Scottish FA were informed clearly, 'We aren't staying there!' and, what do you know, thirty minutes later we'd been upgraded to a five-star Marriott Hotel. A few bottles of wine followed with a nice little bit to eat. Deep down, I just felt sick. There is no way on this planet Scotland should not have progressed to the second round of the 1978 World Cup. Once there, it was straight knock-out stuff and, as we proved against the Dutch, on our day, we were as good as anybody, if not better.

13

HUMILIATED BY CLOUGH

SCOTLAND'S return from Argentina was closely followed by the draw for the European Cup. Liverpool had their sights fixed on joining immortals Real Madrid and Ajax by completing a hat-trick of tournament triumphs after seeing off Borussia Moenchengladbach and Bruges in the previous two finals. They were, quite clearly, the team every other one of the thirty-one clubs wanted to avoid and when I heard we had drawn them in the first round I thought, 'Oh, my God, that's the last thing we need.'

September's forthcoming confrontation between the European Cup-holders and the newly crowned League champions dominated conversation at the City Ground, but first another trophy was up for grabs. Lovely man, Bobby Robson, but he was crushed, in every sense, when Forest took his Ipswich team apart to the tune of 5–0 in the Charity Shield at Wembley, with John Robertson skinning Mick Mills every which way. Martin O'Neill ended up with two goals that day and a reprimand for showboating. He would have killed for a Wembley hat-trick on his cv and started hogging the ball. Clough was so unimpressed, despite our 4–0 lead, that he turned to trainer Jimmy Gordon and said, 'The next time he doesn't lay it off, he's off!'

'You can't do that, Gaffer,' Jimmy replied, and was shocked when Clough warned him about his own position at the club.

'Watch me!' Clough shouted.

The ball reached Martin, he kept possession and that was it, Clough hauled him off and brought on David Needham.

After the final whistle, Robson came into our dressing room to congratulate the Gaffer.

'Well done, Brian', he said, 'but I don't think the scoreline reflects the performance of both teams today.'

'You're quite right, Bobby,' the Boss shot back, 'and if we hadn't been playing at half-pace, it would have been ten-nil.'

Bob Paisley's Liverpool, rest assured, would offer considerably stiffer resistance to a club playing in serious European club competition for the first time, but we possessed at least half-a-dozen full internationals ourselves and, even before a ball had been kicked in anger, I remember feeling confident. If we could get past Liverpool, nobody else was going to stop us, were they? If we could beat Liverpool, we could beat anybody.

The first leg at our place was a belter but I knew one goal might not be enough. A score of 2–0 would give us a cushion, while 1–0 was going to make it that bit harder on Merseyside, so we were all filled with hope and expectation when Colin Barrett banged in a late goal to add to one from Garry Birtles in the first half. Now it really would be game on in the return leg.

Minutes before we left the visitors' dressing room at Anfield, the Gaffer casually told me I would be playing as an extra right-back, tucked in just in front of Viv Anderson. That was news to me, as I was fully expecting to be using my left foot in central midfield. The Boss explained quickly that Steve Heighway and Ray Kennedy both saw a lot of ball and loved attacking down Liverpool's left flank, so he wanted Viv and me to keep a tight grip of things in that area.

Other sides might have worked on perfecting the ploy for a week in training, but that wasn't our style. We never worked on anything. Team patterns, team play, shadow work, it was all so much unnecessary clutter to Brian Clough. His coaching was all done by word of mouth, and woe betide anyone who didn't ensure John Robertson took all the dead-ball kicks. If the Gaffer had faith in me to play right-back, there was no need to worry on my part.

Ninety minutes later after a stalemate, I thought we resembled a heavyweight champion, sagging against the ropes at the final bell but, crucially, we had absorbed every punch Liverpool could muster and defended for our lives with Peter Shilton pulling off a couple of good saves. With the exception of Everton and Manchester United, teams tend to be well received at Anfield and full credit to the Kop. They most certainly respected our defensive performance and clapped us off the pitch at the end.

There was another huge bonus to beating Liverpool, apart from removing the major obstacle in our path to winning the European Cup – and we had the satisfaction of feeling this one in our bank balances. The Boss worked his magic on the notoriously tight Forest committee and got them to cough up £1,000 a man for reaching the second round, where a trip to take on AEK Athens was on the itinerary.

Whether it was Derby in their prime or Forest, we always felt equipped to go anywhere and get a result. Our confidence was not misplaced in Athens, where we won 2–1, but the Greek fans were a totally different proposition from the AEK team. They were distinctly volatile and when we got stuck in traffic outside the stadium, they pelted our team bus with anything they could lay their hands on before making a concerted attempt to roll it over. It was decidedly unpleasant and I don't think anyone on that rocking bus felt very comfortable until the police came to our rescue.

AEK couldn't live with us back in Nottingham at the beginning of November and we trounced them 5–1, giving a terrific exhibition of football. After the first couple of goals, the Greeks lost heart pretty quickly and threw in the towel. They disappointed me, to be frank. You don't get British clubs giving up like that in Europe. We were through to the quarter-finals now and that meant a breather until March when we entertained the Swiss side Grasshoppers Zurich.

The Continent also loomed large for me with Scotland in the shape of the European Championship. Those bitter-sweet memories of what might have been against Holland in the World Cup kept Ally MacLeod in a job for the start of the new European qualifying campaign in September, and I skippered Scotland as we flopped to a disastrous 3–2 defeat by Austria in Vienna after trailing 3–0 at one stage. Ally's position was untenable after that and he was replaced by legendary Celtic manager Jock Stein for our next match, October's 3–2 victory over Norway at Hampden, where I rounded things off pretty neatly with a winning penalty three minutes before the final whistle. The following month brought no joy, merely a 1–0 defeat by Portugal in Lisbon. A lull in international proceedings meant I could give Forest my undivided attention.

All good things come to an end and on 9 December 1978 the inevitable occurred and Forest were beaten in the League. The magnificent year-long, forty-two match unbeaten run, which began with a totally forgettable 0–0 home draw with West Bromwich Albion on 26 November the previous season, was over. Fittingly, the side that turned us over was Liverpool.

They had been lying in wait for us with revenge in mind since our little dust-up in the European Cup. They hadn't beaten Forest in six matches since promotion and Liverpool's 2–0 win was greeted by the Anfield faithful as if they'd won the League. We still had two games in hand over them, but now they had opened up a nine-point lead at the top of the table. By the end of the season we had managed to cut the gap to eight points as we finished in the runners-up position.

I don't think we were ever particularly aware that we were creating history on that record run. It genuinely was just a matter of taking one match at a time and, because it was spread over two seasons, we were never under any pressure. People only really started getting fascinated about the run years later. The mere fact the record stood for so long speaks volumes for it. By anybody's standards, anywhere in the world in a hard, competitive League, to play forty-two matches without losing once is a considerable feat of which everyone involved can feel justly proud. Plenty of old Forest players and supporters were upset when Arsenal beat our record, but I think that is narrow-minded. To complete a thirty-eight match season undefeated in the Premiership in this day and age has far more impact than our achievement, and deservedly so. I can't see it ever being equalled and it was a privilege to watch Arsene Wenger's side develop into such a dominant force for forty-nine unbeaten games before they met their match at Manchester United.

For me, losing to Liverpool was desperate because of the gap it opened at the top of the table. Not many clubs successfully defend their championship, only the great ones. Forest were just very good and Brian Clough was magic. I felt we still had a fighting chance of retaining our league title as we approached April but that month we were obliged to play ten matches and the last two cost us dearly. Liverpool earned a 0–0 draw at our place, then we lost 1–0 at Wolves and the game was up, the title conceded. In fact, we had to win the final three matches against Manchester City, Leeds and, on the last Saturday of the season, West Brom, to overhaul Albion and take second place.

When it came to being hard to beat, nobody did it better. We lost three league games all season – Liverpool were beaten four times – but we allowed far too many opponents to take a point against us. Eighteen draws we clocked up, the pools punters must have loved us.

Meanwhile, Grasshoppers had Peter Taylor hopping about like a cat on the proverbial hot tin roof. Club sides in Switzerland had no great pedigree when it came to doing anything in Europe, but this lot had eliminated Real Madrid in the previous round on away goals, so demanded our utmost respect – as Peter never tired of reminding us. Taylor had been to see them on several occasions, reporting back that they were more than useful and possessed a top-class centre-forward in Claudio Sulser, who had already scored nine goals in the competition that season.

But, hey, we were Nottingham Forest, champions of England and conquerors of mighty Liverpool while they were – who exactly? Despite the best efforts of the management to drum a warning into us, we suffered a nasty shock to the system when Sulser scored in the first ten minutes. I still felt we needed just one goal to get right back into it. We got a couple but Grasshoppers might easily have pinched another and it wasn't until the last two minutes that Larry Lloyd and I scored two more. A 4–1 home win put us on relatively easy street but the scoreline was tough on the Swiss. It was a huge relief to us to win because the match had been a lot harder than possibly any of the players thought it would be. We'd been a bit casual and it had almost backfired on us. Shilton had needed to make a super save from Sulser at 2–1.

We got precisely what we deserved back in the dressing room – a good, old-fashioned rollicking from the Gaffer. 'You're just a bunch of big heads,' he roared. 'You think you can just go out there and do this, you think you can do that and you think you can make mugs out of a side we told you could play. Idiots.' That was the gist of it and, suitably chastised, we went home with our tails firmly between our legs. You win 4–1 and still get a bollocking. I should have been used to it by then.

Four days before the return leg in Switzerland, Forest were back at Wembley, retaining the League Cup with a 3–2 victory over Southampton. As usual before a match in London, we ate at our favourite Italian restaurant by Trent Bridge on the Friday night and relaxed while all the rush-hour traffic faded away before boarding the coach to travel south down the M1.

We booked into our hotel around 9.30 p.m., perfect timing for me to go up to my room, clean my teeth and watch half an hour's TV before getting my head down. I got my room key off Jimmy

Gordon and slipped away upstairs. I've always been a very light sleeper and when it came to the night before a match I just needed peace and quiet and my own space to relax. I roomed with John McGovern for some time and that was almost ideal because he liked his kip as well. The Boss wasn't too keen on anyone having a room all to himself, but I always preferred to be on my own. It was beneficial and he came round to my way of thinking and indulged me a bit. So there I was in bed, watching the box, when the phone rang. It was Jimmy Gordon in reception.

'You've got to get yourself down here, Archie,' he said.

'I'm not coming down. I'm in bed and that's me for the night.'

'You've got to come down.'

'No, I haven't got to do anything of the sort. I've told you, Jimmy. I'm in bed and that's where I'm staying.'

Two minutes later the Boss phoned to command, 'Get yourself down here now.'

Well, talk about an offer you can't afford to refuse. I couldn't very well tell Clough to get stuffed, so I threw on some clothes and descended with a face like thunder, in a foul mood, to discover the games room in the hotel had been cordoned off for the Forest party – and some party it was with beer, champagne and wine flowing to wash down a selection of sandwiches as the lads played crib, dominoes and bar billiards. The Gaffer asked me what I'd like to drink and I replied sullenly, 'The usual, nothing.' I think I managed one glass of champagne before making a move but the Boss caught me sneaking out and snapped, 'You're going nowhere until we've supped this lot.'

It must have been one in the morning before we called it a day, or rather a night. It hadn't been a full-blown piss-up but a few of the lads had clearly enjoyed several beers and never surfaced in time for breakfast in the morning. We went for a walk, had a little lunch and boarded the coach for Wembley. There was no team meeting. We knew who was playing – the first eleven names on the sheet pinned up inside the City Ground on Friday.

Southampton led 1–0 at half-time and we hadn't performed well but I thought I'd been our best player. Still, I got a massive bollocking off both Clough and Taylor. I wasn't doing this, I wasn't doing that and if I didn't pull my finger out I was coming off. I had a particularly good second half, we won 3–2 and Garry Birtles deservedly got the man of the match honours for his two goals, although I don't think I was too far behind him.

Birtles had been at the club since 1975, when he was a carpet-fitter playing non-league football for local club Long Eaton United. He became an overnight sensation soon after Peter Withe cut his own throat by demanding a transfer and Garry went on to join Manchester United for £1.25 million.

Before that, he gave Forest several superb years and never played better than when he helped the club to win the European Cup for the second time. I watched Forest overcome Kevin Keegan's Hamburg 1–0 in Madrid in 1980 on television at home and saw Birtles put in an absolutely incredible shift up front on his own, chasing, closing down defenders and holding up the ball. Garry was so unselfish and would run all day for you. In addition, he was a really nice person.

Maybe I was just lucky, but a good 90 to 95 per cent of my team-mates throughout my career were very pleasant characters. Trevor Francis joined Forest in February 1979 for a million pounds – the first player in Britain to command a fee of that size – and a more modest person you'd struggle to find. Trevor was no problem at all. In fact, he was eager to learn more about the game from the Gaffer, who gave him a tough time to start with, playing him out of position on the right. It was a test of character for Trevor and another example of the Boss teaching a new signing never to take anything for granted.

Another day, another cup, and so to Zurich where Grass-hoppers never had the self-belief to win the tie 3–0 – and they were dead right because it was virtually unheard of for us to concede three goals to anyone, anywhere. A lot of noise emanated from a full house but the 1–1 draw was relatively easy for us.

Just one club scored three goals against us all season and, coincidentally, that was Cologne in the European Cup semi-final first leg a few weeks later. Forest usually prospered because we were very disciplined with good players in the right areas of the pitch at the right time, but we were all over the shop that night at the City Ground and the first forty-five minutes were probably the worst I was ever involved in at the club. The Germans kept catching us on fast breaks, something that just never happened. I tried to get back and defend against the Belgian international winger Roger van Gool, who turned me this way, that way and this way again to the extent I was spinning like a top when I felt my groin tear. I knew instinctively it was more than just a strain. It was sore, I had to go off before half-time and the only consolation was in seeing Forest fight back to draw 3–3.

I was feeling very low afterwards but the Gaffer was upbeat as he casually informed everyone that we would go to Cologne and win. You play like lemons for half the match, concede three goals yet the Gaffer loves you all to death. I should have been used to that by then as well.

Little did I know the injury would have far-reaching consequences, quite apart from robbing me of three international appearances as Jock Stein's skipper against Wales, Northern Ireland and England in the Home Internationals plus a friendly against Diego Maradona's world champions, Argentina, at Hampden.

I flew to Germany with no hope of playing, of course, because of the injury, but the Boss liked to keep everyone together and, after watching the lads train, I managed a little jog. Clough's words to the troops before the kick-off were inspiring. He laid great emphasis on the fact that Forest's great European Cup run had started in the first round when we went to Liverpool and kept a clean sheet. Shilton and Co. could manage that again, surely, and then all we had to do was score once at the other end. None of the British press gave us a prayer and Cologne were so confident of getting through they had already organised the tickets and a fleet of coaches for the final in Munich.

Clough made Forest's task sound ridiculously simple and the 1–0 victory he confidently predicted came to pass thanks to Ian Bowyer's goal in the second half.

I was always going to play against Malmo in the final. Clough told me that if I was fit, I was in the team. What he said was 100 per cent gospel as far as I was concerned and he had never ever given me the slightest reason to doubt his word before. If the Gaffer had said to me, 'Get fit and I'll see what happens,' I wouldn't have stood my ground so much and our relationship would not have degenerated into a bout of cursing, attempted ridicule and medal-flinging, but he made me a promise and he broke it.

I never did tackle the Swedes on 30 May 1979 in the magnificent Olympic Stadium. In fact, I never played for Forest again after tearing my groin muscle against Cologne some fifteen games earlier.

Ten days before the European Cup final, the pinnacle of my club career, I was back in full training, able to go flat out and feeling better and better each day. I knew I was 100 per cent fit then, but a seed of doubt about my selection was planted in my mind a week before Munich in another significant final, against Mansfield in the Nottinghamshire County Cup. I had been building up for ages to play in this one, straining at the leash to prove to anyone and everyone I was ready to return to first-team action. I went to see the Boss on the morning of the Mansfield match. He asked me if I was fit to play, I said I was and Clough said, 'Well, you're starting then, Archie, and that's it. We'll give you forty-five minutes and take it from there.'

I was delighted driving home, but when I returned for the match, I discovered the Boss had decided not to turn up – but worse, far worse, than that, I was down as a substitute. The deal with Clough at Derby and Forest was always that players returning from injury would start and he'd judge just how long they should stay on. They were never left on the bench.

'What's the score?', I complained to Peter Taylor. 'When I left here at lunchtime, I was playing. Now I'm not.'

Taylor replied that he and Clough had had second thoughts and that I would be coming on as a sub in the second half, which I did for the last twenty-five minutes and was delighted with how I performed. I felt nothing from the groin at all in any way, shape or form. My return had been rubber-stamped and there was only one thing on my mind now. I was getting ready to play in Munich and nothing could stop me.

The Gaffer had three dilemmas – how to get Frank Clark, Martin O'Neill and me back in the team. Frank had taken a knock and Martin was suffering from a hamstring injury but I wasn't the least bit interested in them. I was interested in one person and in my mind I knew I was playing.

We arrived in Germany and just walked and talked. It would have been a nasty shock to the system, and totally out of character, if we'd trained or discussed tactics. The day of the match was nice and sunny. We went to the stadium in the morning to get a feel of the place and the whole squad walked out on the running track and round to the halfway line. Clough sat all the lads down, praised the weather and indulged in a spot of chit-chat about the enormity of the occasion for all concerned before announcing the team. He ran through the names in midfield and I wasn't in it.

'You must be fucking joking!' I shouted, in front of the lads.

'What do you mean?' demanded Clough.

'You told me I was playing if I was fit – and I am fit,' I shot back.

'Shut up, you're out,' he said.

More verbals followed before Clough said Taylor would look after me. Pete took me to one side and went on about what a big day it was for Nottingham Forest, blah, blah, blah, what difficult decisions the management had had to make about injured players and I shouldn't rock the boat on this of all days.

'Don't give me all that bollocks,' I shouted. 'You and your mate are shitting on me.'

Out of the three of us, only Frank played. I'm not sure just how disappointed Martin was and whether deep down he maybe knew his hamstring wasn't 100 per cent. In any case, Martin always did have a little bit more between his ears than I did and, unlike me, he realised this was no time to pick a fight. He didn't seem to be as sick as I was. Martin was no shrinking violet but he picked his time to have a go and this wasn't one of them as far as he was concerned.

Back at the hotel, Taylor and I had another big bust-up, which ended with me telling him to fuck off. I was furious as we ate a light lunch and afterwards at the team meeting in the hotel, before we boarded the bus for the stadium, I most certainly let my feelings be known. It ended with the Boss asking, 'Archie, can you go up and get my shaving gear? I've left it in my room.' It was his way of showing he felt I had overstepped the mark and needed slapping down a peg or two.

I refused and he repeated the request, but this time he wasn't so much asking as telling me to act like his little dogsbody. I was humiliated but I also felt I had to back down, so I went up to Clough's room and discovered it in a terrible state. I don't know whether he'd left it looking like a tip deliberately but I had to play hunt the razor here and find the aftershave over there. By the time I got downstairs everybody else was on the bus and I got on to be greeted loudly by Clough enquiring, 'Welcome aboard, Archie, and by the way is that my shaving gear you've got there?' I was beyond caring about the degree of humiliation now. The stunt with the shaving tackle wasn't the worst thing he could do to me. He'd already done that by leaving me out of his European Cup final team.

I sat on the substitutes' bench hating every bloody minute of Forest's 1–0 win. Any player worth his salt who tells you he doesn't mind being a sub is talking a load of garbage. I was a complete misery for ninety minutes, having a right go at the Gaffer and telling him, 'This is total crap, get me on. I can light up this match.'

That wouldn't have been hard. All anyone can remember is Trevor Francis heading in John Robertson's cross. Apart from that, the final was a total non-event, absolutely pathetic as a spectacle. I would have backed myself on one leg to have added a bit of zest and sparkle. Things deteriorated afterwards.

I received my winner's medal, although it meant next to nothing to me, and got back to the dressing room as quickly as possible, sitting on my own for some time and feeling decidedly sorry for myself. The next thing I knew, Clough was walking round the team collecting the medals. He reckoned he needed them to have some replicas made for other people at the club. Equally, he was not in a good mood because Forest had not produced a fitting performance to match the occasion – far from it, in fact.

The lads were not too happy at this unexpected turn of events, and who could blame them? After all, they'd just given their all to win the European Cup and okay, so it wasn't the greatest match in living memory, but those medals meant a hell of a lot to the boys who had played against Malmo.

Clough came to me and said, 'By the way, I'll have your medal, too.'

'You're fucking welcome to it,' I snapped, and threw the thing on to the trainer's padded couch. It fell off.

'Pick it up,' demanded Clough.

'No,' I said.

'Pick it up,' insisted Clough.

'If you want it that fucking badly, you pick it up,' I said and with that, I went for a shower.

The manager then conducted his own presentation ceremony, starting with Peter Shilton. Each of the eleven who had played was given a medal.

I had a horrible time after the match. I was in no mood for a party and felt quite left out of all the celebrations. Betty never went to watch me play and Frank Clark's missus hadn't gone out to Germany, so the two of us went for a meal together and a few drinks. We were joined late on by the Stoke City manager Tony Waddington, who tapped both of us to sign for him. Waddington offered me a three-year contract on better money than Forest were paying me and by 1.30 a.m. I'd more or less convinced him, and myself, that I'd be kicking off the following season in the Potteries. In the cold, sober light of day I decided I didn't want to leave Forest and neither did Frank, but Malmo proved to be his last game as a player, although he didn't know it at the time.

The medal saga wouldn't go to bed and I said publicly, 'On the face of it, this seems an astonishing thing to do, but there must be a logical explanation.'

Clough, inevitably, interpreted that as an attack on him and stormed back, 'I am staggered Archie is moaning. He is showing an amazing lack of loyalty to me and the club. If he's cribbing about not getting his medal, he can have it the second he steps inside the ground. He's been with us long enough to know we believe in making sure that everyone involved in our success gets recognition. The medals have been put in the safe at the Forest ground until we can get replicas made. It seems ridiculous to me that Peter Taylor, Jimmy Gordon and myself should lead a side to the European Cup final and not get some recognition.

'I remember Frank Clark's League Cup winners' tankard being used for replicas. It was some time before he got it back – and no one deserved one more than he did. There's a lot of pride in winning trophies and medals. Although I am invariably the last to get one, it always means something very special to me and my family.'

So that was my European Cup final experience. I was never ever bothered about the medal. Months later, after I had joined Birmingham City, I received a message from the City Ground that the Gaffer wanted to present me with my medal. I went, but the medal means absolutely nothing to me. I'd been a non-playing substitute and I'd been about as relevant to winning the trophy as the man on the moon. See any Forest team photograph with the European Cup and I can guarantee you it will include one very miserable-looking player.

If Clough had nurtured doubts about me, Jock Stein took less convincing and the following week I was back in the Scotland team, leading from the front as skipper as we revived our hopes of qualifying for the 1980 European Championship finals in Italy with a resounding 4–0 triumph over Norway in Oslo.

At least, I had a positive note on which to sign off the season and I came back to Forest for pre-season training in a confident frame of mind, even though Asa Hartford had been signed. The Gaffer was away on his holidays in Majorca and we were walking back to the City Ground having played Notts County in a kickabout on our training ground, when Peter Taylor arrived by my side and said, 'I want to see you in the office when we get back, Archie.'

I went in to be informed by Taylor, 'You're finished here. We've signed Asa Hartford and you will no longer be playing. Birmingham want you – and we want you to go.' Case dismissed. As executions go, it was short, sharp and straight to the point. I couldn't help but think this was the management's revenge for the stance I had taken in Munich. Clough and Taylor had let me stew all summer before putting the boot in right where it hurt.

I was very unhappy that it had come to this and I had another year on my contract to go, so I could have stuck it out, but what would have been the point? My life would have been hell while, after talking to the Birmingham manager Jim Smith, I discovered he was more than happy to offer me a three-year contract and a massive pay rise. I was on £210 a week at Forest but the Blues would be giving me £600 plus a significant signing-on fee. Complete and utter misery in Nottingham for another season or a fresh challenge at Birmingham on excellent money – I didn't need Martin O'Neill's brains to sort that one out.

14

BRUM'S RUSH AND
STEIN BUST-UP

B AYERN MUNICH had just stuffed Forest 5–0 in a pre-season friendly, not that I could give a toss, when the phone rang that Sunday morning at the beginning of August 1979. I was a Birmingham City player by then, wondering what life held in store for me in the Second Division, down the west end of the A38, after a £150,000 transfer. I was up bright and early, busy working in the garden at home in Dean Close, Littleover, a respectable Derby suburb, when Betty shouted from the house, 'The Boss is on the phone, Archie.' I wondered what on earth Jim Smith wanted to talk to me about, especially as it wasn't yet ten o'clock, but of course it wasn't Jim. Brian Clough came straight to the point.

'I've made a mistake', he said. 'Asa Hartford is no good for this team. I want you back. I'm going to talk to Jim Smith and get everything sorted out.'

'Wait a minute,' I countered. 'I'm afraid I'm not coming back. I've signed for Birmingham.'

'Don't be silly,' Clough said. 'I've told you, I made a mistake. You're coming back now.'

I could feel the anger welling up inside me as I retaliated, 'You and your mate shit on me once and you aren't going to get the chance to shit on me again. That's it.'

'Are you sure?'

'Yes, I am sure.'

'If that's the way it is then that's it, son,' he said, and put down the receiver.

Our paths didn't cross again for a few months until Forest staged a modest ceremony so he could present a few of the outstanding European Cup winners' medals to those of us no longer at the club. I went to the City Ground under sufferance and out of a sense of duty I didn't care for. I don't know where the medal is now. My mother or Scot could have it. I'm not even sure if it's the real thing or a replica. Colin Barrett said his was definitely a replica and advised me to check mine. It could be made out of chocolate for all I care. I feel I was let down to an unbelievable extent by the Forest management and now the Boss felt all he had to do was click his fingers and I'd come running. Sorry, pal, it doesn't work like that. He was right about Hartford, though. He'd cost £500,000 from Manchester City but Asa was on his bike to Everton after only three league matches.

I wouldn't have swapped the years I did spend with Brian Clough at Derby and Forest for the world, but there is one other man I would loved to have played for – Bill Shankly. I never did discover what the Everton manager Harry Catterick thought of me, especially after I snubbed him to join Brian at Derby, yet to hear Shanks lavish praise on me sometimes, you'd almost think I had spent a decade on Merseyside at Anfield.

In the autumn of 1979 I thought my Scotland days were numbered, if not stone cold in the ground after dropping down a notch to play Second Division football, and when Jock Stein ignored me for a friendly against Peru in September, everyone was writing my international obituary – not Shanks, though. I'm not vain enough to possess sackfuls of old press cuttings, but there is one I treasure from the Birmingham *Sports Argus* pink after I'd been recalled by Jock to tackle Austria in a European Championship qualifier at Hampden the following month. Shanks, by then retired but far from retiring, was kind enough to tell the famous

Sweet charity – showing off the Wembley silver with Forest skipper John McGovern after launching the 1978 season in style with a 5–0 Charity Shield romp over Ipswich Town.

Game for a laugh – relaxing at home with Scot and Stacey in 1978.

Sitting it out, I resented watching every second of Forest's 1979 European Cup final victory over Malmo in Munich and made sure I was as far away as possible from Clough.

Tight-lipped, I had nothing to smile about while showing off the European Cup with Kenny Burns at a civic reception back in Nottingham.

Above left: Jim Smith gave me a huge wage rise when I joined Birmingham City – and I was delighted to work for him again as Derby's European scout.

Above right: It was a case of friends reunited when I played alongside Colin Todd at Birmingham but, sadly, we fell out much later when he was briefly Derby manager.

Right: Going up again! Birmingham's final match of the 1979–80 season, a 3–3 home draw against Notts County, was good enough to clinch the third promotion place in Division Two.

Revenge is sweet. I pulled a hamstring helping Derby eliminate Clough's Forest 2–0 in the third round of the FA Cup in January 1983 after scoring with a free-kick.

That's my boy. Scot signs for Forest flanked by Nigel and Brian Clough.

'Let's do it this way, Gaffer.' I give the boss the benefit of my advice.

End of an era. Brian Clough stands alone during his final match, against Sheffield United, while Liam O'Kane and I keep our heads down.

Merry Millers, Rotherham United fans enjoy our day in the sun at Wembley in 1996 when we won the AutoWindscreens Shield final.

United at Rotherham – but John McGovern and I expected too much of the players.

Victorious Rotherham players celebrate victory over Shrewsbury Town in front of the royal box at Wembley. *Left to right*: Matthew Clarke, Nigel Jemson, Trevor Berry, Andy Roscoe, Darren Garner and Ian Breckin. Silver-haired Ken Booth watches Andy Roscoe.

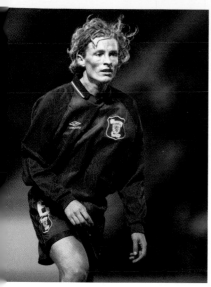

Like father, like son. I felt immensely proud when Scot followed me into the Scotland team and went on to win twenty-six international caps.

Scot left Forest in 1999 and spent five years at Everton.

Flight attendant Stacey (*third left*) and some of her crew.

The gentle touch. My beautiful daughter Stacey makes a new friend in 1997.

Happy family – the Gemmill clan on holiday in Capri.

Midlands sports paper: 'Archie Gemmill would never be out of any squad of mine. You can never leave your best players out. Archie would have been a good signing for any club in the League – and I mean ANY club. I would have taken him to Liverpool a few seasons back had circumstances permitted it. He will do Birmingham City a great favour and I feel he will continue to serve his country well on the field. He was a tremendous asset both to Derby and Forest when they won the First Division championship. One thing in Archie's favour is that he knows all about winning, and winning championships that really matter. He had a lot to do with the successes of both clubs and, at £150,000, he represents the steal of the season for Birmingham. What a shrewd buy.'

My professional career now lay at St Andrew's, where I was introduced to the Rat Pack – alias Mark Dennis, Tony Coton, Alan Curbishley and Kevin Dillon. It seems strange now that three of them have become pillars of the establishment. Curbishley has become an absolutely superb manager at Charlton Athletic, Kevin had a great time as Alan Pardew's assistant at Reading while Tony has used his experience to become Manchester United's goalkeeping coach.

Mark Dennis, meanwhile, became a postman in Southampton and was beavering away in non-league football with Eastleigh in the Ryman Premier League the last I heard of him. One example of the Rat Pack's idea of humour surfaced when Birmingham were staying in a small hotel in Belgium and staff discovered someone had broken into the kitchen and raided a crate of beer plus a leg of lamb from the freezer. Morning came and the aforementioned articles were discovered in one of their rooms, the lamb hanging in a wardrobe. The excuse was laughable. It was nothing to do the with the lads apparently and the beer and meat had been planted. Pull the other one.

Episodes like that happened far too often for my liking and I wasn't too keen on the Rat Pack frequently turning up late for training in cars that had no insurance or road tax. They were just young lads out for a good time and Birmingham was a big enough city for them to lead the life of Riley and get away with it, but it wasn't very pleasant getting changed in the dressing room near Dennis and Frank Worthington sometimes. The place could smell like a brewery after they'd been out on the town and, believe me, Frank did like a good time for all his talent – and his skill and ability were second to none. I don't think I was playing the school prefect. I wasn't walking around pretending to be Mr Goody Two Shoes, but I had come from a strict regime at Nottingham Forest and I wondered what the hell I had walked into.

For all their faults, Birmingham could play a bit and winning promotion in my first season was terrific for all concerned. I was voted Midlands midfield player of the season, which chuffed me no end as some people expected my career to go rapidly downhill after leaving Forest.

In terms of results, Jim Smith was absolutely tremendous at his job, great at extracting the maximum out of other people. He's always enjoyed life, particularly when nursing a glass of good red wine, and seemed happy to turn a blind eye to the antics of the Rat Pack. I didn't think the bad lads were remotely bothered by me and it quickly became obvious that I wouldn't have any success nagging or bollocking them. What I did say at times was geared to trying to get the best out of them, so I was quite surprised, and touched I suppose in a way, to hear Dillon many years later say he wished he had paid a lot more attention to me at St Andrew's.

Jock Stein was paying attention as I bust a gut to become a First Division player again with Birmingham and he gave me carte blanche to do my own thing for Scotland's opening match in 1980. I skippered a Scotland side that included the Liverpool trio of Kenny Dalglish, Graeme Souness and Alan Hansen to a 4–1 victory over Portugal at Hampden in March. That was a handsome result but it counted for zero in the context of the European Championship qualifiers because Scotland had long since blown their chances of making progress. We finished fourth in our group, beneath winners Belgium, Austria and Portugal with only Norway below us.

'You're the boss out there, Archie,' Stein told me. 'If anything needs changing tactically before half-time, just sort it, will you?'

Jim Smith was delighted to see me back in the international fold against the Portuguese and rubbished suggestions that I might be too old to play in the 1982 World Cup finals in Spain.

'Archie will still be playing in the top grade in two years' time,' Jim predicted, 'and if Scotland want him, there's no reason why he shouldn't take in another World Cup campaign. When Archie is playing for Scotland he adds a few inches in height. It means so much to him. He is an inspiring player – just like Alan Ball. Even when such players are not playing, they are vital to have around.'

Jim made a vital signing of his own when he recruited my old Derby friend and next-door neighbour Colin Todd. Flogged off to Everton from Derby by Tommy Docherty for £300,000 in September 1978, Colin did a great job of coming in and organising a defence good enough to win promotion.

Living on the other side of Betty and me in Littleover were a charming couple, Graham and Dianne Rose. Graham, by a lucky coincidence, worked at the big Ford garage in Birmingham and he managed to procure a sponsored car for me, plastered with the words 'Go Go Gemmill' and 'Birmingham City FC' down the side. Colin and I used to take turns driving to Brum and one day, on the way back from training, as I overtook a lorry along the A38, it lost a steel wedge, which shot under my car. Sparks flew and the fuel line was cut, but I managed to haul us over on to the hard shoulder. Colin and I jumped out before my lovely sponsored Ford went up in flames.

'Accidents will happen,' smiled Graham generously when I reported back to him what had happened and he got me a replacement car.

Four or five weeks later, Colin moved house to Devonshire Avenue in Allestree, on the north side of Derby. He lived at the top of a steep road that could be extremely tricky to negotiate during the winter. Around Christmas time, with ice and snow in evidence, I dropped him at his front door and then eased my way down towards the main road home, but a touch on my brakes sent the car sliding into a nasty collision with two parked vehicles. This one wasn't a complete write-off but there was a frozen grin on Graham's face as he said, 'Don't worry, Archie. I'm sure we can get you *another* car,' which he did, even though at this rate I'm sure he was putting his job in jeopardy.

The general madness at Birmingham seemed to affect Colin, too. Normally, he was a quiet, thoughtful soul but he really blew a fuse when Jim had a go at him at half-time on one occasion. It got really heated and ended with Colin ripping off his boots and jumping in the bath, leaving Jim open-mouthed. He asked me to go and coax Colin back into his kit for the second half, which I succeeded in doing.

If things went pear-shaped for Toddy, I felt as if a load of rotten fruit might arrive in my direction from the terraces at any minute the day we played at home to a Southampton side starring Kevin Keegan and Mick Channon. They hammered us 3–0. I went from the sublime to the ridiculous and back again in less than two months over the winter of 1980–81 in the First Division. The day after Boxing Day I scored against Sunderland in a 3–2 victory, but the cheers turned to jeers on 17 January against the Saints. I suspected I might be coming towards the end of my time at the club. I wasn't playing particularly well and it seemed the harder I tried the worse it became. I bore the brunt of the fans' abuse and frustration that day and it was a nasty shock to the old system.

I had never really experienced that side of the game before. At Preston, Derby and Forest I'd never taken much stick. I do like to think I always gave the fans at Deepdale, the Baseball Ground and City Ground good value for money, but those Bluenoses were making my life hell as we trudged off at half-time. There were only about 16,000 in our lowest home crowd of the season and I looked in vain for a single friendly face or voice in the ground as I walked off. I'm a strong character but the abuse was most certainly getting to me and I was praying that Jim Smith would take me off there and then but he shoved me out for another fifteen or twenty minutes before I got the hook. I swear that when Jim summoned me to the touchline that decision got the loudest cheer they've heard at St Andrew's until the day they won promotion to the Premier League. That match is one bad memory that will never leave me. It was the most degrading experience of my playing career.

My strength of character helped me get back in the fans' good books on 20 February when I ran the show in the snow against Norwich and scored another rare goal in a 4–0 win. Birmingham were in no danger of going down now and life was relatively sweet until the night in April when Alan Hansen and Graeme Souness fancied a couple of beers after hours. That night my Scotland career ended up in the gutter.

It must have been almost 11 p.m. when the two Liverpool lads eventually made it to our Glasgow hotel that Sunday. They had been held up for some reason on their journey from Merseyside and Jock Stein had retired to his room for the night, but that was no big deal.

The mood in the camp was bubbly and we were licking our lips at the prospect of getting stuck into Israel in a World Cup qualifier at Hampden. Hansen and Souness were licking their lips, too, at the prospect of an hour or two out on the town. They took some good-natured stick from the rest of the lads, who had already enjoyed a few halves in the hotel lounge and were thinking about heading away to their rooms.

What Alan and Graeme were proposing was no terrible thing, not a hanging offence. They weren't part of any heavy booze culture. At Liverpool, and other top clubs at the time, professionals, by and large, often liked to enjoy themselves with a couple of beers when it was appropriate. I was absolutely sure of one thing, however – there was not a snowball in hell's chance of Jock granting the Liverpool pair's wish. I knew full well that he wouldn't stand for it and told them so. I told them that they were wasting their time but still they moaned, wheedled and pleaded for quarter of an hour until I felt, as Scotland captain, it was at least my place to go and ask Jock if they could go out. I always believed it was part of my job to act as the go-between with the players and the manager. So, reluctantly, I went upstairs, stationed myself outside Jock's room, took a deep breath and knocked gently on his door.

There's a film called *Gone in 60 Seconds* about an expert car thief but I should have nabbed the copyright. That's how long it took for my international career to disappear. Jock had obviously already been to sleep. He opened the door in his dressing gown and blinked as he heard me ask if it would be all right for a couple of the team, without mentioning them by name, to go out for an hour or two.

Jock blew his top, he went absolutely ballistic, ranting and raving. 'How can you possibly even ask me such a thing?' he raged. I was supposed to be his captain, the man who knew exactly what was permitted and what was offside. That's what he felt and he expressed his views very forcibly. I was taken aback a little but stood my ground and argued my corner. I never mentioned that I was making the request specifically on behalf of Hansen and Souness.

I had never seen him so animated. He'd always struck me as a reasonably placid character who liked a little flutter on the horses and dogs, although I'm sure the Celtic boys all knew there was an explosive side to his nature, after all he'd been through in a decade at Parkhead. I took a fearful personal bollocking off Jock that evening, and there was a repeat performance the following morning in public in front of all the players.

Jock wasn't the slightest bit concerned about the identity of the players concerned and never asked. Everything was dumped on me. I knew the regulations, fumed Jock. I was totally out of order. To be fair to Alan and Graeme, they both approached me after that highly charged players' meeting to apologise for getting me into such hot water.

I told them not to worry and that as captain I had a duty to speak on their behalf but I never dreamed things would develop so seriously. Alan I only ever see on the television these days but I still bump into Graeme from time to time at functions and matches. There are no hard feelings. I certainly don't bear either of them any grudges. It wasn't them who had directly incurred the wrath of Jock, they hadn't woken him up and done the asking. That was all down to me and maybe I was silly, maybe I should have told them to drop it.

Jock pulled me to one side for a one-to-one. He finished the chat by saying the episode was water under the bridge, a mistake had been made and that it would never be made again. Now, you can read that in one of two ways. Either Jock was happy to forgive and forget or such a situation would never arise again because, as far as he was concerned, I would never play for Scotland again. At the time, I was relieved and happy because I took Jock to mean it had all been a storm in a teacup and the slate was wiped clean. Big mistake.

Training to tackle Israel the morning before the match went brilliantly. I was involved at the heart of everything, which I expected, with all the free-kicks and setting up of defensive walls. Back at the hotel Jock wanted another private word and in his room he told me that I wasn't playing, that Asa Hartford – the man who took my job at Nottingham Forest, albeit for three matches – was taking my place but that I was still to attend the match.

'I'll make it easier for you, if you like,' Jock said, 'and tell the press boys you've got a slight injury and that I'm not risking you.' My reply was short and to the point – 'Will you bollocks!'

That was the last time we spoke. All the mutual respect we'd had – or, at least, I thought we had – for each other had gone. I was ready to spill the beans and tell the world the truth, the real story behind my axing but Jock Stein always was a canny operator with the press and he quickly got his point over to them. Stories emphasising the '34-year-old' Archie Gemmill suddenly circulated. Funny how my age had not been an issue the previous week. If I was to start creating now it would look like sour grapes, so I went to the match, saw Danny McGrain take my captain's armband and John Robertson score two penalties before half-time. Then I calmly got up from my seat, left the stadium and drove home to Derby.

I never officially retired from international football but that was effectively the end of my Scotland career while Souness went on to win another forty-one caps and Hansen a further fourteen. I think my age was probably used as a weapon to beat me with when the next few squads were announced and my name was conspicuous by its absence. It was a very sad situation. Not for the first time in my life, I had been my own worst enemy, but if people don't treat me correctly, I have to hit back at them. It's just the way I'm made, like it or lump it. I can't hide. I believe it's always better to be honest and up front. I like clarity and hate any form of deception. I live and breathe right and wrong.

I suppose I could have battled on, wormed my way back into Jock's good books and possibly even have skippered Scotland to the 1982 World Cup. Before the Israel match, Jock had taken me to one side and promised me I would captain the team for the Home Internationals the following month, and for as long as Scotland stayed in the World Cup. We even talked about going to Spain and performing well out there.

The Blues finished thirteenth in the First Division, their highest league placing until Steve Bruce guided the club to tenth place in 2003–04. We were a half-decent team with Jeff Wealands or Tony Coton in goal behind a couple of fellow ex-Derby defenders, David Langan and Colin Todd, plus uncompromising fullbacks Mark Dennis, Pat van den Hauwe and Joe Gallagher. Opposing wingers could count their blessings if they met Mark or Pat on one of their merely 'uncompromising' days because the notorious pair's nicknames Dennis the Menace and Psycho were not altogether undeserved.

Alan Curbishley, Kevin Dillon, Alan Ainscow, Ian Handysides and I dominated the midfield places and made the bullets for our main strikers Frank Worthington and Keith Bertschin to fire. Brum supporters still hankered after the goals and glory of Trevor Francis but I think they respected our efforts to provide a decent level of entertainment and results.

We had a sense of achievement, even though our neighbours Aston Villa were crowned champions. Unfortunately, the Villa manager Ron Saunders fell out with chairman Doug Ellis before long, with deadly repercussions for Jim Smith and me.

It was time for a spot of summer sunshine and it brought a grin to my face when a party of us, including my parents and a couple of family friends, flew to Salou in Spain for a holiday. Around our hotel pool each day we were uncomfortably aware of a couple who kept giving Betty the evil eye. Later on in the holiday, with my mum and dad looking after Scot and Stacey one afternoon, I took Betty to a little café for strawberries and ice-cream. The same couple came in and before I could give them a piece of my mind about their rude behaviour, they smiled, said hello and introduced themselves as big Birmingham fans.

The mystery of the evil eye was soon solved as they revealed that staying with them at the same hotel the previous year had been a young lady with a little girl who identified herself as Mrs Archie Gemmill. It turns out she used to put the child to bed every afternoon and sleep with all the waiters! For the past twelve months this couple had fervently believed that I was married to a right slapper, so when they saw the family together they just couldn't work out if Betty was my bit of stuff or what.

Back in the Midlands it was no laughing matter when a championship-winning boss came on the market and the kudos and temptation proved too much for our chairman Keith Coombes, who simply said, 'Sorry, Jim,' when he replaced Smith with Ron Saunders in February 1982.

'Can I have a word, Archie?' asked Saunders. Tommy Docherty had been the first, then came Peter Taylor and now it was Ron's turn to fire the bullet. 'You're far too old. You're totally and utterly finished as this level.' But Ron wasn't about to bomb me out of the club and he added, 'If you're willing, I would like you to stay on and play in the reserves, helping to bring on some of the youngsters.' I thought that was fair enough and good of him.

I'd had a couple of decent seasons at Birmingham. When Jim was sacked half way through the third, it came out of the blue as far as I was concerned because he appeared to get on fantastically well with the chairman. Ron Saunders was very honest with me and I could see his point of view. I was thirty-four and he wanted to build a new Birmingham team using younger players while hoping I wouldn't mind basically concentrating on the reserves and passing on a little bit of my knowledge.

However, I had a short-term alternative. At the end of the 1980–81 season I had gone with Birmingham on tour to South America and injured my Achilles tendon. Although not serious, it was enough to make me wary when Noel Cantwell, who was head coach of the Jacksonville Tea Men at the time, approached me to join him in the North American Soccer League. The money on offer was fantastic – something in the region of £35,000 to £40,000 for two, maybe two and a half months. Footballers used to get a proper summer in those days, perhaps eight, even ten, weeks, to recharge their batteries – not the three or four weeks the top men get now if they're lucky – and it would have been a summer job. I told Noel it was a lovely idea but to forget it because I wasn't fit – end of story.

Several weeks later Betty and I were lying on a virtually deserted beach down at Clearwater in Florida when two figures appeared in the distance.

'I'm sure I recognise those two,' I said to Betty, who thought the sun was beginning to get to me. Sure enough, it was Noel with his right-hand man Arthur Smith. They had somehow succeeded in tracking me down on holiday and now tried their very best to persuade me to change my mind and go to play for them.

'Look,' I told Noel, 'I can't do it. I've got this Achilles problem and I'm not taking anybody's money under false pretences.'

I liked to guarantee value for money – no, make that extra value for my wages. If someone paid me £10 every week, I'd still put in a shift worth £12. It would have been the simplest thing in the world to have signed Jacksonville's lucrative contract but I might have broken down after a couple of games. They would have been paying me well while I sat around for weeks with my leg up, not doing a stroke.

I refused to contemplate robbing Noel and his backers in that way and told him so, but I did promise to get back to him if I finished with Birmingham, by which time the Achilles injury would have healed. Now, after Ron outlined his plans to me, America seemed more and more attractive, so I turned down Birmingham's offer and decided to worry about the future after that.

Ultimately, leaving Forest and going to Birmingham was the

worst thing I did in my career. I wasted my time there. I would have been better employed sweeping the roads. The directors were fine and Jim Smith was very good to me but with so many unprofessional players at St Andrew's, we really had no hope of getting anywhere.

WHITE VAN MAN

SO it came to pass that Betty, Scot, Stacey and I found ourselves living the life of Riley in the opulent Bay Meadows country club in the summer of 1982. Socially, it was ideal. We had a great time and made friends with several families. The Americans are terrific people. When you arranged a barbecue – or cook-out, as they called it – you were 99.9 per cent certain it would go ahead, unlike back home in Derby, where the rain invariably pours down or the wind blows a gale, and that's July.

On the pitch, I played every single minute of every single game alongside such characters as Keith Bertschin, with whom I'd played at Birmingham, Alan Green of Coventry and Peterborough's Jack Carmichael. Sometimes I had to leave Betty and the family for the week to fly to the other side of America for back-to-back away matches in San Diego or Montreal, up in Canada. I was Jacksonville's player of the year and they were very keen for me to stay and play indoor soccer in Phoenix for another shed-load of money, but the Achilles problem was niggling away at me again, and so was the fact that the time had come for Scot to settle down at grammar school. So, with an element of reluctance, I turned my back on what had been an absolutely phenomenal experience.

Back home it suddenly struck me that I was unemployed but that highly unsatisfactory state of affairs lasted as long as it took Larry Lloyd, my old Forest sparring partner, to discover I was back on the market. Larry was manager of Wigan Athletic and very keen to have me at Springfield Park on a pay-as-you-play basis. That interested me not at all and so I told Larry, but he was a stubborn sod, just like me, and refused to let the matter drop, threatening to pester me on the phone again a few days later.

'What are you doing, Archie?' he asked casually when he rang.

'Nothing,' I replied.

'Well, surely playing football and getting paid for it is better than doing nothing,' he reasoned.

Deep down, I knew he was spot on and that you couldn't argue against logic like that. After a chat with Betty and my old Gaffer Brian Clough, I joined Wigan in September. Larry was super. He let me train for a few days each week and then play. I enjoyed a good time at Wigan. They were very nice, friendly people and I'm just sorry we weren't more successful.

I must have been doing something right, though, because suddenly, right out of the blue, Manchester City wanted me. Well, at least, Freddie Pye, the influential Maine Road director, wanted me, let's put it that way. I'm not so sure about the manager, Billy McNeill. Larry rang me one day to reveal City's interest and I thought he was pulling my leg. I couldn't believe they'd be interested in a player of thirty-five but I had a chat with Freddie and we got the wages sorted out. I thought my boat had really come in and it was the big time again, because Manchester City are a massive club, when the deal went totally dead. The rug was pulled from under my feet and I never did get to the bottom of City's U-turn.

I was, nevertheless, on the move in November 1982 and this time my route to work was very familiar. The rot had set in at Derby the day Dave Mackay left in 1976 and it continued through Colin Murphy, Tommy Docherty, Colin Addison and then John Newman. Now Peter Taylor was back on his own and struggling to keep them in the Second Division in a generally depressed era of crowd violence and dismal attendances.

I noticed they were bombed out of the League Cup 3–1 at

Birmingham on Pete's first full day as manager, and he called me within twenty-four hours. My last dealings with Pete had been acrimonious and ugly when he broke the news that I was finished at Forest and virtually shoved a one-way ticket to Birmingham into my hands. I was never going to make it easy for him to get back on good terms and when he phoned to say, 'Come and play for us,' I replied that I was quite happy at Wigan. His manner suggested I should drop everything and come running, which irritated me, but Larry told me I was daft playing hard-to-get and should get myself back to the Baseball Ground. So Pete and I met in the car park of the Dog & Partridge at Tutbury. His opening offer of a deal until the end of that season was not what I was looking for, not by a long shot.

'That's no good to me, Pete. Give me eighteen months or you can forget it.'

'Okay, Archie,' he replied. 'I'll stick you on three hundred a week.'

'Well, you can forget that, too. It's an insult. I want six hundred, what I was earning at the end with Birmingham.'

He told me not to be stupid, but then had a change of heart. Peter Taylor needed Archie Gemmill more than Gemmill needed Taylor. We haggled here and there before shaking hands on a complicated deal. Derby would pay me £300 but if they survived relegation, at the end of the season I would get another £300 a week backdated to November. In addition, I would be given a new one-year contract at £600 a week if Derby stayed in the Second Division, but if they went down all bets were off and I was out on my ear.

I grinned to myself. Derby were in a mess but I thought they would stay up and I was right, even if it was touch and go for some time. I wanted to return to my old club but it had to be on my terms. Pete, with his fabulous dry sense of humour, knew a lot about the game, enough to get by, but he never knew half as much as Clough.

I kicked off in a 2–2 draw with Oldham but we were in a hole, rock bottom of the table, in danger of being cast adrift and hardly able to scrape a win or keep a clean sheet to save our lives. Somehow, we succeeded in piecing together a remarkable four-month unbeaten run of fifteen league games between January and April. Putting one over Clough in the FA Cup third round at the start of 1983 was a considerable bonus. It felt great but strange at the same time. That 2–0 result was the shock of the round as the twenty-second club in the Second Division beat the fourth in the First Division with the help of a rather fine free-kick from yours truly. I curled the ball over the wall and past Steve Sutton. The atmosphere was terrific and Derby played far in excess of their capabilities on the day. As for Forest, they never played at all. Much of that was down to the superb job Gary Mills did on John Robertson, although I was named man of the match and recall getting a standing ovation as I reluctantly left the Baseball Ground mud-heap before the end with a hamstring injury.

Gary was another Forest old boy – in fact, he played for them in the 1980 European Cup final triumph over Hamburg – and he relished the opportunity to get his teeth into Robbo, who was so anonymous that Clough hauled him off with twenty minutes to go. On his performance that day, you'd think Clough might have paid someone to take Robbo away from Forest and that Taylor wouldn't have touched him with a bargepole. Yet that summer, the Dynamic Duo fell out quite spectacularly when John left the City Ground for Derby. Clough was convinced his old pal had done the dirty on him in an underhand manner and totally and utterly blanked Pete from that day on. When you sit down and consider all they had been through together at Hartlepool, Derby, Brighton for a brief spell and Forest, their relationship should never have deteriorated to that extent. The world is a strange place at times.

Still, there was cause for optimism in the spring of 1983. That hamstring trouble kept me out of the next round of the FA Cup –

victory over Chelsea at home – and it took a late goal from Norman Whiteside for Ron Atkinson's Manchester United to eliminate us in round five on their way to stuffing Brighton in the final after a replay. As for the Second Division, it was Mission Impossible accomplished with some ease as Derby stayed up by the impressive margin of nine points.

When it came to renewing my contract, Taylor had changed his tune beyond all recognition from our meeting outside the Dog & Partridge. I was on £600 as agreed but my form had been good enough to earn me a promise of the same for the next season regardless of which division we were in.

Meanwhile, the 1983–84 season, my swansong as a professional footballer, opened in great style at Stamford Bridge – great if you were a Chelsea fan, that is, watching new boy Kerry Dixon help your team crush Derby County 5–0 on John Robertson's debut for us. As omens go, this one couldn't have been clearer. We were crap in the League, although the FA Cup was another story.

In the third round we won 3–0 at Cambridge. Then we had Bobby Davison to thank for a hat-trick that enabled us to squeeze past non-league Telford 3–2. I whacked in a penalty to set up our 2–1 home win over First Division Norwich, who were just starting to fancy their chances of going all the way, and almost out of nowhere, we found ourselves in the quarter-finals, travelling down to the far west to meet another struggling club, Plymouth Argyle.

They were at the wrong end of the Third Division but that counted for nothing and I could never satisfactorily explain how we came home with a 0–0 draw. Plymouth battered us at Home Park, even though we had Kenny Burns on board after his permanent transfer from Forest, and 5–0 would not have flattered them. Back at the Baseball Ground we fancied our chances, of course, but Plymouth beat us 1–0 with a freak goal from their winger Andy Rogers. The ball sailed over our goalie Steve Cherry straight from a corner. It was a shame for Steve, who had been brilliant at their place.

Our exit from the FA Cup was bad enough, everyone at the club was gutted, but what happened next, how Taylor treated me, was inexcusable. Back in the dressing room he vilified me in front of the entire playing staff. I had shot it, I was a disgrace, my legs had gone totally and I would never again play for Derby County. It was almost shades of Tommy Docherty and what he'd told me years earlier in the Midland Hotel when I told him to shove that cup of tea up his backside. I would not have been happy if Taylor had taken me into the privacy of his office the following morning for a bollocking and told me he couldn't see me lasting much longer, but then at least I would have respected him. To bawl me out in front of all the other lads was completely out of order.

The club was in crisis now. They were skint and had already been prematurely eyeing up the proceeds from a semi-final at Villa Park against Watford and maybe even the final itself. Derby were broke, desperate for a takeover but Robert Maxwell pulled the plug on a deal and withdrew his rescue plan. Our troubles on the pitch were reflected in the boardroom with talk of an Inland Revenue winding-up petition.

Two games later, after a humiliating 3–0 home defeat by Brighton and a 0–0 draw at Middlesbrough, Taylor was virtually on his knees begging me to play again. I was summoned into his office and this time he was with his assistant Roy McFarland as he made a half-hearted apology and claimed the enormity of Derby missing out on an FA Cup semi-final date at Villa Park, and all the cash that would generate, had caused him to blow a fuse and berate me. Some things had been said in the heat of the moment and would I very kindly play at Barnsley on Saturday? I looked him straight in the eyes and replied, 'I'll tell you straight now, I'll never play for Derby County while you are the manager.'

The lads got stuffed 5–1 at Barnsley with Derby fans shouting at Taylor that I should be in the team. He was out of a job. Roy

Mac stepped into the hot seat and asked me to play the last few matches of the season, which I was more than happy to do, for him. We beat Palace 3–0 but it all ended in tears at Shrewsbury. The Derby fans ripped plastic seats from a stand, hurling them like frisbees at their own players, including me – the man guilty of missing a penalty. They were bitter. I didn't blame them. Moments later the referee blew early for full-time for our protection. In the dressing room after that disgraceful 3–0 defeat, I pulled off my boots for the last time as a professional footballer – a relegated professional footballer, to be strictly accurate; not something to be proud of on your CV.

It was May 1984 when I called it quits after winning the Derby player of the year award, turning my back on that tidy little £600-a-week contract for one more season. I wanted to go at a time and a place of my own choosing with my good name in the game intact. Losing 3–0 at Gay Meadow in front of 5,500 with a club preparing for life in the Third Division was not exactly what I had in mind. From the champions of England to the Third Division in nine years – what a disgrace.

It's never a manager who gives you the hook for the last time or holds up the board bearing your number. In the end, it's nearly always your body that betrays you. At thirty-seven, I could no longer get there for tackles. I was second-best in that department. I couldn't get round the pitch like I could two or three years previously and it had become harder and harder to train. I really had to push myself through it, asking myself, 'Do I really have to do this?' where before it had all been such a doddle. I used to love training. I was born to run but now my anticipation was slow. The mind was still as active as ever but the legs wouldn't respond.

In a nutshell, I was ideally suited to a team taking the big drop. It was a bitterly disappointing day at Shrewsbury. Derby were already relegated thanks to results the previous weekend when Kevin Keegan, Chris Waddle and Peter Beardsley drove Newcastle to a 4–0 win over us, which took the Geordies up. Still our fans turned out in force in a show of solidarity and we let them down, as we had all season. I had taken more important penalties, massive spot-kicks, all my life and stuck them away with no fuss. If only I could have dredged one up now like the effort I tucked away for Scotland against Holland in the 1978 World Cup. I curse the fact that I missed that penalty with the last kick of my career. In the great scheme of things, it was never exactly going to change the world, but it was important to me. Steve Ogrizovic was in goal and I made it easy for him with a tame effort. We'd been playing for an hour and that goal would have brought us back into it at 2–1. I remember feeling totally and utterly gutted afterwards. I knew that was the finish of my footballing career and I had played crap, and I knew it had been coming.

Derby saw the best of me because I was there for much longer than I was at Forest. It might surprise some people to discover that I made just fifty-eight league appearances for Forest in less than two full seasons. I consider myself to have been extremely fortunate because I was at the peak of my career for seven years, between the ages of twenty-five and thirty-two, and that is a long time compared to some characters in the business who fall victim to injury or don't look after themselves properly.

I played a million games all over the world, at least it feels that way, but only two stand out greatly – big, floodlit European Cup nights at the Baseball Ground with the crowd jammed in like sardines and a tidal wave of noise and emotion as Derby humbled Real Madrid 4–1 and Benfica 3–0. Our game reached majestic heights. For those two ninety minutes, no team in the world could have lived with us. Anyone who was fortunate enough to be there will know what I'm talking about. Otherwise, you'll just have to take my word for it.

Taylor and I had parted company in desperately sad circumstances but we made it up. After I'd signed for him, Betty and a friend went to look for an apartment for us in Cala Millor – that famous Brian Clough enclave favoured by so many Derby and

Forest players. It was miserable grey windy day when Betty chanced to look up and spotted a fabulous penthouse apartment with a 'For Sale' sign on the window. She took the phone number, contacted the Spanish agent and discovered the owner was none other than Peter Taylor. This was good news and bad. I knew immediately that he would sell to me, but also that there wasn't a chance in hell of me beating him down from the £45,000 asking price because Pete was tighter than a duck's arse.

Several years later, Betty and I were strolling from Cala Millor to Cala Bono in the sun when I spotted Pete sitting alone outside a bar, not looking too well at all. We had not exchanged a word since our bust-up in his office at Derby but Betty and I stopped for a chat and a beer. He confessed he'd been out of order with his treatment of me concerning the Plymouth match. We shook hands and Betty and I walked on. The next time I heard anything of Peter Taylor he was dead and I had to prepare for a funeral.

Taylor had told me my legs were gone. I knew that much was true but I made a huge error in the summer of 1984. With the benefit of hindsight, I should have dropped down to a non-league club to get my feet under the table as player-manager, done both jobs for three months and then hung up my boots. Old pros pull that stroke all the time – a little injury conveniently comes back to haunt them or they sign a really good kid in their position and can't possibly stand in the way of this exciting new prospect. But that wasn't me, was it? I wasn't into deception. I was sure I had what it took to go straight into management. After all, I'd spent long enough learning from the master, Brian Clough.

I went for interviews at several clubs over the years including Burnley, Blackpool, Bournemouth, Stoke, Tranmere Rovers, Reading, Notts County and Bradford. In football, it's very easy to find out about someone's character and I had this sixth sense, particularly at Tranmere, that they had contacted someone at either Derby, Forest or Birmingham and the word had come back: 'Don't get Gemmill, he's more trouble than he's worth.'

Tranmere was my first port of call and they asked if I fancied playing as well but I made it clear I just wanted to be the boss, so they made Frank Worthington player-manager. My fellow Scottish international Martin Buchan got the Burnley job instead of me.

Derby were looking for yet another new manager, too, in 1984. Roy Mac couldn't convince people at the Baseball Ground that he could turn things around quickly enough. I went for an interview with the chairman, Stuart Webb, at his house in Derby and thought it went particularly well but Arthur Cox got the job, which was perfectly fair. He was vastly experienced and gave the club a fresh start. Under him, Derby were back in the First Division in three seasons, finishing fifth before another rot set in.

They do say the best way to lose a friend is to go into business with him and I wouldn't disagree, given my unfortunate experience when I became a former professional footballer. How that expression hurt and hit home after twenty years in the game. I suffered three years out of the game between finishing with Derby and joining the Forest coaching staff – and I do mean suffer because they were the three worst years of my life. I was like a bear with a sore head after becoming part-owner of a company. Doesn't that sound grand? The reality was that I was white van man in jeans and a tee-shirt, loading boxes of handwipes, toilet rolls, liquid soap, tea and coffee into the back and delivering them to tiny firms on industrial estates. I had been to the World Cup finals with Scotland and won three league championship medals, and now I saw the scorn in some people's eyes. I took the ribbing as customers, who might once have cheered me from the terraces, gave me a look that said, 'My, how you've come down in the world.' The braver ones would even make a wisecrack and my response wasn't guaranteed to make friends. I would simply shoot back, 'You can shut your face – it's my company.'

I know everything there is to know about tactics but tact is a different matter entirely. Today's Premiership stars can make an absolute fortune inside a decade, set themselves up for life in a business and buy all manner of properties. Good luck to the Robbie Fowlers of this world. For my generation, with the exception of rare characters such as Franny Lee, my old Derby team-mate who made a bundle out of the paper manufacturing business, when we stopped playing we were desperate to stay in the game in some capacity because that was all we knew, pure and simple.

There was an alternative but I didn't fancy the idea of clearing away ashtrays or washing down the spew in the gents at closing time. No, I most certainly was not cut out to be mine host at your local public house. I thought I was good enough to be a manager straight off and my reputation was good enough to guarantee a few interviews.

Meanwhile, Betty and I had bills to pay and while I was looking for a job in football, Rob Sanders, a friend who was running Derby Industrial Power Tools, said he wanted to diversify and he wanted to deal me in. Rob had been to an exhibition featuring a Swedish company that produced handwipes, industrial paper towels and soaps. He thought that sort of stuff would more than pay its way, so we invested £15,000 apiece to become co-owners in J-Speed. George Lyall, one of my oldest and closest friends, came down from Hull to run the show as managing director and salesman while Rob's wife Isobel initially manned the phone, cold calling and taking orders.

George and I had been thick as thieves as players at Deepdale. We hit it off from the word go. He was best man when I married Betty and I did the corresponding honours when Linda made an honest man out of him. Among my possessions is a dog-eared photograph of the four of us innocently playing cards on Linda's bed back in Ribbleton Avenue, Preston in 1967. Talk about the Swinging Sixties!

It was cosy but far from glamorous operating out of a little industrial unit just round the corner from Shaftesbury Crescent, home of the Baseball Ground. To be honest, I wasn't expecting to get my hands dirty. I'd stuck in my £15,000 and was just hoping for a modest return on that investment.

J-Speed started to take off reasonably well and quickly. Rob told me George was over-worked because he had the deliveries to cope with, so why didn't I get off my backside and go and help him? Put like that I couldn't very well argue, so that's how Archie Gemmill the footballer turned into Archie Gemmill the white van man. I thought it reasonable to pay myself £100 a week and I did insist on having more than an hour for lunch if I fancied it.

Betty and I have always been dog-lovers. Sometimes our home is like a hotel for dogs because we often look after our friends' animals when they go abroad on holiday. At the time we had a game little cairn terrier called Zoe, who had a loveable nature second to none. It broke my heart when she died. If you have a dog, it's your responsibility to care for that creature. I can't understand the mentality of people who leave their animals cooped up at home all day. Lunchtime for me meant a good brisk walk with Zoe and if that meant I wasn't on call to J-Speed for ninety minutes or two hours, then tough! Whose business was this anyway? I was miserable as sin, I had to have some perks.

Linda replaced Isobel on the phones, the company was heading into profit but I could sense dissatisfaction in the ranks. George was on a percentage of any profits and thought I was taking money from him by not working to the best of my ability. He also questioned my £100 weekly pocket money.

We weren't without competitors, both in the East and West Midlands, and one day I must have surprised George by returning early from lunch and finding him deep in conversation with a competitor I dubbed the Fat Lad. It didn't look as if many pies were safe when he was about. They quickly made up some story about him wanting to supply us with cheaper materials and chemicals. It was too late, George flushed up and gave the game away with his red face.

My academic qualifications might not be much to write home about but I've got a first-class honours degree from the University of Life and George's embarrassment suggested something fishy was going on. Three or four weeks later the Fat Lad was back and I tackled George directly.

'Is there something going on?' I asked. 'I get the feeling you could be moving.'

'No, no,' George assured me and I gave him the benefit of the doubt. The following week I answered the phone.

'J-Speed, can I help you?'

'Sorry, wrong number,' came the reply but I recognised the Fat Lad's voice immediately and we played out a little charade with me insisting he wanted to talk to George and him asking if he was through to Derby 857613, or some such bogus number, as he tried to wriggle off the hook.

'The Fat Lad's been on the phone for you,' I told George. 'You're leaving, aren't you?'

Still, he played the innocent, insisting again that wasn't the case. That weekend, Betty and I were booked to see a show in London but before we left I contacted Rob and insisted we had to have a meeting first thing on Monday morning to clear the air. I breezed in and told them, 'It's best I start the ball rolling – I'm leaving the company immediately. You can get another driver if you want. I'm not taking anything and I certainly don't want to be accused of affecting George's percentage.'

Ten days later George handed in his notice. He was off to work for the Fat Lad, who had turned his head with a little bit more cash and the promise of shares. I was most upset that a friendship that had endured for over twenty-five years counted for so little in the end and several snide little stories originating from George and Linda criticising me came to my attention. Money got in the way. I could see George's point of view. My heart most certainly wasn't in driving a delivery van and getting asked, 'Didn't you used to be Archie Gemmill?'

George did extremely well for J-Speed for the time it ran and his two successors found it far too much like hard work trying to match his efforts. We'd gone as far as we could and I would have lost a considerable amount of cash, along with a valued friendship, but for Rob kindly stepping in to buy up the outstanding stock and flogging it off to the joiners, plumbers, electricians who frequented Derby Industrial Power Tools.

Business was the last thing I needed to do with the rest of my life. Although I have always appreciated there are people in the world far worse off than me, it's human nature to take things personally. You do feel sorry for yourself and at times when I drove around some of the bleakest parts of the Midlands in that bloody van, I'd be screaming to myself, 'Why me? Why me?'

16

DIRTY TRICKS AND A BITTER END

I WAS playing for Forest Old Boys against a local team in Nottingham in 1987 and, as luck would have it, Brian Clough came to watch a couple of first-teamers recovering from injury whom he had despatched to test their fitness in the charity match. The backroom staff were all there – Alan Hill, Ronnie Fenton and Liam O'Kane. Hill, the chief scout, had a quiet word with the Gaffer and suggested it might not be a bad idea if I came and helped out with the youth team. The next thing I knew, the Boss said to me, 'By the way, you're starting on Monday morning at the club.' So Alan Hill was instrumental in me getting a foot back inside the City Ground but later I believe he stabbed me in the back and played a major role in me leaving the club for the final time.

Initially, the job was for two days a week for the grand sum of £60. I worked alongside Liam to begin with but, in time, I ended up running both the reserve and youth teams. Was I good at the job? At the risk of sounding like Clough, I was bloody magnificent. In six seasons with the reserves, we won the Central League championship three times and were runners up on the other three occasions. As for the youth team, we reached the FA Youth Cup quarter-final in 1987 and the semi-final the following season. It was a hectic period in my life but I loved every second of it.

Coaching success was no great problem because Forest ran like clockwork and I'm proud to say that I played a small part in the development of footballers of the calibre of Roy Keane, Steve Stone, Gary Charles, Steve Chettle, Mark Crossley, Phil Starbuck and Lee Glover.

Just a few characters proved to be a right pain in the backside, principally one Stanley Victor Collymore, Stephen Hodge and an Irish lad from Limerick called Tommy Gaynor, who arrived via Doncaster Rovers. Those three ended up with me in the reserves and were not pleased about it. I tried to reason with them, telling them that the Gaffer had dropped them for a reason and they needed to buckle down and show how keenly they wanted a first-team shirt again, but their attitude and application left a great deal to be desired. I had a right go at them, but they couldn't be bothered and didn't apparently understand that part of my job meant I was obliged to report back to the Boss on just how they were playing.

I had an unbelievable record with the reserves and it should have been better. At the end of one particular season, the Gaffer went off on his holidays to Cala Millor with us nailed on to win another Central League championship. The only problem was that he had allowed several of our big lads to pack up for the season as well, so I was left facing three rearranged games in the space of a week. It was hopeless trying to get a competitive team out. We picked up one point from those games and lost the League. The Gaffer had left with the title in the bag and he was not at all happy on his return, so much so that he suspended me from Forest without pay for a week.

I worked my way up from running the reserves to joining the first team on match days and I couldn't have been happier in 1989 when Saturday, 15 April dawned a warm spring day. Success in the FA Cup had always eluded me, just as it had the Gaffer, and here we were, ninety minutes away from Wembley and facing Liverpool in the semi-final at Hillsborough. I saw scenes that afternoon nobody should ever have to witness.

Eighteen years earlier I had played for a Scotland XI against a Rangers/Celtic select in the Ibrox Disaster Fund match, and I prayed then that football would never suffer a similar tragedy, but here we were again with sport providing the backdrop to a nightmare.

Virtually as soon as the match kicked off I was aware that something was terribly wrong at the Liverpool end. The crowd was unbelievably congested and hands were reaching down from the seats above towards the Leppings Lane terraces, helping some fans to escape the crush. After six minutes, the referee had seen enough of the commotion. It was spiralling out of control and he pulled both teams off the pitch. I know it sounds awful now, but standing in the Forest dressing room at Hillsborough, our only concern in the world was how long it would be before the referee came and told us we could go out and continue, yet outside, ninety-six football supporters were dead or dying. After five or six minutes with no information, the Gaffer sent Liam O'Kane and me to discover what was going on. I truly wish he hadn't. Bodies were lying everywhere. It was like a scene from a war zone. I walked slowly back to that dressing room with my head bowed, went inside and told the Gaffer, 'The lads can go in the bath now – there's no way we'll play again.'

When the semi-final was staged again at Old Trafford a month later, only one team was ever going to win and that was Liverpool. They had to win that match for the ninety-six dead fans and go on to win the FA Cup. It was their destiny if you like, while Forest were in a no-win situation.

I had to fight Alan Hill's ignorance to make sure my son, Scot, wasn't bombed out of Forest in January 1990. Hill most certainly didn't fancy him as a player, not that he ever had the nerve to tell me that straight to my face. Just to make certain I knew the score, Liam and I set him up. After training, the coaching staff used to change in the referee's room at the City Ground and we put our plan into operation while Hill was taking a soak. With me in perfect earshot, but hiding out of sight, Liam casually said, 'I see young Gemmill might be getting a contract,' to which Hill spat back, 'He's got as much chance of making it in football as flying in the air. He will never, ever make it.'

Hill's acumen is such that Scot progressed to make over 300 appearances for Forest in nine years, twice helping the club to promotion to the Premiership and scoring twice at Wembley in 1992 in the Zenith Data Systems Cup final victory over Southampton, the last trophy Brian Clough won as a manager. In addition, Scot won twenty-six Scotland caps and later spent four enjoyable years at Everton before moving on to Leicester City.

Still, I knew what to expect when the Gaffer summoned me into his office and quizzed me, saying, 'They're not greatly in favour of giving your son a professional contract. They don't think he'll make it, you know.'

'I have no doubt whatsoever that Scot will make it, Gaffer,' I replied.

That was good enough for Clough. He respected my opinion.

'The boy better get a three-year contract, then,' he said, and the meeting was swiftly concluded.

Scot had started off playing football at Ecclesbourne Grammer School in the well-to-do village of Duffield, north of Derby, and progressed to turning out for Chesapeake FC in local football. He always looked about three or four years younger than his age, but one or two clubs were chasing him while he was still at school. Betty was insistent that he should complete his GCSEs and, by then, I had been working for Forest for a while. I had a word in the Gaffer's ear and Clough was happy enough to take Scot on YTS terms to discover whether he was going to be a chip off the old block. Scot had eighteen months to prove himself and he played regularly for me as I was the youth team manager.

I picked him but he was never our outstanding player by any

stretch of the imagination, yet I had no qualms, when it came to the crunch, in promising the Boss that Scot was worthy of his first professional contract. He had a good footballing brain, could pass the ball and showed good appreciation and awareness of what was happening around him. Those were three crucial criteria as far as I was concerned. Scot was never going to win header after header like Roy Keane, he didn't possess the physical attributes to boss midfield in the manner of Keane, Billy Bremner or Bryan Robson, but I was 100 per cent certain he had enough to make a decent career for himself in the game and he has never, ever let me down. I'm very proud to call him my son.

Liam has long been a loyal and trusted friend but we fell out for the first and only time in April 1991 on the occasion of Scot's debut at Manchester City. The Gaffer didn't name the team this time, just the squad, because he didn't want Scot to know he was playing and possibly fret about it instead of getting a decent night's sleep. Saturday morning arrived and after a cup of coffee we went out for a stroll. Brian gave me the nod that Scot was playing, so that I had time to ring Betty and arrange for her to come up from Derby to watch him on this momentous occasion. I didn't tell anyone else, of course, and Liam was most upset. He was Forest's first-team coach and adamant that I should have confided in him.

Liam got over it, though, and that was the only time we exchanged cross words. If only the same could have been said of my dealings with Hill, my life would have been so much calmer and less stressful. Starting with the 3–1 win over Luton in the 1989 League Cup final, Liam and I made it to the Twin Towers on six occasions. The Gaffer had his day in the sun, too, and a long overdue FA Cup final in 1991 when Forest went down to Spurs after Des Walker had the great misfortune to score a headed own-goal and Paul Gascoigne wrecked his knee in a kamikaze assault on Gary Charles.

During all that time, working my way through from the kids to the first team, I never had a single job offer from another club and it didn't bother me one iota. I wasn't remotely interested in anything else because I truly believed that when the Gaffer eventually retired I would fill his shoes.

Towards the end of the Gaffer's reign, bitterness surfaced among the Forest staff, unnecessary evil, deceit and backbiting. It was like the last days of empire with characters desperate to settle old scores before everything changed for ever. They were out to impress the chairman Fred Reacher and safeguard their jobs. Life was anything but harmonious. People were jockeying for position and the shit flew around left, right and centre – much of it involving Hill.

I wanted Brian Clough's job at Forest when he called it a day in May 1993 and I was convinced I was both good enough and ready. Sadly, my interview with Reacher lasted just ten minutes during which time he must have asked me at least six times, 'What would you do if Nigel Clough or your boy Scot were playing badly?'

'Obviously, if they don't play well, they're out. It's as simple as that,' I replied, bewildered that Reacher wasn't apparently interested in my plans to take a relegated club forward and exactly how I'd get us back in the fledgling Premier League.

Reacher only had me in out of courtesy, because I had applied and was on the staff. He was obsessed with Nigel Clough. It was crystal clear in my mind, however, that I could lead Forest after what I had achieved at the City Ground since hanging up my boots professionally in 1984. I know I was highly respected by the players, many of whom I'd nurtured right through the ranks from the youth team.

So Brian Clough went, I had that ten-minute farce with Fred Reacher and Frank Clark took over. Eighteen months later he sacked me.

There was friction from the moment Frank brought in Pete Edwards, a fitness coach with whom he had worked at Orient. It

178

was by no means as scientific as it is today but Pete had a lot of new ideas and training methods involving weights, harnesses and hurdles. Liam and I didn't exactly embrace these innovations with open arms. Liam was frightened that Pete would take his job. Both of us were 'old school' for want of a better phrase and we reacted very badly to this new kid on the block.

Routine day-to-day training, as far as I was concerned, was basically a jog, stretches and a few little sprints followed by keep ball. If it didn't resemble what you had to reproduce for ninety minutes on a Saturday afternoon, I wasn't interested. That served me well enough throughout my professional career and it also helped Forest win a thing or two. If it ain't broke, don't fix it – that was my motto and I was happy to argue the toss with anyone who'd listen that football wasn't played with harnesses and hurdles.

Granted, Forest had been relegated and were now out of the Premier League but that state of affairs was down to the players and the Gaffer losing his grip rather than any fundamental problems on the training field. Liam and I made Pete's life hell, I'm none too proud to confess, as we rebelled against his methods.

Eventually, I believe I was set up and fell for it hook, line and sinker and got the sack. Someone put the poison in for me, though I could never prove it.

Now Pete was small in stature but strong, an unbelievable weightlifter, and Hill was involved in a scene in his office between the two of us that threatened to get out of hand. It would have been an ugly scene, too, because I was right up for it but something clicked in my brain, like an electric light being switched on, and I thought, 'Hang on a second, old son. There's something wrong here. Something's going on.' I backed down and afterwards apologised to Pete. We had a good chat, in fact, became firm friends and I'm still in touch with him.

We were fortunate to have the services of a physiotherapist, Graham Lyas, who was better at his job than I was at mine, and I was exceptional. Graham was a genius in my opinion yet Hill told two of our injured players, Steve Stone and young Gary Bowyer, to go to Frank Clark and complain that they weren't receiving the correct treatment from Graham. However Stone and Bowyer disagreed and ignored his instructions.

Pete provoked many differences of opinion, particularly in the field of rehabilitation where he wanted Forest to apply his up-to-date methods, but Graham told him to keep his nose out, which didn't go down at all well with Hill.

I was happy to escape this distinctly unhealthy atmosphere for a few days and took the opportunity of joining John Perkins, who was then in charge of the youth team, to see how Forest's young lads were progressing at a youth tournament on the Continent, while Graham stayed behind to look after several long-term casualties. The rest of the management and coaching staff went off to Tenerife for an end-of-season wind down and it was there they had a night of the long knives and decided our fate. Graham and I were getting the sack. Other people on the Tenerife trip, whom I trust and respect, have told me that Hill was instrumental in those decisions.

Just before I left with the kids, Richard Money turned up to have lunch with Frank and I thought he might be after a scouting job. On my return, Liam and I were undergoing the none too thrilling task of sorting out all the assorted training kit and bits and bobs to assess what needed replacing when a phone call came from Frank's secretary to tell me, 'The manager wants to see you, Archie.' I never had an inkling what was coming. I thought he wanted a chat about how the lads had got on. Give my old team-mate Frank his due, though. He didn't mince his words.

'I'm letting you go, Archie. I want my own man in,' he said, and it dawned on me.

'That'll be Richard Money, then.'

'Well, that's got nothing to do with you,' Frank replied, and he was right. I simply got up and left. Frank had made up his mind.

Money was in as reserve team coach for the start of the next season, but Frank didn't last too long as Forest manager before getting the sack. He ended up at Manchester City with Hill just after Christmas 1996 and learned of his sacking from there while he listened to the car radio driving to the training ground the following February. They had taken Pete Edwards with them but he was soon out of Maine Road because he grew to dislike Hill.

Hill didn't like me because I was outspoken, very outspoken according to some at the club. Allen Clarke, Forest's youth development officer at the time, maintained I had a love-hate relationship with Brian Clough and was one of the very few who could stand up to him or contradict him. I recall one pre-season practice match, near Mansfield, shortly after Roy Keane had joined us from the Irish club Cobh Ramblers in the summer of 1990. Keane formed a midfield three with Steve Stone and Scot, and very tasty that trio looked, too. As we walked across the pitch for a half-time cup of tea, I seized the opportunity to promote myself to the Boss.

'Well, you know I've brought Stone and Scot through,' I said. 'I think I should stay with them this season.' The Boss was less than impressed. 'Shut up,' he replied tersely.

I wouldn't and had another little bite. It ended with Clough turning to Allen Clarke with this withering warning: 'Tell your friend to shut up or I will sack him.'

Hill could be a charmer but I felt there was also a more underhand side to his behaviour, with lots of cloak and dagger stuff. Hill always thought he would become the Gaffer's assistant manager and when Ronnie Fenton was appointed, he was furious and walked out in a huff to Notts County – big mistake, and he soon knew it.

181

Allen Clarke acted as the go-between with Clough to get Hill back on board at a time when the Boss was seriously considering taking the Wales job. Clarke has remained a good friend but I told him then in no uncertain terms that it was the worst thing he ever did for Forest.

17

BLOODIED BUT UNBOWED

FOREST, to their credit, paid up £30,000 straight away in settlement of the year I still had on my contract when Frank Clark decided my face no longer fitted at the City Ground in 1994.

The Blackpool job looked distinctly promising. The interview lasted ninety minutes and afterwards Billy Bingham, who was a director, confided, 'That went really well, you came over terrifically, Archie. I'm going to do everything I can to see you get the job. We won't be in touch for three or four days, though, because we've had a lot of applicants.'

Three days later I answered a phone call from Blackpool's lady chief executive, Gill Bridge, thinking, 'Yes! This is it,' only to be brought swiftly down to earth as she related the news.

'I'm very sorry, Archie,' she said, 'but we've given the job to Sam Allardyce.'

Then there was Bournemouth. I went down to the south coast for talks at a lovely golf club in the country but it was a similar story. I felt fairly confident but then came the call a few days afterwards – they had appointed Mel Machin.

There's no shadow of a doubt that I have been my own worst enemy and made things difficult for myself. When you have the aura of Brian Clough, enjoy the amount of success he enjoyed and are idolised all over the world, you can say anything and do anything. I simply don't have his presence

– and I also refuse to 'play the game'. Chairmen invariably like to have the final say on things, but if I don't agree with them I find it impossible to bite my tongue. I will always argue my corner. It's a fact that a lot more people dislike me than like me in football. Perhaps it's because I'm so totally and utterly 100 per cent up front.

I was struggling to contain my enthusiasm back in September 1994 when the invitation to join Rotherham came out of the blue from their chairman, Ken Booth.

'Would you be at all interested in becoming the club's next manager?' he asked over the phone.

'More than interested, Mr Booth,' I replied. So it was I dressed to impress for the interview at Millmoor – best bib and tucker, collar and tie, the works. I wanted this job and I wanted it badly. I hadn't been out of work for very long but my detour into the business world outside football had been a disaster and I had no intention of returning there.

Booth explained that the team was not doing too well under the present manager, Phil Henson, he'd heard good reports of my work, he loved Brian Clough and what we had achieved during Forest's era of success and he thought I could do the job. So far, so good. Then Ken dropped a little bombshell into negotiations. I wouldn't mind working with the staff who were already at Millmoor, would I? Now if football has taught me anything, it's that if you are to succeed, you must surround yourself with people with whom you are comfortable, people who put you at your ease and whom you can trust implicitly. John McGovern and I had a pact – whichever one of us landed a top job, the other would join him. Quite apart from being my best friend in football, John had already enjoyed a taste of management with Bolton and also up in the north-west with non-league clubs Horwich RMI and Chorley. He was currently down at Plymouth Argyle, as assistant manager to Peter Shilton.

I told Ken that I wanted John to come in as my assistant and he replied, 'I don't think we can do that,' to which I countered, 'Well, if that's the case, I don't think I can take the job.' The talks continued, Ken was hooked now and he eventually suggested one contract for me as manager on a shade under £40,000 a year and another for John on less money. On went the haggling. Ken hadn't made his pile from a scrapmetal yard next to Millmoor by being a soft touch over the years. Eventually, we shook hands on a deal that brought both John and myself £30,000 and the title joint manager. I celebrated by making a phone call to Plymouth. 'We've got the Rotherham job, partner,' I said.

First impressions were brilliant – and misleading. Before we officially kicked off with a 2–0 win at Hull, John and I watched our new team play exceptionally well in a 1–1 home draw on the Tuesday night against Birmingham City, which left us purring with enthusiasm. We couldn't stop ourselves bursting into the dressing room after the final whistle to tell 'our' lads how well they'd done and that all fears of relegation would fly out of the window if they maintained that level of performance. It soon dawned on us, however, that turning around Rotherham's fortunes would be anything but easy.

Bobby Davison was our first signing, on a free from Sheffield United. I knew him well from my days at Derby. He had bags of experience and I believed Bobby couldn't fail to score goals at this level. He was usually good for fifteen goals a season. Shaun Goater was already at Rotherham and he was a twenty-goals-a-season man if ever there was one in my book. With Goater and Davison up front and Andy Roscoe flying down the left to provide the ammunition, if we could tighten things up at the back, chances were John and I could relax and enjoy our debut season as bosses. It never turned out that way and we had a particularly hard first campaign.

Five clubs went down that season and with transfer deadline

day looming, we were aware that it was becoming too close to call as we hovered just a couple of places above a relegation spot. We pulled off a master stroke then by signing Gareth Farrelly and Nathan Peel on loan from Aston Villa and Burnley respectively. Farrelly rejuvenated the midfield while Peel made an instant impact on his debut with a goal as we completed the double over Hull. When the dust settled, Rotherham were still standing in the Second Division, in seventeenth position, eight points clear of the drop.

John and I had worked flat out. My day started with a forty-five mile drive from my home in Derby to be at my desk between nine and 9.15 a.m. After training, I'd go to a film at the massive Meadowhall Centre in nearby Sheffield before either going back to Millmoor to watch the reserves or taking in another match elsewhere. I'd arrive home at around 10.30 p.m. John was most certainly putting in the hours as well, although I did sometimes envy him because he and his wife Ann lived almost 'over the shop' in Sheffield. We were treated reasonably well by the fans but as time went by and we weren't winning matches, you could sense the frustration mounting.

Whether you're Rotherham United or Timbuktu United, you're going to get slated by some people in the crowd if things aren't going your way. I accept that supporters are entitled to a little moan here and there but I attend matches now when a player can have a patchy fifteen to twenty minutes, give the ball away and 10,000 people in the crowd are keen to crucify him. The level of verbal abuse has gone right off the scale and none of it helps the victim. He's out there trying his hardest to get it right.

The Millmoor fans fell short of physical demonstrations of disapproval but I needed a few stitches in my head the day Imre Varadi came out of his corner at Rotherham, swinging punches and cursing. He never tagged me. That really would have added insult to the injury I suffered ducking one of his flailing fists and catching the edge of the treatment table. There was blood on the dressing room floor but fortunately none of mine on the chairman's office carpet – although some people at Millmoor might have preferred to keep Varadi rather than John McGovern and me.

We knew a vast improvement was required following a disappointing first season together in the hot seat. Nobody could quibble with Varadi's goal-scoring record at Rotherham, even if they were suspicious of a career that had already taken him to both the nearby Sheffield clubs, Everton, Newcastle, West Brom, Manchester City and Leeds. Booth, to his credit, backed me 100 per cent and Varadi was packing his bags again – this time for Mansfield – after his contract was cancelled for that stupid assault on me.

The seeds of trouble had been sown weeks earlier when Varadi injured his back getting out of his car. That was unfortunate and a bit freakish but I could accept it. People do innocently find that their backs lock when they climb out of their cars – rare, I grant you, but not unheard of. One of the press lads asked me what was wrong with Imre and I told him the truth. Varadi was furious and let me know I should have concocted some feeble lie about a training ground injury. Maybe he thought I was accusing him of malingering.

Fast forward to a Rotherham reserve match against Swansea. Varadi was playing to test his back. To be honest, I was more concerned about a name on the opposition teamsheet – John Williams. Here was a big lad so fast I swear he caught pigeons. I had nasty visions of what Williams would do if he played on the shoulders of our young back four and turned them, so before kick-off I drummed into them how important it was to drop back and play deeper than normal, keeping dangerman Williams at arm's length.

The interval arrived with Swansea leading 3–0, all three goals stemming from Williams' blistering pace. I didn't mince my

words and, with an expletive tossed in here and there for maximum effect, I told our defenders that if they weren't prepared to
listen, they would never progress any further in the game and
might just as well start preparing for life in non-league football.
Varadi piped up from his corner, 'That's no way to treat youngsters,' to which I tersely replied, 'Piss off!' and with that the gloves
came off and he rushed me like a bull in a china shop.

The biggest mistake I made in 112 league and cup games in
charge at Millmoor with John McGovern was to expect too
much from the players. I should have made greater allowances for
their lack of talent and ability. I will hold my hands up now and
confess it was wrong to expect Second Division performers to
produce what I was used to seeing from players in the top
echelon. I didn't see it at the time but it certainly hit home after
I got the sack.

I was blinded to some extent by the ability of team-mates
during my own playing career. Andy Roscoe was a perfect
example. From the word go, John and I recognised that we
needed someone with a bit of pace to give us balance down
the left. Roscoe came to us on loan from Bolton and four
months later, in February 1995, we paid £70,000 for him and
he did fairly well for us. I never had any complaints about
Roscoe's level of commitment, but what let him down was the
final ball.

The crucial difference between a good player and a very good
player is delivery, making a pass to someone in the same
coloured shirt, and it's been that way in football since the year
dot. I was lucky enough to play the bulk of my career next to
Alan Hinton and John Robertson, two men who can stand
comparison with the best crossers of a ball the game has ever
seen. When Hinton and Robertson went scurrying away down
the left, you could put money on the delivery being exceptional.
Seven or eight times out of ten, the cross was accurate. With
Roscoe it was two or three times out of ten. He would get

himself into some marvellous positions only for his final ball to betray him and count for absolutely zero, but he was a game lad and never stopped trying.

Brian Clough once told me this story, which illustrates the point of how a manager must be aware of his players' limitations.

'I was at that level to start with at Derby County where I could still play ninety minutes in testimonials and stuff,' said the Gaffer. 'That's how I got on with everybody, they could sense I was on their level. I went to Middlesbrough for my first job in football and Raich Carter was manager. Now Raich Carter was up there and I was down here, and in the talks I had with him, Raich Carter used to tell me, "I can't get my players to do this, do that and the other." I was listening, no talking in those days. One of the things he came out with was, "You get a ball here and I tell them to switch it to the outside right if it's on your left foot – stick it thirty-five to forty yards. Come Saturday, can they do it? Can they hell!" And I said to him, "Mr Carter, do you realise how hard it is to do that?" That was the gap, you see, between him and the players he had, me as well.'

The lesson I should have absorbed from Clough was never to demand more from any player at Rotherham than he was capable of. Before Varadi attempted to punch my lights out at the start of the 1995–96 season, we had a clean sweep and brought in Gary Bowyer from Forest, Darren Garner, the former Plymouth player, from Dorchester Town, Mike Jeffrey from Newcastle and Paul Blades from Wolves.

Blades was a central defender. I had played with him at Derby and he had also gained a little bit of decent experience at Wolves. I was convinced he would be ideal for us but the chairman took some persuading and it was quite a while before I managed to talk him in to giving us the go-ahead. I didn't blame Ken Booth because £100,000 was an awful lot of money for Rotherham to pay for a player. As it turned out, it was not money well spent. Blades never quite recaptured the form I was expecting him to show and he wasn't a great success. He gave of his best but it wasn't the standard I was looking for. I was looking for a dominant character to organise the back four and I was looking in vain at him.

Ultimately, managers are judged on results and by the quality of the players they bring in and I don't think Blades ever did himself, or me, justice. John picked a good 'un in Garner, a nice, competent player from the word go who has gone on to enjoy a long career at Rotherham. Bowyer was another player I felt I knew well from our days together at the City Ground but he picked up two or three injuries and never figured as prominently as we would have wished. As for centre-forward Jeffrey, he looked a likely lad at Newcastle but was another who never fulfilled his potential with us.

I'm not blaming the players for me getting the sack. That would be totally wrong. It was the responsibility of John and myself to get the best out of them. We failed and paid the price for that. Our league form was disturbing and if ever there was a sackable offence it came when we went to Wrexham and lost 7–0 after crashing out of the FA Cup 5–3 at Rochdale.

We were a knockout in another cup tournament, however, which kicked off with 774 fans watching Roscoe clinch a 1–0 win at Chester in the Auto Windscreens Shield. Wigan were eliminated in a penalty shoot-out thriller, then we stuffed York 4–1 and beat Carlisle home and away in the northern area final. Millmoor attendances for league matches might have been down to 3,500 but everyone in Rotherham, it seemed, wanted a ticket for our Auto Windscreens Shield final against Shrewsbury Town and we were roared on by a 25,000-strong red-and-white army at the Twin Towers.

John and I knew our way to Wembley blindfolded, and we also knew it was going to be an absolutely terrific experience for everyone connected with the club, especially the players who, almost to a man, had only ever been there as spectators. We also appreciated from experience just how much more satisfying the weekend would be if Rotherham could reflect on it as winners. Wembley is no place for losers.

John and I tried to keep everything as low-key and relaxed as possible. On Friday afternoon, we arrived by coach at Sopworth Hall. The plan was to train at Bisham Abbey but the weather was foul, raining and windy, and we called it a day after practising a few set-pieces and having a little five-a-side kick-about. A glass of beer or wine was on the menu with the evening meal, something Clough always endorsed. I scrapped plans for a light training session on Saturday morning, granting the lads a lie-in and, following breakfast, we all enjoyed a stroll in the country.

Tickets to see a top match in London were, I felt, quite in order and Rotherham United were represented en masse at Stamford Bridge to see Chelsea hammer Leeds 4–1. A little trip to the cinema was next on the agenda. I don't know if it was a lucky omen or not, but 'my film' was selected by the lads – *Trainspotting*. I took some fearful ribbing from the lads that night but they were in a great mood.

John and I sensed we would win at Wembley on Sunday and we weren't disappointed. Nigel Jemson scored both our goals in a 2–1 victory. Ken Booth was obviously delighted, and cock-a-hoop when I presented him with the winner's trophy. A few months later he was returning my P45.

Our league form picked up with the Auto Windscreens Shield on the sideboard at Millmoor and we finished in sixteenth place. The previous summer John and I had earned some cash from a few promotional bits and pieces and we had put some money in the kitty for the squad to unwind on holiday in Cala Millor. Unfortunately, a few of the lads had a drink too many one night and complaints were made in our hotel about their behaviour. This year, Auto Windscreens Shield winners or not, we weren't going to risk a repetition and so it came to pass that the coaching staff ended up in Tenerife, where John had an apartment.

Normally, when a manager gets the bullet he leaves the club but this hadn't happened to Phil Henson – quite the reverse in fact. He'd been at Rotherham man and boy and was appointed chief executive when we blew into town, so he was on the Tenerife trip with us. It was late one night, John had retired, we were playing pool and Phil had enjoyed a drink or two when he casually informed me, 'If I'd had the last two years that you two have had, I would expect to be sacked.' Now Phil had everybody's ear at Rotherham, particularly the chairman's, and while I'm not suggesting he was the reason for John and me leaving the club, it did set me thinking.

I told John first thing the next morning what Phil had said and that if we didn't hit the deck running in August, I felt we were on our way out, even though we'd taken the club to Wembley and given them the biggest day out in their history. As for Phil, he came up a little sheepishly to apologise and say he'd been out of order for some of the things he'd said. I've learned in life, however, that people in drink often reveal their true thoughts.

I felt as if the rug was being pulled from under our feet when the chairman sold Goater and Mattie Clark, our goalkeeper and captain, during the summer. They were two of our bigger players and while I understood that money was tight and we got £325,000 for Mattie from Sheffield Wednesday, I didn't want to lose either of them. Ken said they had to go because he wasn't prepared to keep raiding his own savings to keep the club going. I couldn't shout the odds too much because I was allowed to bring in two new strikers – Lee Glover for a club record £150,000 and Junior McDougald.

I thought they guaranteed goals, loads of lovely goals, and that if someone else could weigh in with a few, we would be good for fifty goals from our front three, enough to make sure we were comfortably in the top half, maybe even pushing for promotion. Optimism gave way to pessimism when Junior was injured in pre-season and then Glover also picked up a knock.

After beginning with an encouraging point at Walsall, we lost our next seven matches, including a League Cup double-header with Darlington. Six of those defeats were by a single goal and the crunch came on 14 September 1996 when a two-goal lead at home to Bristol City evaporated into a 2–2 draw days after we'd been beaten 1–0 at home by Chesterfield.

Losing a derby is never good at the best of times, and now it looked fairly disastrous. The chairman came into our office and asked John, bold as brass, 'Would you like to resign?' and I said if that was what he felt was best for the club, then I would go too. I knew our results just weren't good enough. Equally, I knew we would turn things around given time but Ken's head had already been turned by Danny Bergara.

There had been a spot of nonsense before the parting of the ways when the chairman tried to split us up and actually accused me of employing 'verbal psychological warfare' against one of our young players, Carey Williams. I had John to thank for that! We were training in this lovely landscaped park with trees and a hill at the far end. I was barking the instructions, trying to get the strikers to make decent runs, when the midfielders played them through. Carey was very quick, but not on the uptake, and when he asked, 'Can you tell me where to run, boss?' John was exasperated and couldn't resist pointing to the horizon and telling Carey, 'You see that hill. Up there – and keep going.' Carey duly set off and he took some getting back, I can tell you!

I did give John a bollocking once, though. Our centre-half ducked a clearance but it struck him right on the backside instead and the ball rebounded inches wide of a post. John collapsed in stitches, the crowd were killing themselves with laughter but I was just angry that a slapstick moment had almost cost us a precious goal, and I let John know my feelings in no uncertain terms.

There was more slapstick under Bergara. The Millers suffered the worst season in their history and were relegated to the Third Division with four matches still to play.

18

TAXI FOR MR GEMMILL

I WAS not a happy soul following the sack from Rotherham in September 1996 and for fifteen long and tedious months could be found mooching around the house, doing the odd-job here and there and restoring the garden to its former glory. I might have been seventy-nine rather than forty-nine, and I almost drove poor Betty mad.

December 1997 rolled around and Derby County's annual Christmas party promised to be a belter. Jim Smith had taken the club into the Premier League where they were comfortably holding their own and on course to finish in ninth place. Emotional ties with the Baseball Ground had been severed and there was a smashing new stadium at Pride Park as a potent symbol of progress. I always enjoyed the Christmas get-togethers and was usually invited onto a table with a dozen friends. Jim was there, of course, holding court and chatting happily to supporters before the two of us fell into conversation, which swiftly turned into business. I was all ears.

Jim had two jobs on offer. He was looking for someone to coach the Under-17s and another face to scout throughout Europe. The game was changing, he argued, and Derby could not afford to be left behind in the race to sign quality foreigners at a time when players at home were over-priced. The Continent was where to look and Jim had quickly struck gold by unearthing a couple of classy Croats in Igor Stimac and Aljosa Asanovic plus Jacob Laursen from Denmark.

My record with the young boys at Forest suggested to Jim that I would be ideal to groom Derby's Under-17s, which I was, but I'd been there, done that and bought the tee-shirt. The European job, however, was a totally different kettle of fish and one that appealed to me immensely as a fresh challenge. I was sold on that idea and Jim could see how enthusiastic I was. Within a week the job was mine and I kicked off 1998 on a European adventure that took me regularly to France, Germany, Finland, Sweden, Austria, Spain and Portugal. I ventured beyond Europe, too, to Argentina and Costa Rica.

Arguably, my greatest success while scouting for Derby came from that most romantic of outposts, Carlisle. There were never ever any airs or graces about Rory Delap but the boy could play. Soon after I started, Jim was eager to tap into my time at Millmoor to discover whether much talent was knocking around in the lower divisions.

'There's one, Jim,' I said confidently, 'and he's a bloody belter.'

Delap had played for Carlisle in both legs when Rotherham knocked them out of the Auto Windscreens Shield, and also against us in the league. He was still a lad but possessed the physique of a man and was so versatile. In three matches against Rotherham, I think Rory played right-back, centre-half and centre-forward, and looked the business each time. Jim needed little further persuasion to agree a fee of £500,000 for Delap, and Southampton splashed out a club record £4 million for the Republic of Ireland international in July 2001 – a very tidy profit indeed for the Rams.

The real nature of my business was abroad, of course, and the beauty of spying on Derby's behalf was literally not knowing what the mission might uncover. It proved to be a heady mix of the fascinating and the frustrating. Take my first trip in January 1998, to France. We were in the market for a left-sided defender and Ghislain Anselmini of Lyon came recommended. I flew to watch him at Strasbourg and while Anselmini was comfortable on the ball and tactically aware going up and down, he showed nothing that led me to believe he was any better than Chris Powell, the player already filling the position back home at Pride Park. No follow-up worthwhile, I reported back to Jim Smith. However, another player did catch my eye – Olivier Dacourt of Strasbourg. Now there was an excellent midfield man, comfortable with both feet, who compared favourably with Paul Ince in style. He was definitely one worth keeping tabs on. Dacourt was only twenty-three and possibly out of Derby's price range, given the £4 million Everton paid for him six months later, but he has gone on to establish himself in the French team and transfers totalling over £21 million have taken him from Goodison Park, through Lens via Leeds United to Roma.

The following week found me in Belgium, running the rule over Lierse's left-back Nico van Kerkhoven against Anderlecht. Then it was back to France to see if Franck Rabarivony of Rennes might be the one to fill Powell's boots long-term.

Often it was the characters who got away who proved more interesting than the subjects of my initial visit. Rabarivony did catch my eye but solely because he had an absolute stinker against Auxerre. He looked a soft touch in the air and did his marking job relatively poorly, but his mate, the Rennes centre-forward Kaba Diawara, was a good 'un, strong and athletic with a good first touch. He was worth following up if ever a forward was required. A year later, Arsene Wenger paid £2.5 million to take him to Arsenal. Meanwhile, the Auxerre left-winger Bernard Diomede had a superb left foot plus good pace and awareness. He worked extremely hard for the team and I wasn't surprised to see Liverpool paying £3 million to bring him to Anfield in June 2000.

One left-sided midfielder particularly impressed me and I duly informed Jim that Laurent Robert's in-depth knowledge and understanding of the game was plain for all to see and that he definitely warranted another look at Montpellier. Unfortunately for Derby, Paris St Germain were looking in Robert's direction and he went there before making a £9.5 million move to Newcastle United.

One early trip to Argentina was with Raul Cascini of Independiente in mind but, as I was there for five or six days, I took in another couple of games. One of them featured Rosario Central's Horacio Angel Carbonari and he looked an absolutely superb defender with a shot like a cannonball. Carbonari had all the attributes to play in the Premiership, including strength in the air and on the ground, and he was very dangerous at all set-pieces. I reported back to Jim, 'We've got to have Carbonari,' and Jim flew to South America himself to check on the player after being impressed by a tape of Horacio in action. Carbonari came to Pride Park for £2.7 million in May 1998, the fans loved him and he would have been an even greater success but for injury.

That month of May was a cause of personal celebration and deep personal shame. If helping bring Carbonari to Derby was a champagne moment, nothing could match the sobering effect of being banged up overnight in a cell in Ilkeston nick for drinking and driving – a nightmare end to what had been a beautiful evening chewing the fat with Martin O'Neill and John Robertson. You might have thought that all those years I devoted to ensuring Brian Clough got home from Nottingham in one piece would have put me off booze for life, let alone mixing it with driving.

That afternoon I'd had a thorough work-out in the gym at Breadsall Priory, my local hotel and country club, but then I made the gross error of having nothing to eat before jumping in the car and driving down the M1. My destination was Leicester City and a function promoting that summer's World Cup finals in France.

I arrived at Filbert Street and downed two glasses of champagne before dinner, alongside George Cohen and Frank Worthington. It was a splendid meal and I was seated between the esteemed Celtic manager and his assistant. Martin, John and I indulged in our own version of the very good old days at Forest, along with some red wine to oil our conversation. My glass was topped up by a waitress, so it was impossible to judge precisely how much I had. Probably three glasses, a maximum of four.

I thought I was okay to drive home although a shadow of doubt crossed my mind as the Leicester Post House appeared on the horizon. Should I book in there for the night? It would be so easy to get my head down and I could still be up and home in time for breakfast. Nah, I felt fine, the M1 was virtually deserted and I could be safely tucked up in bed at home inside forty-five minutes.

I was no more than a mile from my front door when I approached a roundabout and became aware of the lights of another car pulling out on my left from a road leading to factory units. Moments later those lights turned into a police car. Had I done anything wrong, officer? Was I breaking the speed limit? No, it was just a random check at 12.40 a.m. and, oh, by the way, have you had anything to drink this evening, sir? Yes, I've had a few glasses of wine. Well, would you mind blowing into this bag, sir?

Sitting in that police cell was the most degrading, shameful thing that has ever happened to me in my life. The police refused to allow me to make a telephone call but, to be honest, I was quite grateful for that because it would delay an inevitable massive dressing down from Betty.

I was allowed out of my cell at six in the morning and given a cup of tea at which point I summoned up the courage to phone Betty. She was so distraught at the shame of me having been caught drinking and driving that I think she would have preferred it if I had been involved in an accident. I had to tell my mother and father about it as well. All in all, it was a very humiliating time in my life.

My case didn't take long to be scheduled for Ilkeston magistrates court. The people I spoke to all reckoned a twelve-month ban was inevitable and I was advised to be represented by a solicitor but I thought I would defend myself, believing I might help myself in some way. That just shows how naive and stupid I could be at times. How could I contemplate getting a lesser ban or fine? Who was I kidding?

I pleaded my case – thirty years careful driving, not a hint of an accident, two minor speeding offences, job on the line, that sort of thing. The chief magistrate took everything into account before simply asking, 'Were you driving the car?' and the next thing I knew I was facing a twenty-month ban with a £500 fine. Good old Archie, he knows best!

Derby's club solicitor thought twenty months was excessive and that I could get it reduced on appeal. So did I and I soon had an appointment at Derby Crown Court after agreeing to pay almost £1,400 for a barrister. My brief did his best but, almost uncannily, it ended with one question from the judge – 'Who was driving the car?' I had to put my hand up again. Case dismissed. Appeal rejected. Next please.

Jim Smith was magnificent the way he stood by me in my hour of need when it would have been the easiest thing in the world to dispense with my services. I am eternally grateful to him.

It almost sounds like a joke, doesn't it? Have you heard the one about the European football scout banned from driving for twenty months? If the club were trying to economise, I had just made myself virtually unemployable. When I raised my fears with Jim, he said, 'Leave things to me, Archie.'

I have gone on about always providing extra value for money when I've been in the game, yet I cost Derby County a small fortune in taxi fares. Heathrow, Manchester, Birmingham, East Midlands airport – I got there to the lot of them and back by taxi with the club footing the bill. Every time I got in a taxi I was reminded of the stupidity that made my night out in Leicester memorable for all the wrong reasons. I've learned my lesson the hard way. Now all I'll have is a glass of wine if I'm with friends. I never even drink at home unless we are having a dinner party, and then I'm more interested in Betty's food. She is an excellent cook. If the two of us are going out on a social occasion, there's only one of us ever going to drive home and you don't need to be a genius to guess who that is!

I'm sure Jim downs a decent glass of red now and again, and occasionally wonders how much longer he would have stayed at Derby had Carbonari and another of my discoveries, Branko Strupar, stayed fit.

I spotted Strupar playing in Belgium for Racing Genk and knew immediately he was exactly what we were looking for. If Derby had a weakness it was their lightweight attack, but Branko was a huge man with the ability to hold up the ball and the strength to take a lot of weight off the front line. In and around the box, he had an admirable goals-per-game ratio and looked value for money at £3 million. Branko's big weakness was in the pelvis, and injury robbed him of virtually two of his three seasons at the club.

Brian Clough had a neat way of dealing with anyone who praised or criticised one of his new purchases to ensure he wouldn't carry the can. The Gaffer would say, 'I always sign the good ones and Peter Taylor signs the bad ones.' Jim took the lion's share of the praise but he also took the brickbats.

Then there were the ones who got away – notably Michael Mols at Utrecht. I was very taken with Mols. In fact, I thought he was as good as any forward I had seen since Kenny Dalglish. Mols was immensely powerful physically and could turn defenders inside out. I urged Jim to buy him but there was a lot of competition and Mols was out of our price range.

William Gallas was absolutely outstanding when I saw him and another to follow up – but perhaps not at the £7–£8 million that he eventually cost Chelsea. Jim was very close to signing Sylvain Distin and bid £1.4 million for him. Distin had been given a free transfer by Paris St Germain as a kid and swore he'd never go back there. He swallowed his pride, though, and decided to return to

Paris, to our great frustration, before pitching up at Manchester City years later.

I did my share of homework when Jim was looking for an attacking midfielder and was keen on Per Frandsen at Bolton Wanderers. I went to cast my eye over the boy and thought he was a little bit short. For brief periods he'd look like a million dollars and you'd think he was a world-beater, but then it might be thirty or forty minutes before he was involved again. Frandsen spent too long on the margins of the game. That was what put me off him.

Watching Bolton was no waste of my time, though, far from it, because they had Eidur Gudjohnsen in their ranks and I considered him to be a terrific player for a twenty-year-old, even if he could do with shedding a few pounds from around his midriff. Colin Todd was in charge of Bolton, the deal was set up and Derby were getting Gudjohnsen for a reasonably small fee before Todd was suddenly sacked and his replacement Sam Allardyce, the old shrewdie, whacked a £4 million asking price on Gudjohnsen's head. If Todd had stayed at Bolton, Eidur Gudjohnsen would most definitely have become a Derby player.

Some trips ended with me eager to string up our tipster from the nearest lamppost. From what I was told, I had high hopes of a twenty-six-year-old Dane, Diego Tur, when I set off to watch him at Brondby but he turned out to be a central defender who lacked pace and couldn't read the game to save his life. Not only did he refuse to get involved physically, everything Tur did for FC Copenhagen on the night was distinctly average. Sadly, this Diego turned out to be more of a turkey than a Maradona. Then there was Djibril Diawara – later destined for Everton – whose distracted performance was so wretched when I watched him for Monaco against Metz that his coach hauled him off after half an hour.

Occasionally, I witnessed a player who was simply class personified and way out of our league. Take a bow Vicenzo Montella. I had turned up in Italy to look at a decidedly average Empoli midfielder and stayed to marvel at the Sampdoria striker. Montella was exceptional, demonstrated good close control, made intelligent runs, turned defenders both ways and topped off his performance by scoring two quality goals. When Sampdoria were relegated, Montella stayed in *Serie A* because Roma rated him highly enough to pay 25 million euros, and Montella soon made his debut for Italy.

By the start of the 1998–99 season Jim wanted a new striker and Ibrahim Bakayoko from the Ivory Coast was a name that cropped up. I saw him play for Montpellier, but didn't fancy him that much – certainly not at the £4.5 million Everton paid for him a couple of months later. Sylvain Wiltord at Bordeaux was top class, though, and I went to see him twice in quick succession. I filed my first report after he destroyed Grasshoppers Zurich, telling Jim, 'Wiltord was excellent. He has good pace, great awareness and the ability to find space for himself. Scored twice and could have had more.'

Jan Koller at Lokeren in Belgium was another centre-forward I rated highly on the strength of a single match and I told Jim that if his proposed move to Anderlecht fell through, he would be a strong contender to join us. Koller moved to Anderlecht in the summer of 1999, however, became the Czech Republic's most prolific international marksman and earned himself a megabucks move to Borussia Dortmund.

I was a big fan of Norwegian striker Rune Lange and twice made trips to see him do the business for Tromso. I felt he would be in our price-range. Big, powerful and a strong runner, he was in his early twenties and coaching could only improve his first touch.

What a team Derby could have put together with limitless cash and me alone watching the cream of the Continent in action. What a shame so many rival clubs had bigger chequebooks and greater pulling power. I don't know how much Bordeaux might have been prepared to accept for Wiltord in November 1998 but I do know they received £12 million from Arsenal twenty months later.

One week took me from the ridiculous to the sublime and demonstrated the extremes to be found in my working life, clocking up the air miles. First came a trip to watch the Cameroon striker Patrick Mtombo, who was playing for Cagliari in Italy, but it was impossible to assess his strengths and weaknesses because what I witnessed was no more than a training session against an amateur team in appalling conditions. The pitch was waterlogged, the temperature around freezing point and the players fully rigged out in tracksuits, gloves and woolly hats.

Then came the sublime. I don't know how long Manchester United had been aware of Ruud van Nistelrooy, but I first caught up with him a few days later, playing for PSV Eindhoven against FC Twente. At twenty-three, van Nistelrooy already had everything required to be a top-class forward. He was big, strong with adequate pace, a good first touch, made excellent runs and finished to a very high standard. As for weaknesses, I felt it would have been extremely pedantic to search for any, such were his strengths. Sir Alex Ferguson's faith in spending £19 million on van Nistelrooy has been totally justified. I heard Brian Clough call the Dutchman 'the best player in the world'.

Ferguson was also keenly aware of a Finnish player whom I had marked down as superstar material from the moment I saw him in an international against Germany. My intended target was Jonatan Johansson but he was very disappointing, apprehensive and tentative with no appetite whatsoever for the game. Teemu Tainio, on the other hand, then a nineteen-year-old front player, could not have been more different. Exceptionally bright from start to finish, he worked non-stop, running at the Germans and putting them under pressure. As well as that, he was in possession of a superb football brain and two good feet. On that showing, he warranted constant scrutiny in my book.

The big problem with talent such as Tainio's is that you'll never keep it to yourself and it wasn't long before he was off to Auxerre, then United for a two-week trial where he scored four goals in two games for the reserves. A spell of national service and a spate of niggling injuries disrupted Tainio's career but he looked destined for the very top.

United's signing of Eric Djemba-Djemba in the summer of 2003 for £3.5 million came as no great surprise. I'd seen the lad from Cameroon almost two years earlier, aged twenty, when he turned in an eye-catching display in central midfield for Nantes against Lazio and reported, 'He has strength, mobility and good awareness. Djemba-Djemba is very comfortable on the ball and looks like a fabulous prospect. I would have no hesitation in taking him.'

If the weather was bad in Italy the day I went to see Mtombo, it was even worse in France for a clash between Nancy and Sedan, whose Brazilian defender Eduardo Oliveira dos Santos had come to our notice. Again, the appalling conditions made it impossible to judge anyone. Driving snow, rain and gusting winds meant the ball was out of play more often than it was on the pitch.

The standard of first-class Dutch football fluctuated wildly, I found, and produced a couple of dreadful matches. When NEC tackled FC Twente I was obliged to report there was not a lot to inspire me in a very poor contest littered with poor passing, poor play and poor movement. Another to get the thumbs down was AZ Alkmaar v. Den Bosch, a decidedly average match with not a lot happening, while I wrote off RKC Waalwijk v. SC Heerenveen as a particularly low-class affair.

When I went to Norway to take in Lyn v. Stromsgodset, I had to apologise to Jim and tell him that he wouldn't be receiving a detailed summary of our target, striker Christer George, because the ball was simply launched into orbit at every available opportunity. It was like watching two Wimbledon teams from an earlier decade playing each other and a bonus if any player had more than a couple of touches.

A few eyebrows were raised when Jim paid Sheffield United £3 million for Lee Morris in October 1999. The lad had a nightmare with injuries at Pride Park and never lived up to his price tag before being quietly shipped off down the road to Leicester five years later for a nominal fee. I had slight reservations about Morris when I saw him against Crystal Palace in March 1999 and reported back that his crossing was poor, although it was certain to improve with coaching and experience.

In one amusing incident, I turned up to watch Kevin Ellison play for Altrincham against Rushden & Diamonds. I obviously caught him on a desperately bad day and, for a wide player, he took up lousy positions. Afterwards, I had to suppress a grin as the Altrincham chairman, no doubt visualising a bundle of pound notes from Pride Park going up in flames, pleaded with me that Ellison was far better than he'd shown in this, his worst game of the season.

At least Ellison gave me ninety honest minutes on which to judge him, which is more than can be said for Spanish centre-half Jean François Hernandes. His contribution for Rayo Vallecano against Real Betis – and my interest in proceedings – ended abruptly after twenty-five minutes when he was sent off for a second bookable offence with Rayo so totally in command that it had been impossible to judge whether he could defend or not in the first place. That was stupidity bordering on the criminal.

Sometimes I had to sympathise with a man undergoing a temporary crisis in his career. We fancied Martin Albrechtsen, a young Danish defender, and I couldn't understand why he looked a shadow of himself in the Copenhagen derby between the two clubs, AB and OB. Anyone judging Albrechtsen on that display alone wouldn't have touched him with a bargepole. He was beaten very easily both on the ground and in the air while his distribution was dismal before he was hauled off by the AB coach midway through the first half. I was mystified, but all became clear when the AB general manager confided that Albrechtsen had been playing for the previous month with an ankle injury that required pain-killing injections and had pleaded with the coach not to play when he was so patently unfit. Albrechtsen became West Bromwich Albion's record signing, briefly, when they paid £2.7 million for him in the summer of 2004.

I could also feel for Aston Villa when Bosko Balaban turned out to be such a dead loss for them, because the Dynamo Zagreb player gave a thoroughly good account of himself when Croatia drew a friendly in Belgium and looked every inch a pedigree international forward.

Mistakes, I made a few. One wrong turning took me down to watch a French midfielder called Mario Espartero playing for one club you are unlikely to have heard of against another that scores a load of points at Scrabble. Louhans Cuiseaux against Gueugnon it was, a Third Division friendly and nowhere near the standard required for Premier League football. Espartero wasn't Super Mario – or even a game boy, come to that. His overall performance was abject, lacking any desire, and his work-rate was poor. I noted physical contact was not in his game-plan at all. That wasted weekend proved how deep Derby and I were prepared to dig in the quest for an uncut diamond.

Watching some matches abroad was an almost surreal experience. Take one trip to Belgium, for example. I'd been tipped off by our man on the ground that Anderlecht had a tasty midfield player in Patrick van Diemen, who had lost his first-team place through injury and couldn't break back into the side because they were doing so well. Well, I thought he was worth a punt but when I got to the ground for a reserve match, there were more athletes training around the pitch than fans watching, and van Diemen wasted my time with a distracted display. I had a bit of sympathy for him. In circumstances like that it takes great motivation to play anywhere near your best – and some of those Belgian girls in shorts were rather attractive.

I made a big play for Bernt Haas in the spring of 2001 when he was approaching the final year of his contract in Zurich. The defender was twenty-three at the time and could boast a fine pedigree. I discovered he'd been playing for Grasshoppers since the age of seventeen and had more than 300 first-team appearances under his belt plus Swiss international caps and European Champions League experience. Bernt was very pleasant and level-headed when I spoke to him and he told me he fancied a crack at the Premier League some time. I urged Jim, 'Now's as good a time as any!' but nothing came of it and Bernt went on to sample life at the top with Sunderland and West Brom instead.

Le Havre had a rare pearl playing for them in nineteen-year-old Jean-Alain Boumsong and five years before he arrived in Scotland with Rangers, via Auxerre, I noted that the precocious central defender had all the ingredients to become an exceptional player. He will serve Newcastle United well.

Lucien Mettomo was another number five with all the attributes required to play at the top level and, on the strength of his performance for St Etienne against Lens, I had no hesitation in recommending him as one worth pursuing. Daniel van Buyten represented the other side of the coin. The fax from his agents at PMS Sports International had me eagerly anticipating a colossus in the Standard Liège line-up against Beveren. Indeed, during the warm-up he appeared to have tremendous physical presence at 6ft 6in and weighing in at over 13 stone. That was as good as it got for van Buyten, though, on a night when he was beaten in the air as many times as he headed the ball, was caught ball-watching on numerous occasions trying to play the offside trap, and looked distinctly uncomfortable in possession. Here was a central defender who fell into my bye-bye rather than buy, buy category.

However, it was Jim Smith saying the farewells when Derby began to struggle and things turned sour for him. Colin Todd was recruited to assist him and I don't think the partnership worked particularly well. 2001–02 was a truly dreadful season. Derby had three managers and ended up with John Gregory in charge of a

First Division club. It wasn't a barrel of laughs for me, either. I got sacked and a thirty-year friendship with Colin Todd disintegrated.

I think Jim was on borrowed time from chairman Lionel Pickering from the opening match. That was encouraging enough, a 2–1 home win over Blackburn, but we hadn't won another league game when Toddy was promoted to manager in October 2001 and Jim was given a hefty shove sideways. Pickering wanted Jim to become director of football, but when Jim asked what the role entailed and Pickering admitted he wasn't exactly sure, a definite parting of the ways was inevitable. It should have been handled so much better.

Jim was upset, and rightly so, when Todd banned him from the training ground. Jim had been instrumental in building the club up from nothing much to shout about in the First Division and here he was now, expected to work in a little office at Pride Park, which clearly wasn't going to suit him. You could understand Todd's point of view, though, in not wanting the previous manager hanging about the place.

Colin recruited new players and different people to work for him but I was still doing the European scouting, although things didn't feel right. Three players arrived from France, for instance, and I knew nothing about them. Well, that's not strictly accurate. I checked an old teamsheet and discovered the name Pierre Ducrocq. He must have played in a Paris St Germain game I watched in France but he made no impact or I would have remembered him.

Todd was sacked with indecent haste, out on his ear after just twelve matches, and I followed twenty-four hours later on Wednesday, 16 January 2002. Most of that day was spent deep in discussion with acting manager Billy McEwan and goalkeeping coach Jim Blyth about keepers, although I did disappear from the training ground after lunch to take delivery of my new club Toyota. I never got the opportunity to put much mileage on the clock of that car. A call came to see chief executive Keith

Loring and I went along innocently, sure he wanted my input on a new keeper, only to be told, 'I'm sorry, Archie, there's no easy way to break this – you're sacked.'

I demanded to know the reasons and was told they were strictly financial. Derby must have been even worse off at the bank than they were on the pitch because they tried to fob me off with a fortnight's money, although I was entitled to three months' compensation.

Things were bad – and now they were about to turn ugly and personal. There was poison in the air and dark rumblings about agents and backhanders. During Todd's brief reign of three months, Derby had signed those three from French football, Ducrocq, Luciano Zavagno and François Grenet. Personally, I didn't rate any of them. I made the point that Zavagno, an Argentinian, and the two Frenchmen were nothing to do with me when asked the question directly by the local evening newspaper. Colin called to sympathise with me losing my job and I told him about the article and what I'd said. He was calm about everything, reassuring me, 'Don't worry, Archie. I'll back up anything you say.'

I had submitted reports to him on precisely fifteen matches: Leeds v. Troyes, Piacenza v. Brescia, Genoa v. Piacenza, RCSC v. Genk, Nantes v. Lazio, Austria v. Turkey, Poland v. Cameroon, Monaco v. Marseille, FC Karnten v. SV Salzburg, Blackburn v. Manchester City, SV Salzburg v. VFB Admira, Feyenoord v. Vitesse, Genk v. Westerlo, Standard Liège v. Charleroi and Rennes v. Le Havre.

In truth, that little lot hadn't produced a vintage crop of possibles, let alone probables, worth pursuing. Whoever persuaded Colin to sign Ducrocq from PSG, Zavagno from Troyes and Grenet from Bordeaux, it most certainly wasn't me. For conspiracy theorists, I think it's worth pointing out that Zavagno joined Derby on 16 October and it was two days later that I watched his old club Troyes getting whacked 4–2 at Elland Road in the UEFA Cup.

Still, Derby's dirty linen was about to be hung out for a national audience to crow over. Early one morning the phone rang and it was Colin's wife, Jennifer, screaming, 'Have you seen that article in the *Daily Mail*?' and accusing me of stabbing her husband in the back. My take on the French signings had been twisted and spun. I was on to the *Mail* like a shot in an effort to trace who was painting me in such a bad light. The reporter responsible would only admit to acting on a tip off 'from someone in the higher echelons at Derby'.

I called Jennifer back to set the record straight and tell her that, in any case, Colin was already aware of my feelings, but she was having none of it. 'You've stabbed him in back,' she insisted.

If the club could prove someone had taken backhanders on Ducrocq, Zavagno and Grenet, Derby would certainly save on compensation money at the very least. I got my three months' cash in the end, but not until I'd survived Pride Park's version of the Spanish Inquisition. Again and again I was quizzed about the French signings. What did I know? Which agents did I use? How much did I get? In the end, it got so bad I almost replied, 'Watch my lips – they were not my deals.'

Try telling that to the Derby public, too. It was bad enough Jennifer Todd going round town slagging off Betty and me to all and sundry, including our mutual friends, but now rumours were working overtime that I'd been taking backhanders. It isn't very nice when you're talked about like that. I could live with it, though, because I knew the truth. I even kept my temper somehow when an irate Derby supporter lurched up to our table as Betty and I were trying to enjoy dinner and demanded, 'How much money did you get for the Frenchmen, Gemmill?'

The Todds were not to blame for the article and neither was I. The saddest aspect is that Jennifer and Colin actually believed that after thirty years of friendship and watching our sons grow up together, we would do such a thing to them. They wouldn't believe us when we said we hadn't spoken to the national press. It's very strange how friendships can collapse after so long.

Some years earlier, when Colin was manager of Bolton, I was struggling for work and Jennifer put me up for the job of chief scout at Wanderers. I met Colin at the Post House, Stoke and we went to see a match at Wolves. We quickly agreed wages and length of contract. I only had one small doubt – I didn't have a bulging contacts book. Yes, I can be an introvert and confessed to Colin that it would take me a little while to get my feet under the table, ring a few people and ask for their help.

Colin reassured me that wasn't a problem as far as he was concerned. He dropped me off in Stoke with the promise there would be a contract ready for me to sign at Bolton within a few days. It was three years before I had any contact with him again and, funnily enough, there were no regular weekly phone calls from Jennifer to Betty either.

19

FROM FINNEY TO ROONEY

I F there's one thing guaranteed to make my blood boil, it's the clown who pipes up, 'Of course, Tom Finney, Stanley Matthews and Duncan Edwards wouldn't be able to play in today's football.' That is such a load of garbage, so stupid it's embarrassing, yet some characters peddle that tripe on the evidence of those grainy black-and-white newsreels from half a century ago.

Granted, football now makes the game then sometimes look slow and ponderous. That's because today's pitches are immaculate, comparable to bowling greens, and surrounded by a multitude of ball boys to keep the action constantly on the move. Yesterday's heroes, though, would have been immense in any era. They were all supreme craftsmen, masters of their art who could beat an opponent, cross the ball and score goals. There was nothing Duncan Edwards could not do, I am led to believe, after winning possession with a tackle like a bear-trap, and he was particularly adept at reading the game.

Finney grew up in an era when professional footballers consumed pie and peas on a Friday night, drank three pints of heavy and smoked ten Woodbines. The beer wasn't the only thing that was heavy. So, too, were the thick shirts, baggy shorts, clumpy boots, quagmire pitches and especially those leather footballs, which, after a downpour, were more like cannonballs. Now it's all pasta, sparkling mineral water, specialist stretching exercises and computerised training regimes before changing into lightweight kit and soft leather boots as comfortable as bedroom slippers to kick synthetic balls – and that's great. Make no mistake, I'm all for it.

Pele, Franz Beckenbauer and Diego Maradona would be better now than they were twenty or thirty years ago if they were around to take advantage of all the technological training and dietary advances. Colin Todd was in his prime at Derby thirty year ago and his speed then would be sufficient to hunt down Thierry Henry today over twenty-five yards more often than not.

Sven-Goran Eriksson calls David Beckham 'the most famous footballer ever, along with maybe Maradona, maybe Pele.' That's most certainly true. Beckham is the most popular player in the world, especially from a merchandising point of view. When it comes to shifting perfume, razors and sunglasses, I think he has done a particularly astute job. With advertisers, he is the undisputed number one, but in terms of footballing ability, Beckham is nowhere near to being bracketed in the same class as Maradona and Pele. He has worked very hard to get the maximum out of his limited ability. He's never really had the pace to go past people and it was very clever of David, his agent, or maybe even his dad, to realise what his strengths were and suss out that he didn't need to beat opponents physically. For three or four years in his prime at Manchester United, week in week out, Beckham could land the ball on a sixpence from thirty to forty yards and get himself into good positions to send over crosses. His skill from set-pieces and trademark spectacular goals for United and England became known and feared world-wide and played a very large part in his success.

A few years ago Beckham came over on television as thick as a brick wall, but he has managed to create a very attractive image and is much more intelligent than most people give him credit for. I'm sure there is a bit of jealousy within football because Beckham has made himself so highly valuable as a commodity, making much more off the pitch than on it. At his best, fully fit, motivated and scandal-free, Beckham has it in him to be what passes as a 'great' player these days, but how much does he need football with all the commercial work and film offers?

Although England are always there or thereabouts when the big tournaments arrive, I don't see that they have any world-class players. The term has been abused over the years to such an extent that some merely consistent internationals can find themselves promoted to 'world-class' level.

When I use the label, I'm thinking about Zinedine Zidane. He is nearing the end of his career, but in terms of skill he must still be as good as any footballer on the planet. Second best player in the world? I'm struggling to find one outstanding individual from a collection of Andriy Shevchenko, Pavel Nedved, the two Brazilians, Ronaldo and Ronaldhino, and Thierry Henry – purely on the strength of the Arsenal form he has displayed over the last five years and regular twenty-goal hauls each season. At international level, Henry has not been as explosive and there are those who claim with some justification that Thierry goes missing on the big, high-pressure occasions.

England's best three players are their two major central defenders, Rio Ferdinand and Sol Campbell, and Frank Lampard, who has enjoyed a tremendous couple of years with Chelsea and on the international stage. Michael Owen I have never considered to be world-class in any way, shape or form. His control is unremarkable and he has no great awareness of what is happening around him. Owen has scored goals because he's played in dominant teams, particularly at Liverpool. When you're getting eighty or ninety chances a season, you should be scoring twenty goals or so, which is what he's done with those little darting runs of his. Owen's clean-cut image is world-class but to be a world-class footballer you at least need to know how to control the ball. Play it up to Zidane from any direction at any height, speed, to any foot, and nine times out of ten he can kill the ball stone dead, turn and be away. Play it up to Owen and he will be successful maybe 50 per cent of the time. That is the gulf between them.

If Owen isn't already looking over his shoulder at Jermain Defoe in the England team, he should be because I've always had a lot of time for the Tottenham forward. Defoe has got a lot going for him and is one for the future.

Unlike Owen, Wayne Rooney does have the capacity to pull me to the edge of my seat. He doesn't need a great deal of coaching in the traditional sense from Sir Alex Ferguson and the staff at Manchester United's Carrington HQ – he needs coaching between the ears. Rooney is still a baby, yet I thought he was England's outstanding player in Portugal during the European Championship finals in the summer of 2004 and who knows what the team might have achieved but for his broken foot.

Wayne was born with footballing talent, the game comes naturally to him. Footballers generally have a lot of rough edges when they begin their careers and coaches can help them by emphasising when and where to pass the ball and when to hold it. Awareness can be coached but a player must have the aptitude to get to the top and Rooney has it by the bucketload. The whole package is there – two excellent feet, a genuinely impressive, sharp footballing brain, the ability to create space for himself, pace and power. He is also good in the air and can score goals, of course, while it looks as if there isn't an ounce of fear in his body.

If Wayne dedicates himself 100 per cent he will find himself in the world-class bracket without a shadow of a doubt. The big question mark against him is can he steer clear of controversy in every area of life? He has so much potential it would be nigh-on criminal to squander it. He's only a young lad and United can't exactly lock him up in a monastery when he's not playing. Going out with his mates now and then isn't so bad. Visiting prostitutes isn't such a clever career move.

Then there's his temperament. He can be volatile on the pitch and will find life considerably easier when he learns to curb that temper of his. Otherwise, he's going to find himself no stranger to red cards.

If Wayne Rooney needs an example of what can go wrong, he should look at England old boy Robbie Fowler, a fellow Scouser who seemed to have the world at his feet. Fowler had four or five unbelievable seasons at Liverpool, where the crowd adored him and he scored goals for fun. Then Robbie went off the rails a bit. He picked up several bad injuries and that seemed to depress him. Watching Robbie Fowler playing for Manchester City compared to his halcyon days at Anfield is chalk and cheese, like comparing a beggar with a king.

Never delude yourself into believing the Premier League is the best in the world. I watch more Premiership football than is good for me and saw a lot of top-level games abroad when I was Derby's European scout. Without hesitation, I can tell you that both Spain and Italy have better leagues than England. Take Arsenal, Manchester United and Chelsea out of the equation and, depressingly, there is very little to get excited about despite Liverpool's astonishing Champions League Cup final victory over AC Milan. The days when English football ruled OK, from 1977 to 1982, are long gone. During that time the European Cup was claimed by Liverpool twice, Nottingham Forest twice, Liverpool again and Aston Villa.

Liverpool became masters of Europe with an absolutely fabulous team. They had been well organised and great competitors under Bill Shankly, and everything kept ticking like clockwork with Bob Paisley and Joe Fagan in charge. Since those days, though, the major tournament has been dominated by other nations, recently the Spanish and Italians. Arsenal, Manchester United and Chelsea have got through the opening group stage easily enough but faltered against better European teams with better players.

The image of the game at home has never been whiter than white. Dodgy agents, backhanders, boozers and drug-taking allegations were not unfamiliar in the 1970s and 1980s. It's all just a lot more high-profile now. Top performers receive an awful lot of money and the publicity it brings and doors it opens means the players must be on their best behaviour constantly. Five years ago, speculation that the stars would be paid £100,000 a week would have got you some very strange looks and a call for the men in white coats to take you to the funny farm, but we're getting there, thanks to the millions ploughed into football by Sky TV. During my playing days, reporters usually concentrated on what was happening on the pitch. Now the emphasis has shifted. A new breed of journalist devotes time to tracking players, eager to get them into the papers for all the wrong reasons. You know things have gone too far when a few of the tabloids have dedicated David Beckham correspondents in Madrid, there to report on his every move, preferably off the pitch rather than on it.

The press certainly played their part in the demise of Berti Vogts as Scotland manager. A foreigner in charge of the Scotland team, is nothing sacred? A German as well – it's the end of civilisation as we know it! Some small-minded bigots were waiting, if not hoping, for Berti to fail from the moment he was appointed in February 2002 until he resigned in November 2004. That has to be wrong. Take Charlie Nicholas, for example. He was a good player in the 1980s who won twenty international caps and scored a hatful of goals for a very fine Celtic team – sometimes it seemed they scored ten every week and he'd get four of them – but things didn't go nearly as well for Charlie when he moved down south to Arsenal. Now he has a platform as a TV pundit for Sky Sports and he used it, if not abused it in my opinion, to go over the top regarding Berti Vogts. Had Charlie wanted to criticise the Scotland players, have a go, by all means. He was entitled to do that, but Charlie really needed to have been a top-notch manager for seven or eight years with a trophy or promotion medal to show for his efforts before I was going to take what he had to say about Berti Vogts very seriously.

Some of the flak aimed at Berti was really very personal and, eventually, he got sick of all the bile flowing in his direction and said, 'Enough is enough.' I read one headline after his final match in charge, a 1–1 draw in Moldova, which proclaimed: 'Berti, Berti, Get Tae F***'. Charming.

At least when he played, Charlie had to beat defenders and a goalkeeper to score. Now cheap shots are the order of the day. Until you've had a go in management yourself, you can have no inkling of just how difficult it is, getting your team selection and tactics spot on and juggling with twenty or so egos in the dressing room. Alex Ferguson didn't look too clever that time he was days away from getting the sack in January 1990 when Manchester United came to the City Ground in the third round of the FA Cup and I was on the Forest coaching staff. We absolutely paralysed them that day, but they hung on, their substitute Mark Robins scored the winner, and they went on to win the Cup. I know from running the youth and reserve teams at Forest, and from my time at Rotherham, how easy it is to make cock-ups when you pick the wrong team or plump for the wrong system.

While I feel Berti would accept that one or two mistakes were made in terms of team selection and sometimes substitutions, nobody should ever criticise his application and professionalism. He stepped down after a torrent of abuse – and other nasty things flying out of bitter mouths – in the wake of that draw in Moldova, where Italy, incidentally, only scrambled a 1–0 win. At least four key players were missing – Steven Pressley, Christian Dailly, Jackie McNamara and Nigel Quashie. I'm not belittling the replacements, who obviously gave of their best, but take away a third of your team and you know it's going to be difficult.

Graeme Souness said Berti was coaching 'the least talented group of players' the country has ever had. I wouldn't go as far as to insult the internationals we do possess like that, but I accept that Graeme was sympathising with Berti's predicament. I still feel he was totally out of order.

219

When Graeme and I were Scotland team-mates, we played alongside an awful lot of good players but our time has long gone. I am sorry it all went wrong for Berti. I got on well with him and I do know nobody could have worked harder or tried harder to get it right. Did he care? He cared like hell but things just didn't go his way and his luck with injuries was nothing less than appalling. Sometimes in life you don't get out what you put in. It looked a sound appointment at the time. Berti had done it all in football, both as an international world-class player and a manager. He had all the qualities.

The critics were quick to put the boot in but Berti had successes, notably recognising and promoting the youthful talent of Darren Fletcher and James McFadden. Paul Dickov and Nigel Quashie were no spring chickens but they came in and did a good job, while McNamara returned to the fold and looked the part. What a huge plus Dickov has been for the Scotland squad. Paul's not the greatest player by any stretch of the imagination but he's got to be one of the gamest and a superb example to any youngster coming into football. His attitude and do-or-die spirit has taken him to the highest possible level.

Developing a consistent, winning Scotland team is a monumental job. I've got a couple of roles with the Scottish Football Association and I'm doing them to the very best of my ability to ensure Scotland have a deeper pool of players to choose from in the future.

After Derby paid me off in January 2002, I picked up a job for petrol money at Sunderland, where I was on good terms with their chief scouts Tony Book and Mick Walsh. I knew Mick and he phoned out of the blue one day to commiserate about the Derby business and to offer me the chance to do some talent-spotting for Sunderland.

'At least it will get you out of the house, Archie, and people will see you're not dead!' he argued. Football can be a cruel game when you get older, and it's very easy to be forgotten. Mick and

Tony suffered a similar fate to me when Peter Reid left the Stadium of Light.

Life was chugging along when Berti Vogts got the Scotland job and I had the bright idea of firing off a letter to SFA chief executive David Taylor, offering my services, complete with CV and a note of everything I'd achieved within the game since retiring from international football. I reckoned that I was ideally placed to run the rule over all the Scots plying their trade south of the border and that the manager might well welcome an extra pair of eyes and ears. I was right and I had an excellent relationship with both Berti and his right-hand man Rainer Bonhof, who took charge of the Under-21s.

One weekend might find me flying off to compile a report on rivals, such as Italy before Scotland took them on in a World Cup qualifier. Then I might be asked to check the form of specific players, and I might hear a whisper that a likely lad was bursting to play for Scotland. One such tip-off brought Michael McIndoe of Doncaster Rovers to my attention and he went on to represent the Scotland Future team. I am also in the business of ensuring that every club knows I'm interested if they have got a player with Scottish blood in him making progress through the youth ranks. This is particularly important to me because in September 2004 I was appointed the new Scotland Under-19 manager. The aim is to bring through internationals such as Fletcher and McFadden.

Berti Vogts first asked me to have a look at Fletcher when Darren made his Premiership debut for Manchester United at Leicester in a 4–1 win. The highest compliment I can pay him is that he didn't look out of place that day alongside seasoned professionals including Ruud van Nistelrooy, who got a hat-trick, Paul Scholes and Ryan Giggs. I would have defied anyone to pick him out as a young lad coming through the ranks unless they knew his identity. Sir Alex Ferguson seems happy to use Fletcher on the right of midfield but I believe he will develop into a central midfielder of rare quality for club and country. He has a fabulous career ahead of him.

Vogts wasn't helped by the reluctance of Sir Alex and Everton's David Moyes to play Fletcher and McFadden more often. They are Scotland's two best young players to my mind. I will be shocked if Fletcher doesn't make an excellent player, while Everton's McFadden has got the ability to be exceptional in years to come. James oozes talent but has taken some time to learn how to play the game, when to pass and when to run with the ball.

Scotland will never seriously improve until the number of foreigners employed by Scottish clubs is limited and we inject more native talent at an early age. Berti could go and watch a Rangers-Celtic match and see maybe three players qualified and equipped to represent Scotland if he was lucky. Here you run right, bang, smack into the impenetrable brick wall of a club v. country stalemate.

Everybody with half an ounce of common sense knows the Old Firm outgrew Scottish domestic football years ago and now they crave success in Europe, primarily the Champions League. The financial rewards can be huge and Glasgow's giants are not exactly what you might call debt-free. To achieve their aims, they want the best available players immediately and that means foreigners. European law means the Scottish Football Association can't suddenly pass a new ruling to restrict clubs to, say, four imports apiece, which I think would be reasonable. Maybe Hearts, Hibs, Aberdeen, the two Dundee clubs and others might accept an informal, but binding, agreement among themselves to kick-off with a minimum of seven Scots in league matches, but asking Celtic and Rangers to play ball would be as rewarding as asking turkeys to vote for Christmas! Until Scottish football can boldly grasp the nettle and find a way of forcing more youngsters through into the leading clubs' first teams, we will continue to struggle to make progress. There's no magic wand. I can't emphasise enough how quickly my first take of Scotland

Under-19 players might improve if they could play regular first-team football, particularly Scott Cuthbert, Rocco Quinn and Charlie Mulgrew at Celtic, Steven Naismith (Kilmarnock), Marc Fitzpatrick (Motherwell) and goalkeeper Euan McLean (Dundee United).

There must always be room in British football for the world's top talents but too many clubs have signed too many average foreigners simply because they have been cheap and available. Nobody should underestimate the impact of Eric Cantona, an absolutely magnificent Frenchman who was the touchstone for Manchester United's string of trophies, even if he did have a few little demons running around in his head, and consider how much poorer the game would have been without Dennis Bergkamp, from Holland via Inter Milan. The £7.5 million my old mate Bruce Rioch persuaded Arsenal to shell out for Bergkamp in 1995 has certainly been money well spent. He's such a technically proficient player and exciting, too. I can't speak highly enough of him.

I have nothing but the utmost respect for Arsenal's unbeaten forty-nine match run between May 2003 and their 2–0 defeat at the hands of Manchester United at Old Trafford in October 2004. It was a phenomenal achievement and going through a complete Premiership season without losing is something I never expect to see repeated. Fantasy football is not something in which I often indulge, but it did cross my mind that it might be fun to see if I could select a composite team from former colleagues to tackle, and beat, Arsene Wenger's finest. So after no little soul-searching, here are Gemmill's Greats (4–4–2):

Peter Shilton (Forest and England); Viv Anderson (Forest and England), Colin Todd (Derby and England), Roy McFarland (Derby and England), David Nish (Derby and England); Bruce Rioch (Derby and Scotland), John McGovern (Derby and Forest), Archie Gemmill (Derby, Forest and Scotland), John Robertson (Forest and Scotland); Kevin Hector (Derby and England), Charlie George (Derby and England). Subs: Kenny Burns (Forest and Scotland), Martin O'Neill (Forest and Northern Ireland), Ian Bowyer (Forest), Tony Woodcock (Forest and England), Garry Birtles (Forest and England).

Shilton must rate as a better goalkeeper than anyone Arsenal have called upon since David Seaman hung up his gloves, and I would pick Anderson over Lauren at right-back. My toughest job was perming two central defenders from five outstanding candidates. Dave Mackay just missed the cut because, although he was an enormous influence at Derby, Dave was approaching the twilight of his marvellous career when I played with him. If Kenny Burns and Larry Lloyd are still speaking to me after this, I'm sure they will both express their disappointment. The Forest partners were good enough to win the European Cup twice, but I maintain that McFarland and Todd possessed a bit more finesse – and I would have to fancy Todd to neutralise the pace of Thierry Henry.

David Nish was an extremely accomplished footballer in every sense. You could play him in virtually any outfield position and he wouldn't look out of place. He wore number three for Derby and was not far behind Arsenal's Ashley Cole when it came to mastering the art of playing in that position.

Wide on the right of midfield, I would have to go for Bruce Rioch, who scored goals much as Freddie Ljungberg does, while I would have the utmost confidence in John McGovern looking after whomever he faced, be it Gilberto or Cesc Fabregas. Who gets the plum job of going head-to-head with Patrick Vieira? I'd fancy that, any time, even if it would be more shades of head-to-chest given our discrepancy in inches. You didn't seriously think I'd miss a match like this, did you? I would be perfectly content with Alan Hinton on the left wing but John Robertson gets the vote. I don't think there's been a better crosser of the ball in Britain in the last twenty-five years and Robbo in his prime was at least the equal of both Robert Pires and Jose Antonio Reyes.

Arsenal can lay claim to a couple of unbelievably good strikers in Thierry Henry and Dennis Bergkamp, a pair who can most certainly both score and create goals. They have the edge in this department and are a bit in front of Derby's front two of Kevin Hector and Charlie George, although it would be a very good contest. Hector, or King Kev as he was known to the Derby fans, was a supreme, unfussy goal-poacher while Charlie can lay claim to a European Cup hat-trick against Real Madrid, something I imagine Henry and Bergkamp can still only dream about. As a former Arsenal man himself, Charlie would relish the notion of trying to eclipse Henry and Bergkamp.

I suppose I have to choose a manager, which is not exactly an onerous task. Imagine the scene in our dressing room, a mood of great anticipation as we prepare to challenge Arsenal. It's ten to three, suddenly the door bursts open and in walks Brian Clough, 'Forty-nine unbeaten, is it?' he says. 'Well, that lot won't make it fifty!'

Scotland have seen better days, it goes without saying. I wonder what Walter Smith would give to be able to field this side today from players of my vintage:

Alan Rough; Danny McGrain, Gordon McQueen, Alan Hansen, Willie Donachie; Bruce Rioch, Billy Bremner, Graeme Souness, John Robertson; Denis Law, Kenny Dalglish.

That little lot would give the boys from Brazil, Argentina or anywhere else you care to mention a run for their money. Donachie was a very good player who enjoyed a wonderful career;

Gordon McQueen was an excellent centre-half, and I still can't quite put my finger on why his partner, Alan Hansen, didn't win more than twenty-six international caps. He should have had far in excess of that number because he was an absolutely fantastic player. Alan couldn't lay claim to any great pace but he was so comfortable on the ball and read the game so well. He led by example. Mind you, this is virtually a team of Scotland captains in itself and I'd have top quality back-up on the substitutes bench in Willie Johnston and Don Masson, to name but two.

Jock Stein and I weren't on speaking terms when he blew the final whistle on my Scotland career in 1981 but I fancy he would have been the manager to get the very best out of my select eleven, and they would have given their all for him.

20

GONE BUT NOT FORGOTTEN

I STILL expect the phone to ring and to hear a familiar voice asking, 'Are you coming round this morning, or what?' Straight to the point and quite demanding – that was Brian Clough from the moment he signed me on 22 September 1970 until the day he passed away, aged sixty-nine, on Monday, 20 September 2004 surrounded by his family in ward 30 of the Derby City Hospital.

I was privileged to count myself a friend and was privy to some of his darkest moments before he won his biggest battle against the booze and emerged from that particular tunnel of despair with a liver transplant and the chance to smell the roses in his garden once more. The successful operation gave him a wonderful new lease of life for another twenty one months after he'd been given weeks to live.

He always did have bags of style and came out of the Freeman Hospital in Newcastle boasting about a massive eighteen-inch scar on his belly, shaped like an upside down Mercedes Benz badge. I shivered the first time he showed me the scar in hospital, partly because I had been told that during his illness, the consultants had found 'something else' down there – the stomach cancer that ultimately claimed his life.

A cup of tea and a natter in his immaculate front room became a matter of routine for the pair of us after Brian retired. It's difficult to articulate quite how much I miss those home fixtures. We'd chew the fat over the previous night's football on television, marvel over a Ruud van Nistelrooy goal and maybe discuss our plans for a midweek trip down the A38 to watch his son Nigel's Burton Albion. Sometimes he would play music by the Ink Spots, Ella Fitzgerald, Matt Monro or Frank Sinatra – you'd be guaranteed to hear them all during the season if you walked into the secretary's room on your way to the Boss's always-open office door – and talk about his favourite comedians, the Marx Brothers, Morecambe and Wise, Tommy Cooper and Chic Murray.

He's gone now but will never be forgotten by the disadvantaged whose wheelchairs he purchased, the hospital wards he visited, the pensioners he cooked for, those soup runs he made, or the old lady in his local butcher's who complained about the price of meat and found a tracksuited figure behind her, saying, 'Hey, don't worry. I'll get that for you, love.'

He won't be forgotten either by my fellow professionals at Derby County and Nottingham Forest. They won't forget the Gaffer because, together with Peter Taylor, he turned two ragbag groups of young nonentities, journeymen professionals and creaking veterans into medal winners, champions of England and champions of Europe.

He loved you if you were playing and he loved you if you weren't. Injured players were in for a treat. Some spent the first week on the treatment table and the next on holiday in Majorca, with their wives and children, at Brian's expense. More than anything, he appreciated the importance of a happy family and he was devoted to his wife Barbara, daughter Elizabeth and sons Nigel and Simon plus a host of gorgeous grandchildren.

I played badly for him a few times, so imagine Betty's delight when she opened the front door and took delivery of a beautiful bouquet of flowers or a splendid box of chocolates with this message: 'Cheer up, next week will be better!'

For the dinner held in Nottingham to celebrate the twenty-fifth anniversary of the club's first European Cup triumph, every Forest hero was there, either in person or on video. There were little clips of each of us in our prime but the Boss was very quiet, almost as if he didn't want to intrude on our personal moments of glory. Afterwards, they asked him to do five minutes and he had the 600-strong audience eating out of his hand. They virtually had to drag him off after half-an-hour. His brain was razor-sharp.

What motivated the boss? His innate belief in himself, I think. Not only did he believe he could always get things right, he was convinced he always *was* right. Somehow he managed to instil the same level of confidence in his players. We really did believe we could win every game under him. He knew football inside out and possessed a wonderful knack of bringing the best out of a group of players, making them feel they were the best sixteen or eighteen in the business. Brian was a wizard at blending very different personalities, which is how he was able to create two great teams. John McGovern was his biggest individual success. Brian took John under his wing bringing him from Hartlepools United to Derby for £7,000, then to Leeds and finally making him captain of the Forest team that ruled Europe.

Brian's man-management skills were of the very highest order. Gamblers, tramps, boozers, womanisers – he embraced them all if he thought they could do a job for him, if they showed talent on the pitch.

One of my team-mates got into terrible debt to the tune of thousands of pounds. The Boss was not impressed when he learned some heavy characters were chasing the player for money. Something like that could affect a player's form and that would never be tolerated. Many managers would have washed their hands of the player and put him straight on the transfer list but the Gaffer had a much more humane solution – he opened his own chequebook and, hey presto, the debt was completely cleared and potential disaster averted.

At Derby, fridges, cookers and colour televisions would turn up on various players' doorsteps – replacements for broken appli-ances and all paid for by the Gaffer. In those days, a decent wage rise was £10 a week and players were much closer to the working man in the street. The Boss didn't have spies all over town, just people who would keep him informed if there was a problem, or one was likely to develop. He knew how to keep on top of things.

Derby were nothing when the Gaffer went there, scraping by on gates of 8,000 in the old Second Division. A few seasons later they were Football League champions and giving Juventus a scare or two in the European Cup semi-final. It was exactly the same at Forest. From the depths of the Second Division, they rose to win the title and go on to conquer Europe not once, but twice. Arsenal have been in the top division from the year dot while Manchester United are a simply massive club, an institution, even if they have had their occasional ups and downs, but Sir Alex Ferguson and Arsene Wenger had just one European Cup between them when the Boss died.

What Brian achieved with Derby and Forest is impossible to repeat. Just consider how much newly promoted sides struggle in the Premiership. Imagine West Bromwich Albion, for example, winning the Premiership and going on to lift the Champions League twice. That stretches credulity a bit but it does give a modern-day illustration of what the Gaffer achieved at Forest.

Would he have had a problem handling Rio Ferdinand or Kieron Dyer? Are you joking? Brian admired those players for their talent, but not for some of the stuff they got up to off the pitch. Of course he would have coped with them, mainly because problems would never have been allowed to arise in the first place. It's an insult to question whether he would have been a successful manager, pushing Arsene Wenger and Sir Alex for the Premier-ship title season after season, and how he would have loved a verbal joust with Chelsea's Jose Mourinho, a character with almost as much self-confidence as himself.

Brian had an aura that can't easily be explained, a quite marvellous ability to radiate cheer, hope and goodwill the mo-ment he entered a room full of sick kids or the elderly and infirm.

He was idolised by many and rightly so. With that new liver inside him I knew he would find the strength of character to resist the drink again.

I wouldn't say he was coping for a spell, thriving would be a more accurate description as he dashed around Derby and Nottingham, opening this and that and presenting prizes at schools, or popping up at the most unlikely non-league grounds to watch Burton's pre-season friendly matches. I sometimes acted as Brian's unofficial chauffeur and was delighted to see him accompanied everywhere by a small plastic bottle of still water. That became his official tipple but it wasn't easy for him when he went to functions and the place was awash with wine and champagne. Some people would have loved to claim they had enjoyed a 'proper' drink with the Boss.

He wouldn't take one drink because he knew that then it would be two, three and four glasses and you never remember numbers five, six and seven. When he was on his feet again after the liver transplant, the Clough clan went off on holiday together for the first time in many a long year to their old haunt, Cala Millor in Majorca. That was a test for Brian because he used to do some seriously heavy drinking there in the good old, bad old days. But he was happy, relaxed, the family he adored was with him and he was in no mood to throw everything away. The operation gave him a second chance, and he was far too shrewd and canny to toss it all away. He became again a man in total control of his faculties, and looked twenty years younger than he did before surgery. All his natural healthy colour returned – the red-faced character on show towards the end at Nottingham Forest was unrecognisable.

They say drink wrecks your memory but that was most certainly not the case with the Boss. He remained tremendously articulate to the end and could talk with authority on a wide variety of subjects for as long as you wanted – sometimes even longer! I can remember three or four members of the St Mirren team I started out with in the 1960s but Brian could still recall all the

Middlesbrough teams he played for as a teenager aged seventeen, eighteen and nineteen, the names of their wives and what they were doing.

He wasn't ever going to fall off the wagon because he had far too much going for him and far too much respect for the liver donor's family. When I get over to the 'other side' I fully expect him to have the team set up and a place in it for me. Keep my boots warm for me, Boss!

INDEX

Lyall, Linda 169–71
Lyas, Graham 180
Lytham St Annes 20

Macari, Lou 114, 118, 121, 123
McDermott, Terry 104
McDougald, Junior 192–3
McEwan, Billy 209
McFadden, James 220–2
McFarland, Roy xii, 23, 37, 48–9, 52–3, 57, 62, 72–5, 78, 107, 164–5, 168, 223–4
McGovern, Ann 186
McGovern, John 33, 36–8, 40, 51–2, 55, 58, 65, 102, 104, 107, 110–11, 135;
joint manager of Rotherham with AG 190–1, 193–4; 223–4, 229
McGrain, Danny 154, 225
McGregor, Ewan 125
McLean, Euan 223
Machin, Mel 183
McIlroy, Sammy 105
McIndoe, Michael 221
Mackay, Dave 34–7, 57
  succeeds Clough at Derby 74–6, 88, 224
  his signings 77–8, 82–3
  sacked from Derby 90–1, 160
McKay's café, Nottingham 105
MacLeod, Ally 94, 95–6, 113–21, 123, 132
McNab, Jim 27
McNamara, Jackie 219–20
McNeill, Billy 160

McQueen, Gordon 89, 114, 226
Madeley, Paul 53
Maitland, Betty see Gemmill, Betty
Malmo FF 88, 95, 138, 139–41
Manchester City 8, 34, 53–5, 57, 65, 67, 77, 80–1, 93–4, 102, 133, 146, 160, 181, 202, 217
Manchester United 11, 40, 49–50, 53, 71, 87–8, 105–6, 126, 128, 133, 136, 147, 163, 205, 214, 216–7, 221, 223, 230
Mansfield Town 138, 187
Maradona, Diego 126, 214
Marchetti, Gianpetro 63
Marsh, Rodney 19, 54–5
Maryhill FC 2
Masny, Marian 84
Masson, Don 114–5, 119, 121, 226
Matthews, Stanley 213
Maxwell, Robert 164
Mee, Bertie 55
Mettomo, Lucien 208
Metz 202
Middlesbrough 80, 83, 189, 232
Middleton, John xiii, 97–8
Miljanic, Miljan 84
Millport 12
Mills, Gary 162
Mills, Mick 129
Millwall 19
Millward, Doug 12
Milne, Jimmy 15, 21
Mols, Michael 201
Monaco 202

Moncur, Bobby 45
Money, Richard 180–1
Montella, Vicenzo 202–3
Montpellier 197, 203
Moore, Bobby 35
Morgan, Willie 40
Morris, Lee 206
Morton 10
Mossvale YMCA 2
Mourinho, Jose 230
Moyes, David 222
Mtombo, Patrick 204
Mulgrew, Charlie 223
Murphy, Colin 91, 93, 96, 160

Naismith, Steven 223
Nantes 205
Nash, Ernie 9
Neal, Phil 104
Nedved, Pavel 215
Needham, David 104, 110, 130
Neeskens, Johan 122–3
Neill, Terry 106
Netzer, Gunter 84
Newcastle United 75, 109, 165, 189, 198, 208
Newman, John 160
Newton, Henry 73
Nicholas, Charlie 218–19
Nish, David 67, 72, 79, 88, 223–24
Northampton Town 11
Norwich 22, 102, 151, 163
Notts County 103, 167, 181
Nottingham Forest
  AG transfers to xiii, 96–8
  rivalry with Derby County 39, 51
  win Championship and League Cup